Mortar in My Blood

An Italian Odyssey

by

Frank Mauro Puzio

DORRANCE PUBLISHING CO., INC.
PITTSBURGH, PENNSYLVANIA 15222

To My Mother

For My Children and Their Children

To Arnold:

A learned friend, true to his profession.

Frank McTizJe

Easter · 1997

Contents

Peruse me O reader,
if you find delight
in my work,
since this profession
very seldom
returns to this world,
and the
perseverance to pursue it
and to invent
such things anew
is found in few people.
And come men,
to see the wonders
which may be discovered
in nature
by such studies.

LEONARDO DA VINCI
MADRID I 6r

Foreword

"Past things shed light on future ones; the world was always of a kind; what is and will be was at some other time; the same things come back, but under different names and colors; not everybody recognizes them, but only he who is wise and considers them diligently."

Francesco Guicciardini (1482–1540)

This is not the book I had intended writing. That book was to be entitled *Italian Gestures and Gesticulations*, a serious study of the sign language and facial expressions commonly used in Southern Italy which are fast disappearing in America. More accurately, that book should be entitled *Neapolitan Gestures and Gesticulations*, for the people of Naples gave birth to another form of communication, a delightful extension of the art of talking.

I knew the purpose for writing that book from the beginning. It pained me to see that my children, and many other children of Italian parentage, possessed very little knowledge of this lost art, an acknowledgment of the loss of identity threatening them. I see I retained the purpose if not the content of that original book when I reflect that I dedicated this book to my children and their children.

What happened to that other book? I have acquired source material for over thirty years and still have it. I will get around to writing it, even though I now know that writing is hard work (at least for me), something I would not acknowledge for many years.

"Dal dire al fare c' è mezzo d'un mare" (from saying to doing lies half an ocean).

This present book began early one morning as I lay in bed, thinking about the people I had met and known, many of whom I had loved, in the masonry and building businesses that had been my life. I thought too of the fascinating microcosms of life of which these people had been a part. Some of these recollections were funny, some sad. So I decided to make a list. By 10 A.M. I had compiled forty-nine reminders of stories I could relate. My enthusiasm ran wild! I concluded that a compendium of short stories, something like *All Creatures Great and Small*, but about people and experiences in the construction industry, would make an interesting legacy for my children.

This book is not an autobiography; it is more the recordings of an observer of human nature.

But was it possible to do this in my sixty-fifth year? I had been trained as a civil engineer, not a writer! I figured that hard work alone could overcome the deficiencies in my education, but I was only partly correct. I soon learned there are techniques to writing well; and intertwined among the bare facts of storytelling have to be the threads of living personalities. So as I began to write, I discovered what professional writers must know by instinct, that if you want to hold interest, you must talk about real people.

I found out, too, that I had many important things to say about my people and their privations, character, and immigration to this country. A burning desire came upon me to make other ethnic groups understand my forefathers and the values they gave us, those qualities which make us tick. It was easy for me to realize that I was protesting the unfair judgments and malignities to which my forefathers had been subjected. So the book began to take on a character all its own.

But as I continued to write, and discover, I began to despair. How could I possibly put all this together and attain a sense of continuity? I hit a low point, one of many. A friend, though, had told me that when the creative juices don't flow, there is no alternative but to put the project aside temporarily. These respites helped me regain my enthusiasm.

Along the way I found it useless to deliberately avoid technical talk about bricklaying, and ultimately I decided that maybe a primer on brickwork would not necessarily be fatal. I figured I would try to write about masonry work in such a way that the reader would not be bored. A few friends have told me they like what I have written.

You will find as you read my book that I switch quite freely from proper Italian to dialect, especially where I quote proverbs. First, I think writing in dialect is necessary to prevent the loss of nuance, for only in dialect do the attitudes of a people come through. The old saw 'It loses something in the translation' is more than accurate where dialects are concerned. I am happy to relate, however, that the many dialects of Italy, long derided and officially discouraged, are now making a comeback. The sterile insistence of Mussolini's Fascist regime, that dialects be banished because they are *cafonata* (in low-life taste), is being reversed. The Italian government has at last joined scholars in encouraging the revival of the delicious and true-to-life color of provincial languages.

You will find that I frequently extol the virtues of my people, particularly when talking about the simple, wholesome peasants and small-town artisans I knew. You will also find that there are feelings and experiences I found very difficult to confront, and I felt uncomfortable writing about them. You will spot them.

Acknowledgments

No one can write a book without recognizing the debt owed to those who lent encouragement.

Foremost among these is my wife, Emily, who lent constant encouragement, and another of whose contributions was the exclusive use of her Italian country kitchen. I worked there from the small hours of the coming day, and the trussed ceilings, bricked ovens and Emily's collection of hanging herbs warmed me.

Accompanying me in silence was our contemplative Siamese, Cel the Fel, who raised no objections to having his name diminutized from the original Celery. He was loyal for more than four years. Without his presence my writing suffered the last year.

Many years ago Uncle 'Nick' (Ruotolo) used to give me his old copies of the *National Geographic*, and thus opened up the world in which I am still happiest.

"Thank you" seems woefully inadequate.

There was a gentle man who insinuated into my being the more worthy values of life. That was 'Grandpa,' about whom you will read here.

Undoubtedly there were compulsions, silent though they were, emanating from my children, Emilie-Mary and Frank, as well as my two granddaughters, Amy and Vanessa.

I do not forget Mom, my mother, to whom elsewhere I dedicate this book.

Then there was Father Joe (McNamara) whose splendid humanity rejoiced with me and for me.

And finally, Helen Rauch of Manasquan, New Jersey, who typed every single word because I would not use a word processor.

Grazie Mille
Frank M. Puzio

Italian Pronunciation

An *i* in Italian is pronounced like a long *e* in English, as in *sleet*.

Conversely, an *e* in Italian is pronounced like an *eh* in English, as in *sled*.

There is no *k* in the Italian alphabet. The *k* sound in Italian is obtained in two ways:

Before *e* and *i ch* is added, so that you procure *chi* (who) as in English *key*.
And
Che (what) as in English *keh*.

Ca is exactly as in English *ca*.

Co is exactly as in English *co*, as in *cooperate*.

Cu is exactly as in English *coo*, as in *coo-coo* or *cuckoo*.

Chapter I

La Famiglia

My father was a bricklayer, and my grandfather was a bricklayer. My father's brothers—Uncle Louis, Uncle John, and Uncle Joe—were all bricklayers, too. Only Uncle Al, the youngest, escaped. He eventually became a mechanical engineer, but, like me, he was a bricklayer on Saturdays, some Sundays, and all summer vacations. He and I were what were known as "boots," unfinished and sloppy bricklayers who had mortar all over our shoes. My brother was also a bricklayer before he became a successful real-estate developer.

My father had three sisters—Aunt Rae (Raffaela), Aunt Mary, and Aunt Florence. Aunt Rae married Uncle Dominick, who was a bricklayer, naturally. They had five sons, all of whom were bricklayers. Aunt Mary married Uncle Andrew. Uncle Andrew thought he was a young apple farmer from the Hudson Valley in New York State, but when *la masciata* (a compact) was made between the families of the now serious young lovers, it was decided that Uncle Andrew should become a bricklayer, too. The family taught him bricklaying, and he became a good layout man.

Years later, *la famiglia* (the family) all helped to build Uncle Andrew's and Aunt Mary's new, all-brick house high on the hill of a farm in Marlboro, New York; the family worked together just like when we rebuilt Uncle Dominick's and Aunt Rae's house on 204th Street in the Bronx. It was all family scrambling about. The boys, the young grandchildren of Mastro (Master) Mauro, as well as his sons, cousins, and nephews, all of whom were destined to become bricklayers, were the laborers. As we carried the mortar up ladders and cut our shoulders on the loaded hods of brick, our hands peeled, cracked, and bled from the drying of the mortar. We were also the water boys, the scaffold men, and the cleanup men.

Some of my cousins were older and stronger than I, and my body ached with strain and exhaustion. Sometimes I cried inside. But I couldn't "let people talk." How that had become a part of my life! You see, my father was the oldest and strongest of the sons, the one evolutionally selected to be the leader of the family, and I was his son. I could not bring shame upon him. My mother watched worryingly from Grandma's house across the street in the Bronx. Later, she and Grandma would minister to my hurts, though not in my father's presence.

My cousins Tony, Morris, Mikey, JoJo, and Rudy, who were Aunt Rae's sons, Sonny and Jamesie, who were Uncle John's sons, and Louis and Jimmy, who were Uncle Louis's sons-in-law—all of whom were bricklayers-to-be—were testing me, just as they tested each other. When my head pounded from the exhausting work, I had only to look up and see the warning, piercing, hazel eyes of my father cautioning me "not to let people talk."

Later I will tell you more about "Don't let people talk," a way of thinking that has a lot to do with the immigrant philosophy and one of the reasons, I think, America became so great. Many paid the price and reaped a thousandfold in return from this way of thinking.

But I haven't told you about my great-uncles, my father's uncles. They were *muratori* (stonemasons or wall builders), too. There was Zi Giuan, Zi Antonio o'Lungo (Uncle Stretch), and Zi Pascale (the father of Uncle Andrew, the hopeful apple farmer). Of course, in our enlightened state, we know that in proper Italian my great-uncles would have been known as Zio Giovanni,

Zio [1] Antonio il Lungo (the Long One), and Zio Pasquale, respectively. The Neapolitan dialect, however, rolls across the tongue like the caress of warm caramel, and I still like it better.

These three were Moscas. All my life I have respected them and their memory, for when my grandfather Mauriello (little Mauro), a Puzio, was orphaned in Naples, the Mosca family took him in. They were not blood relatives, just neighbors. The social worker hadn't yet been born, so there was nobody to tell them what to do. There was no court to yank my grandfather from his *paese* (town) and send him off to an orphanage. The Moscas solved the problem in a different way. They simply took in the young boy, put him to bed with their sons, and the next day shared their bread with him. And so it was that my father grew up respecting Zi Giuan, Zi Antonio, and Zi Pascale as true uncles.

Many years later my grandfather's adoption into the Mosca family caused a serious and interesting problem when the young lovers, Mary Puzio and Andrew Mosca, wanted to marry. The issue was that it is a sin for cousins to marry because the resultant children will be grotesque, or worse. Happily, my father settled the matter before Neapolitan passions could destroy young love.

The osmosis of time had blurred history and had to be set straight. People had forgotten my grandfather was not a true Mosca. "There is no blood relationship; therefore they are not truly cousins," so spoke my father, the new patriarch. And it was fascinating for my young eyes to observe how my aging grandfather had relinquished his authority to his strongest son.

"Court" was held on Reservoir Oval in the Bronx, where we lived. This was just across Mosholu Park from the little Italian community of Saint Philip Neri Church and Villa Avenue. My grandparents lived downstairs with my great-grandmother and their unmarried children, Uncle Joe, Uncle Al, Aunt Florence and Aunt Mary. Every Sunday *la famiglia* gathered. Around nine in the morning, all came to Nonna's house (except the new wives and mothers). Everybody drank Nonno's wine and ate Nonna's mounds of *polpette* (meatballs), and problems like Aunt Mary's marriage-to-be (or not) were aired. Then all the men and boys

---

1. Zi and zio both mean uncle.

played pinochle or *briscola*, a partners' three-card game where wile is at a premium.

Grandma and her mother, Marossa (dialect for Mama Grossa, meaning Big Mama), took care of the house and the cooking, and the daughters, my aunts, helped. They were the experts on capping the tomato bottles. Actually, Marossa was not big at all. She was "Big Mama" because she was "Great Mama." Paradoxically, she was tiny, about four feet eight inches tall, and never weighed more than eighty-five pounds. But she was a force to be reckoned with; nobody ever violated her dignity. We buried her when she was ninety-seven, and she was still as tiny and as imposing as ever. Cholesterol problems were unknown then. No wonder! The constant hard work not only solved the family's problems, but it also helped dissolve cholesterol—something we have only recently learned.

Nonna, Marossa, and my young aunts also picked the vegetables, but they did not tend the garden. That was Nonno's job after work each day and on Saturday. We always had our own fresh tomatoes, arugula, parsley, basil, and escarole. Nobody in the family bought tomatoes for the pasta sauce. We bottled the plum tomatoes for a whole year's supply; these were the San Marzano genus from outside Naples. In that frenzied once-a-year operation, huge cauldrons, some sterilizing bottles and Mason Jars and others cooking luscious tomato pulp, boiled away on the cast-iron stoves. Extra fires and pots were set up in the backyard. Every jar had bits of fresh basil in it. Nobody escaped work those days—not nieces, nephews, cousins, uncles, or aunts.

But our elders forgot to tell us bottling tomatoes was work. It was fun, almost as much fun as stomping purple-footed on the grapes for Nonno's annual wine making in October. Years later, when I became one of the affluent Westchesterites who played golf every Saturday, Sunday, and holiday, I would often reflect on how different my week-ends were from those of the old days. Which were better? I know. Can you guess?

Every one of my cousins became a bricklayer. My sister, Theresa, married a bricklayer, Jim Lionelli, the son of bricklayer Vicinze (Vincenzo) Lionelli. Jim, as well as his two brothers, Sparky and Louis, also became bricklayers. And we were all "related." Jim's mother was a Mosca. They had all come from

Afragola, a small *paese* near Naples. Today, those deceased Puzios, Moscas, and Lionellis would never recognize their own childhood alleys. Afragola is now a high-rise section of Naples.

But the bricklayers do not stop there. One of the many admirable traits of these immigrants was an innate obligation to help your neighbors and, of course, *la famiglia*. A result of this was the *compare* and *comparillo* system, a heartwarming but now almost completely forgotten arrangement of society that had been born of necessity.

A man became a *compare* and a woman became a *comare* in several ways. You could be best man or maid of honor at a wedding; you could be godfather or godmother at a baptism; or you could be the sponsor of a young adult at the sacrament of confirmation. The recipient was a *comparillo* if a boy and a *commarella* if a girl. In proper Italian, the words are *comparino* and *commarina*, respectively. The obligations of the *compare* and *comare* were taken seriously because they acted as another security blanket against the ravages of fate. In the event of the death or incapacitation of one or both parents, the *compare* or *comare* would assume a serious measure of responsibility for the child. The roles they played were especially important in an alien world.

I think it is a pity that many sponsors (*compari*) of confirmation today are strangers to the confirmees. A satisfying warmth resulted from the tacit safety-net arrangement, which extended even to the families of the two principal players, all of whose members became *compari* or *comare*. My own godparents were *compare* Arthur Blank, lawyer and boyhood pal of my father, and *comare* Mary DePonte, favorite cousin and childhood girlfriend of my mother. My parents taught me and my siblings that our godparents were special, and all holidays required some demonstration of our filial respect for them.

For as long as I can remember we used (and still do) another definition for the words *compare* and *comare* which has to do with extracurricular sexual activity. To infer that a man has a *comare* (or a woman a *compare*) is to suggest a relationship that does not quite approach that of the English words mistress or lover. The nuance attached to the two Italian words suggests an arrangement of convenience, a less overwhelming passion, and thereby less of a threat to the inviolable marriage state of either of the players.

It is easy for me, as an Italian reared so close to immigrant households, to understand how these particular words were selected to describe the whispered relationship of the participants. Let me explain. A *compare*, in the process of fulfilling his obligations as an overseer of the welfare of a *comparillo* or *commarella*, would visit the household of the child's mother when she was widowed. You can see how the opportunities for emotional involvement multiplied.

I am certain that many invented scandals did not in fact exist, but the words *compare* and *comare* began increasingly to assume a new additional definition. Today, with the original societal obligations of the players no longer required, the words begin to approach mistress and lover, but, happily, not quite. They are lighter and more reserved for joke-telling, but still very much in use to this day.

My father was a popular *compare* when his four children were very young. By this time he had graduated from bricklayer to contractor. The young men who had selected him as their would-be *compare* were assured of several things: a champion of their welfare, the opportunity to learn the bricklaying trade, and a gold pocket watch. The pocket watch and gold chain became a standard expectation, and later, when I made my own confirmation and my sponsor was a stranger selected by the pastor at Saint Brendan's, I inwardly resented the fact that I didn't get a watch like my father's *comparilli*. All those watches gone to waste!

I think a young man's selection of a *compare* is very interesting and worth remembering. The scenario must have been innate, for it never varied, or so it seemed to my young mind. The young man's approach to his would-be *compare*, in this case my father, was always made on a Sunday. The youth was accompanied by his father, and both were attired in more than their Sunday best. My mother greeted them with much good grace and invited them into the parlor, where anisette or homemade cordial with bottled cherries was served. The young man and his father (or on several occasions the young woman accompanied by her mother) were offered the Sunday *dolce* (sweet), usually a simple homemade, sugar-coated *taralla*.

We four children were summoned to be introduced to our guests and to divert the young person while the adults talked. The subject was not a surprise, despite the fact that the visit had been unannounced. Certain harbingers had hinted at the reason for the visit. To begin with, ambassadors for the youth had made discreet inquiries (the beginning of *la masciata* process), combined with what in Washington is known as a "leak." Also, the dress and deferential manner of the parent reflected his (or her) fear regarding the possibility of being rejected. The nosegay (usually home-grown flowers) which the youth presented to my mother was another sign. The clincher, however, was the fact that the parent was accompanied by the child.

The approach was always discreet. To blurt out the reason for the visit would be considered *cafonata* (in low-life taste). The uneasy parent, therefore, talked about inconsequential subjects, including the weather and generalities about the state of the world. Then, my mother would excuse herself and suggest we children take our young visitor outside. Finally, my father would say something to the parent like, "But I can see, Gennarino, that you came to talk about something important. Tell me what it is."

And the parent would respond with something like, "It would do our family great honor if you would agree to be *compare* to our son. He admires you, has heard people speak highly of you, and would very much like to be your *comparillo*."

"*Tengo piacere*" [2] (It will be my pleasure), would be my father's response, followed by an obsequious embrace. My mother would reenter, graciously extending her hand and offering her own "*compare*." The young person, kissed by my mother, was put at ease, and expected to greet his new *compare* and *comare* with recently practiced bows.

The deed was done. After the religious ceremony some months later, we all went to dinner at the home of the new *comparillo* (or *comarella*). At that time, my father presented the gold watch.

On one occasion my father sponsored seven *comparilli* at confirmation! I have four—two boys and two girls—but my father

---

2. In proper Italian, one would say, '*Sarà piacere mio.*'

had a total of seventeen! My mother had two *commarelle*. I know at least six of my father's *comparilli* became bricklayers, some of whom went on to be top-notch foremen in the trade. Tony Barbarino, Vinnie Lombardi, Jimmy Funicello, Totò (Salvatore) Campaniello, Achille Mosca, and Aniello Lunedi became part of the family work force. I am not certain whether Joe Rocco, Joe Laparuta, and Mike Tuccillo eventually became bricklayers, but they were *comparilli* and filled in on the jobs during the summer time. Another was Andrea Daniele, *o'panettiere's* (the baker's) son. For many years my mother sent me to buy bread at Andrea's father's store. Andrea and a brother later inherited the huge brick and stone oven in the basement as well as the grocery store above. Over five hundred loaves could be baked at one time inside the brick-arched chamber. The paddles needed to rotate the loaves were over twenty feet long! The oven had to be placed at the rear of the basement so that there was room to remove the long flapping paddle.

In addition, there was Vince Basicano, who later became a top labor foreman for us; Guy Mosca, son of Zi Antonio o'Lungo who became a good all-around artisan; Uncle Al Puzio, my father's younger brother; and Uncle Nick, my favorite uncle and my mother's younger brother. It was not unusual to be called to be *compare* to a younger brother, which is similar to a brother being asked to be best man at a wedding.

The picture should become clear. The *compare* and *comparillo* system worked. A superb work force was available to be tapped, and, on the other hand, employment was almost guaranteed, earned as a result of the expert, proper training wrought.

For centuries, in Italy the stonemasons were known as *muratori*. *Muratori* built the Pantheon, Hadrian's tomb, and the Colosseum. Their descendants are the bricklayers and masons we know today. But bricklayers do not work alone. They must be attended by those who deliver the materials to them. Moreover, the mortar has to be mixed, the bricks stacked, the scaffolds built, and miscellaneous iron and steel parts built in; in addition, constant cleaning and inventory control is required. The men who perform these jobs are known as mason tenders, *manuali* (hand workers or laborers), *scaffaioli* (scaffold men), and *calciatori* (mortar makers). The *compare* and *comparillo* system assured not only a supply of bricklayers and stonemasons, but a wealth of related *manuali* who were not required to develop the expertise of the *mastro*.

It was a soft summer evening in June on Reservoir Oval in the Bronx, and I know it was 1933, for I distinctly remember I was twelve years old. My mother, father, and I were standing with Zi Giuan and his wife in front of their house after having paid a visit to *la pergola* (the grape arbor) and backyard garden overlooking Saint Brendan's Church on Perry Avenue. Zi Giuan's house was only 500 feet away from Grandpa's house, from which my family had moved because we needed more room to separate the four growing boys and girls. You will remember Zi Giuan was a Mosca, my father's uncle by devotion, and one of my father's most reliable foremen.

My parents had paid deserved compliments to Zi Giuan and his wife for the splendid state of their growing grapes, tomatoes, and salad greens. The horse manure was showing its amazing effect on the growth and gloss of the entire garden. Fortunately, manure was plentiful; it was cars that were scarce.

I don't remember exactly how the subject finally came up. but it was decided that evening that starting the next morning Zi Giuan would be my first mentor in the Bronx on Boscobel Avenue, where Uncle John was running a job for my father in the University Avenue section. This old tenement was to be a four-story apartment building, with new stores on the ground floor.

I had been chomping at the bit to turn twelve years old, for in my mind that was the magic age to start work in the summertime. I didn't know it at the time, but as I look back now, 1933 was the heart of the Great Depression, the year of bank closings, bread lines, and apple hawkers. This is not to say I was ignorant of these problems, but, being young, I was not fully aware of the depth, duration, and cataclysmic impact the Great Depression had on our people. Who among us doesn't know now? But back then, the scarcity of jobs was not to me a source of fear, though it was to those with whom I was to work.

I can still feel the excitement of that night. My sleep was fitful, and I lay awake all night long so that I would not sleep through my 5:00 A.M. awakening. But I need not have worried. My mother was not going to have me start out unprepared. We had laid out my working clothes the night before. The stoutest old shoes were selected for my first day, with the express understanding that the money my mother had pinned to the inside of my trouser pocket was for one purpose only—to buy the highly respected working shoe as soon as the nearest Army-Navy store opened that Monday morning. I will tell you more about working shoes later. They were an important part of life. This privilege to leave the job site would be accorded only once—son of *il padrone* (the boss) or not.

Getting up was no problem. My father was still not able to break his bricklayer habit of arising at 5:00 A.M., and my mother's life wrapped around the early morning preparations necessary to send my father off to work sated not only with the full-meal breakfast, but with "o lunch." If ever I were asked to create a logo for the Italian working man in America, it would have to be "o lunch." *Il panino*, as it was called in Italian, was no *panino* at all; it was a *panone*—usually half a loaf of an eighteen-inch round loaf or a full loaf of the *spoletta* type, a more muscular version of French bread that is scooped out and filled with the delights of imaginative peasant cookery, mostly vegetable. Favorites were eggplant parmigiana, zucchini and eggs, peppers and eggs, sautéed broccoli *di rape* (bitter), escarole, tomato salad, endive and arugula, potatoes and eggs, and many other leftovers from Sunday's dinner. Hot cherry peppers were a favorite garnish.

In any event, my mother was up early, engaged in creating my "o lunch," and in the process of seeing to it that I was awake. My father had already checked on me so that we didn't "let people talk." At 5:30 A.M., I was down in front of the house, my father's Model A Ford providing a convenient seat for me as I awaited Zi Giuan. He came out at 6:00 A.M. and declared, *'Mettiamo a mano alle sette'* (We start work at seven). Literally, the idiom is, "We put our hands to." Since we had only a twenty-minute ride, he was telling me softly that there was no need for me to wait for him so early in the morning. Zi Giuan was a quiet man, yet there was a suffused source of strength within him that warned the fire ran deep. There would come a day when I would hurt this honorable man. My skin still cringes at the embarrassment.

Uncle John was accompanied by his son, who had the proud name Achille (Achilles), but whom, sadly, we all called Caggy. Caggy was a bricklayer, plasterer, cement finisher, plumber, hardware man, and whatever else you wanted. Not too many years later this marvelous talent was to be wasted; Bacchus possessed him, and the fruit of the vine eventually overwhelmed him. He died a young man.

In short order, Zi Antonio o'Lungo (Uncle Stretch) came along with his sons, Raffaello (Ralph) and Gaetano (Guy). Guy drove the ancient Hupmobile. As we piled in, I stole a glance up at our second-floor porch windows. Sure enough, my mother was hiding behind the curtains.

I couldn't wait to get to the job. When we did, my grandfather was already there. Also, there was Andrea Acierno, a Charles Atlas in miniature. This perfectly muscled little man was a gentle creature who taught me a lot starting that day. I didn't know it, but he must have decided I needed a friend to protect me from myself, as well as from the extra burdens I would carry as the son of *il padrone*. I was to enjoy that protection for many years.

My Uncle Joe, who was twelve years my senior and twelve years junior to my father, was there, too. He would later be my partner in the business. Uncle Joe already was an accomplished bricklayer, having served part of his apprenticeship with the LaSala brothers, who, at that time, were one of the largest mason contractors in New York, and very demanding of perfection.

Also, there were some of the young *comparilli*, the lucky recipients of the gold watches my father distributed at Confirmations. Later in the day, it would be a question as to whether they were so lucky. Not only did the sun beat down on them unmercifully, but under the relentless gaze of my grandfather and all the other "uncles," there was no time for youthful nonsense. Practically everybody was a relative or a near relative.

The perpetuation of constant work would be assured only by my father's ability to be competitive in an economy which was in shock. And it was up to these men, *la famiglia*, to keep it that way. The Great Depression had not come as a surprise to these people. Hadn't life always been that tough? Centuries had well prepared them. These men put their hands and backs-to, tightened their belts another notch, and put their faith in *la famiglia* to pull them through. Had they not come across oceans to survive? "This, too, will pass." *Pazienza* (patience)!

It would be several years before I would be permitted to keep a trowel in my hand. To learn, I was to start at the bottom as a *manuale*, a laborer. In those days we mixed mortar and even concrete by hand. I was told to help Raffaello, Uncle Stretch's older son, and to watch how the mortar was mixed.

It surprised me to see that the proportions of lime, sand, and Portland cement were determined by counting the shovels of each. I had expected a more precise method of determining proportions. Later I would understand that making mortar was like being a good chef—it was a matter of "feel." Too many variables went into the mix to rely on weight or volume alone. The amount of loam (impurities) in the sand, as well as the percentage of fines (crushed ore or sand) and water already contained in it, were some factors. Raffaello started my education by adding, when needed, a half shovelful of sand, a cup of hydrated lime, a splash of water, and a quarter shovelful of cement. He mixed this for two more minutes with a hoe, then finally folded and refolded the calcia, the eternal pastiche of masons, with a shovel.

In a short time, the mortar had dried on my shoes, my face, my hands, and my arms; it had even grayed my hair. It had not yet gotten through the skin, but, aware or not, by the time I went home that night, the mortar had oozed into my blood—forever.

Raffaello taught me how to swirl the mortar with a counterclockwise, up-and-over motion of the shovel, constantly working from the perimeter of the circular pile inward. These motions would create a more homogenous, lump-free mix.

Most people do not know that shovels come in two types, pointed and square-end. The pointed shovel is used for digging and excavating soil by hand. A mason's shovel, known in Italian as *la paletta*, has a square edge, which is designed to grab a fuller load of mortar or sand. Years later my other grandfather would teach me a lesson about "counting other people's money with *la paletta*."

By that afternoon, Raffaello had me making batches of mortar myself. The old hand-mixing process was backbreaking but fun. You always started by taking about forty shovelfuls of sand from the truck-delivered mound and forming them into a conical pile. Then you pushed *la palleta* down through the peak of this tiny mountain, spreading the sand until you formed a circular dam. To this you added the Portland cement and slaked lime, in proportions of one part of each to six parts of sand. Later you would add water.

The Portland cement came in ninety-four-pound linen sacks. When you had unloaded 200 of these from the delivery truck, you knew you had already burned up your lunch. The only trouble was that your body was so exhausted you could not eat your lunch! Part of the mortar man's work is to unload the trucks, and that's what we had to do that day. Raffaello took pity on me. My twelve-year-old body was having a tough time handling the sacks; they were slipping to my knees. He had the truckdriver hand the sacks down to the edge of the truck and had me form the first layer on top of the spruce mason's planks. I noticed the truckdriver had built himself a stairway as he went, eventually piling the sacks over his head. It took me several years of summer work before I could lift those sacks over my head.

Piling cement sacks is not done by strength alone, but by fluid motion, using inertia and momentum to assist the body. The mortar man must think like an athlete. An athlete must keep his body balanced and relax his muscles, for relaxed muscles can overcome a series of poor techniques. Athletes never abuse their bodies with unbalanced motions and neither do *manuali* when they pile cement sacks.

"Wash up," Raffaello called out to me.

The unexpected relief came out of me like an escaped bag of wind. Why? It was yet half an hour to noon! So I sat on the pile of screened sand, too tired even to wet my hands. My body would have to get used to the pain. Would it ever?

Raffaello then said, "This afternoon we're getting a load of brick. You will have to help unload them."

I nodded in assent, too tired to raise my head or to eat the lunch my mother had lovingly prepared. I knew she had packed a delicious omelet of potatoes and eggs stuffed into the torpedo-shaped *spoletta* bread.

Lunchtime passed all too quickly. Raffaello and I were back to work at noon, again half an hour ahead of the others. I had spent my entire lunch break in an exhausted daze. In those days we worked nine hours. Later, the time would be cut to eight. Today it is seven, or even six for some trades.

One of the most important factors in bricklaying production is the condition of the mortar. If it begins to set up, the masons cannot spread it. If it is too soupy, it falls off the trowel, which makes for all kinds of problems, including weak and porous walls, besides sloppy results and lost production. Mortar that sits through a lunchtime becomes unworkable. But tempering with water the mortar in each tub can be reconstituted into a smooth, workable mass. This was our job. Mortar tempered more than once is unusable because the chemical process is abused and the mortar loses both its adhesive properties and compressive strength.

The mortar box is an important part of a mason's life. This rectangular-shaped box is made of scaffold planks, including the floor. Scaffold planks are exclusively made of spruce, a wood of long grain, which is necessary for the flexible strength required safely to span across the putlogs or cross supports.

The long grain of the Sitka spruce is superior to the Eastern spruce, but the best of all spruces for strength and flexibility is the Western White spruce; as a result, it is more expensive. In later years, we bought these planks in loads of thousands at a time, and never did I see a load come to the job without the labor foreman nervously looking over the planks. The foreman entrusted this chore to no one else, for his men's lives depended on the condition of these thirteen-foot-long planks. For years I had seen Uncle Stretch and later Guy Vallese, Vince Basciano, Ralph Belloise, and Frank D'Angelica carefully examine these planks. These men chose four or five planks at random, propped them up on one end, and then bounced on them like trampoline performers. They treated the planks that had knots with extra care, and the fracture of any one plank made the whole load suspect. The men then hand-picked the planks and returned the rejects immediately. This expensive procedure was never violated, for the welfare of *la famiglia* depended on the integrity of these planks.

That afternoon, as Raffaello had promised, the load of face brick arrived, about seven thousand of them, neatly stacked in long rows on the body of a long flat-bed truck. This was in the days before brick were palletized and off-loaded with forklift trucks. The plank platform had been prepared along the curb, and it was elevated to permit rain or street water to pass below. Soaked brick, especially the hard-burned kind, are very difficult to lay and keep from "swimming," and the resultant loss of production and leaning walls are simply unacceptable.

When the truckdriver saw I was to be the receiving end of the unloading partnership, he said, "Wait a minute," and went into his cab. He handed me a peculiar pair of "gloves." They were two slabs of laminated rubber, with two holes at the top, through which wrist thongs were passed. Only the wristband was attached to me; the rubber slabs flapped in the breeze like the flippers of a seal. At first I thought they were cumbersome and a waste of time. Not so later.

Raffaello and the driver laid out the start of the rows, working to unload enough brick from the ground in order for the driver to get up on the truck. Then he started passing the brick down to me. When he saw I couldn't handle six at a time, he kindly cut it back to five. The secret was to slap the brick together between the flippers. That was not too hard—to begin.

As the driver worked farther into the pile, the distance between us grew. There was no more handing down.

"Catch!" he said. Then five brick came flying at me, perfectly thrown, inertia permitting them to arrive unseparated. Instinctively, I reached for them, one flipper on each side of the pile. I was more surprised than he was. Catching the brick didn't hurt, and my fingers weren't smashed! I then realized how regular gloves would have never protected the palms of my hands.

The driver let me catch my breath. "Ready? Go!"

His aim was unerring, at my side, above my knees, and away from my head. As soon as I realized I could catch the brick constantly, the exhilaration I felt let me forget my fatigue. Raffaello then spelled me for a while. By late afternoon the deed was done. I felt my first day had been a success, especially since my father had arrived unexpectedly and caught me hard at work.

Dominick Belsole, a dear friend about whom you will hear more later, had told me that when he ran the yard for Colonial Sand and Stone Company, located on the Harlem River at 139th

Street, barges of brick used to come down from the upper reaches of the Hudson River and were unloaded there. He said that crews of these men used to fling up to seven bricks at each other. That must have been a sight!

By only the second day I felt my body hardening. In another day the wracking pains were gone and my sleep was the sleep of satisfaction.

Andrea Acierno offered encouragement every day. He taught me how to make myself an integral part of the wheelbarrow. When I was young, wheelbarrows didn't have pneumatic tires. These old-style wheelbarrows often tipped over, and the steel wheel had a tendency to dig itself into the ground. Andrea showed me how to move into the wheelbarrow, like into the stirrups of a horse, with my arms slightly behind my body while my hands gripped the handles. He also showed me how to load the wheelbarrows carefully to equalize the loads of brick or block on each side. The handles are not to be raised more than is needed to clear the ground, the arms and back are to be kept straight, and short steps should be taken.

The next day "Goldstein the Iron Man" came to the job. He had no first name or other identification that I ever knew about. He was just like "Johnny from Brooklyn," another one of those men who were given names that sounded like run-on sentences. I'll tell more of that relative and father of eighteen later.

On the day Goldstein the Iron Man came on the job, you could hear the sighs of relief, for I had been sent to the telephone for several days to call him. We were getting to the point where we needed the steel lintels (the supports which span over the windows and doors). Without them the brickwork could not continue. We also needed the columns that would support the steel frame for the floors above.

I still don't know whether Goldstein the Iron Man could read, but he knew figures. There never was anything but a handshake between him and my father. This was not all that unusual an arrangement in those days, as well as a tribute, I think, to the simple honesty among immigrants which easily replaced the need for formal education and formalities. At the end of the job, Goldstein the Iron Man would tell my father how much was owed him, and I never heard my father question it. How my father himself had estimated the cost of these items, I don't know. But these brother immigrants from different parts of the world solved their problems together.

After Zi Giuan pointed out the openings needing steel, Goldstein the Iron Man made a few cryptic notes—most were in his head—studied the concrete mats requiring columns, and then jumped aboard his truck. I jumped on, too. I was not going to let this man out of my sight.

Actually, to call that vehicle a truck was a distortion. The "flat" body sloped downward from front to back, riding just above the solid rubber wheels, and the bed wrapped over the end like the U-shaped handle of a cane desperately reaching for the ground.

His shop was in a red brick building, which still survives, one block west of Webster Avenue, immediately north of where the Cross-Bronx Expressway leads to the George Washington Bridge. There was no Cross-Bronx Expressway in those days, though.

The shop was awfully quiet. Where were Goldstein the Iron Man's men? He unlocked the pair of large swinging doors to expose a dirt courtyard that served as a driveway, loading platform, and storage area for much of what looked like discarded pieces of cut-off junk steel—all of it rusty. The left side of this courtyard contained an open shed which ran the depth of the whole lot, with the roof resting on the lot-line wall. The only decent-looking lengths of angle irons and channels were piled on the shed floor.

What I saw depressed me. Nothing was ready for our job; surely Zi Giuan's men would get stuck. I did not need to be told that Goldstein the Iron Man had no men of his own. And there was no crane. I didn't expect to see a fancy one like I had seen in the movies, but at least something that ran on a rail to lift the steel onto that so-called truck.

But I hadn't yet reckoned with Goldstein the Iron Man's survival instinct and his desire—that one ingredient that can also be called willingness. I have come to know that willingness gives birth to perseverance and far outranks education in getting things done in this world. Even intelligence pales in comparison to willingness.

Goldstein the Iron Man was physically equipped for what he

had to do; he was six feet two inches tall, with the frame of a blacksmith, which in reality he also was, as I was to see in short order.

The first thing he dragged from under the shed was a simple A-frame of pipe which grudgingly rolled on two steel wheels. From the top hung a thick mariner's tie rope, which I was later to discover was what prevented this homemade crane from falling over. When he had tied the rope over an overhead rail, his makeshift crane was ready. A winch wound a cable that he used to drag shapes of steel over to himself. This dilapidated truck was alongside, and the fury of one-man action began. I stayed out of his way.

First, Goldstein the Iron Man pulled over long steel channels, which looked like a toboggan with short, straight sides. In erection these channels lie on one of their sides, not flat on their back. With a quick glance at his scribbled dimensions, he started burning off the different measured lengths needed, always in pairs. The flame of the acetylene torch was blue-hot, and he sliced through the steel as if it were mashed potatoes. I had originally thought some kind of huge blade cut the steel.

Lintels are comprised of three, four, or more steel sections assembled with bolts, depending on the thickness of the walls to be supported. Each lintel has a simple angle iron attached to the front, which is where the face brick course will lie as it crosses over the openings.

Goldstein the Iron Man knew exactly what he was doing. To assemble the sections, he burned bolt holes through them and used short, already-prepared pipe sleeves that would both accept the bolts and keep the sections separated. I wondered how he was going to attach the angle iron so that the masons could have some latitude in moving the lintels up or down in line with the brick courses. Easily! He drilled the bolt holes as vertical slots rather than round holes. The bolts could then be tightened after the angles lay on the brick below. In no time at all he was assembling his babies, flying like a whirlwind.

"Load the plates," he said and pointed to a pile of rectangular steel plates about a quarter inch thick. These plates, which do not rest directly on the masonry, would be set in mortar to distribute the load over the width and breadth of the wall below. I threw about thirty onto his truck.

He started loading the now-assembled sections, some weighing as much as two hundred pounds. I realized again how much Goldstein the Iron Man knew his business. At the end of each section he had burned an extra hole. He then inserted the clevis hook at the end of the cable of his homemade derrick through these holes so he could easily drag the sections onto his truck.

In less than two hours since we had left the job site, Goldstein the Iron Man had fabricated enough steel to keep us going for a week! In another half hour we were back on the job. What better scene could have greeted me than to see Joe McGinness and my father awaiting us!

What a perfect setup! I had returned a hero in my mind. They already knew I had not allowed Goldstein the Iron Man to get out of my sight. That was initiative, and my reward was much, enough to let me remember fifty-five years later. From my father I got a smile of approbation, a scarce commodity, especially in front of the men. From Mr. McGinness, I received even better. He said, "Your father is proud of you." I thought life was perfect!

Sometime the following week, Nonno beckoned me in that uniquely Italian gesture, the motion of which looks like a hand scratching the back of a dog's neck. This gesture is done by shaking the right hand, palm down, in exaggerated, jagged motions, containing all movement in the fingers and forearm. I responded by jumping up on the wooden-horse scaffold. He then handed me a brand-new Ditson trowel, a nine incher, and motioned me to lay brick. There was no preamble and no instruction; I was to just go to it.

I had observed more than I thought. I went through the showy maneuver of turning the blade over and furrowing the mortar, point down, then concentrating it in the center of the pan. I did this to loosen my nerves as well as my wrist, for I was aware that everyone was watching me, and I hadn't even laid a brick yet! I dug my trowel in with my right hand as I picked up a brick with my left. The mortar I put on the brick was excessive, poorly distributed, and ended up mostly on my shoes. (I would soon learn to caress and flatten the mortar with the edge first and not dig in with the point.)

Fortunately, Nonno had selected the right kind of wall, a wide one, for me to begin. Brick are laid in wythes, that is, thicknesses of one, two, three, or four bricks. Since a brick is nominally four inches wide, walls became known as four-inch, eight-inch, twelve-inch, and sixteen-inch. Nonno had wisely chosen a sixteen incher for me. Only two sides of a wall are ever exposed to view. In a sixteen-inch wall, however, two wythes are buried in the middle, and since these wythes will never be seen, a bricklayer can take considerable liberty with how he lays these hidden brick. Brick-layers practically throw these brick into the wall and then slush them over with mortar so that all the sins are hidden. These thick walls became my favorite that day and have remained so, though they are rarely built today.

I started filling in the two wythes in the middle. Others had already laid the two courses defining the outsides of the wall. My job wasn't too difficult, especially since the "fill" was dry. The brick that are laid in the middle are placed diagonally in a herringbone shape, but little attention is given to consistent spacing between them. I noticed the men picked up at least four brick at each bending for this fill. Then we "slushed up" by filling the spaces with mounds of mortar. The next step is to roll the trowel across the herringbone. But before we did this, we cleaned our shoes and scaffolds of previously dropped mortar and put this excess on the inside brick, thereby hiding more sins.

I saw Uncle Johnny looking over at me and then at his father. He reached down into his bag and came toward me while his father's back was turned. He handed me an old, beat-up trowel with rounded edges and point. It was only about six inches long and felt so much better than the nine-inch "shovel" Nonno had given me. My young wrist could handle this smaller trowel, and not as much mortar ended up on my shoes as a result.

I was to enjoy Uncle Johnny's kindness for over fifty years. He was a simple man who found success within himself. He was a hard and pleasant worker who paradoxically loved to fight with his "dukes." More than once I saw him use that clean left hook to the gut. He settled arguments quickly, though no ill will ever lingered. Frequently his opponents, often men from other trades, became his lunchmates atop a pile of bricks. If the whole world were full of people like Uncle Johnny, I think it would be a better place. He exited this world the way he lived—without fanfare. His two bricklayer sons, my cousins Sonny and Jamesie, had preceded him.

I lay my first brick on the next exposed course and immediately made a mistake. I broke bond, that is, I failed to start my brick over the middle of the brick below. That meant that one of the men working on either side of me would end up with an extra piece of brick on one of the exposed wall sides, an error which defeats the purpose of laying out the walls so that pieces end up only at the end and against window jambs.

Vinny Lombardi, a *comparillo*, and Curly DeRoberts on the other side, tried to cover up for me by quickly sliding my brick to proper bond. Too late! Nonno turned and saw immediately. He walked over, beckoned me to hand him the trowel, reached for my right hand, turned it over, and silently cracked the edge of the trowel right into the middle knuckle. The skin split and turned purple against the white bone. In all my life I have never felt pain like that. My arm went limp; I didn't know how to separate it from me. So great was the pain that momentarily even my humiliation before the men took second fiddle.

Nonno did not have to say aloud, "That's lesson number one; come back in two generations, and I will have time to teach you lesson number two using more 'progressive' educational methods."

This lesson in the learning process was to be almost duplicated a few weeks later. My cousin Sonny (Maurice for Maurizio) and I were in a race on the same wall. Sonny was a year older and no longer had to get off the wall to do laborers' chores like me. There always was a lot of competition between us, but already he had been on the wall a year, so there was no way I could keep up with him. I tried to make up the difference by flinging in brick and mortar mixed with wind and fury, with little attention to care, and the result was a mess.

Suddenly, a cry rang out: '*Sporcaccionne!*'

A *porca* is a pig; add *cionne* and you've got a big pig, and place an s in front and you've got the biggest pig in town! Nonno was right. There was mortar all over my shoes, the planks, and the wall. As Nonno reached for my brick hand, I deflected his trowel with my own. There was no way I was going to have a repeat of lesson one. In the process, his trowel sliced into the fatty part of my hand. I remember the neat strip of blood was a rather attractive shade of red.

'*Farmi vedere*' (Let me see), he demanded. I let him examine my hand as I detected a note of regret in his voice. Then he said, '*Va pisciare copp' e mani.*'

I often heard this strictly dialectical command, "Go piss on your hands." The disinfectant qualities of urine were highly recommended and, to my observation, quite effective in preventing infection. Where were you going to get iodine or Mercurochrome in Afragola or Arabia?

The hands of masons are not only tough and calloused, but the skin's constant exposure to the mortar, lime, and brick dust give the epidermis a shiny, impervious surface, almost distinct from the flesh below. When boys first begin mason work, the drying effects of the first few months of exposure result in constant peeling, itching, and painful cracking of the skin on the hands. Some are more seriously affected by an allergic infection. The standard cure is to urinate on these sores, and eventually they heal. The dry skin and callouses are a minor purgatory through which neophyte bricklayers must pass. You see, the wearing of gloves was disdainfully avoided—a good bricklayer just didn't do it. Actually, brick cannot be laid expertly with gloves. Later, when out-of-towners displayed gloves, these workers immediately became suspect to the foremen.

This might be a good time to debunk some old wives' tales about how many brick a day the old-timers used to lay. I have heard many uninformed experts venture opinions, especially about the reasons why. It was always blamed on the bricklayers' unions and the daily quotas they supposedly dictated. But this is not so! Never did I see or hear any such direction from a union delegate or anyone else.

Now, it is true that over the past fifty years daily bricklaying production has diminished dramatically, from the three or four thousand the "experts" talked about to six hundred or so today. What really changed, though, were the conditions under which brick were laid, especially the types of walls. Earlier I talked about the thicknesses, or wythes, of brick walls. Today we have mostly "skin" jobs, consisting of only one wythe of brick (nominally four inches) as a wearing surface. The "skin" is exposed to view and accordingly needs to be carefully laid and finished, then pointed up and brushed down, for it is forever thereafter subject to critical review. The thick, "wall-bearing" jobs, like the first wall I worked on, where a great percentage of the brick laid requires little attention to precision of placement, are scarcely built these days. This is the main reason for the dramatic reduction in production. Moreover, as previously noted, the number of hours worked per day has diminished through the years, from nine or more to today's six. Another consideration is the great increase in the number of openings now built into modern buildings for light, air, or specialized equipment. Each opening, with two jambs, a sill, and a steel head, requires several interruptions in the planning and detail process of bricklaying. The faster process of just "throwin' 'em in" is simply not possible. Lastly, of course, is the actual deterioration of the work ethic, a fact of modern life not exclusive to the bricklaying trade.

Chapter II

Corner-Man

It was the summer of 1939, and I was eighteen years old. The war in Europe had not yet started. Little did we know that in a few short months the world would be engulfed in a horror heretofore without equal.

We were in Allentown, Pennsylvania, building semi-attached houses—all solid brickwork. My father and Uncle Joe were partners on a job for M. Shapiro and Sons Construction Company, builders in New York. I was on vacation from my first year's studies in civil engineering at New York University, and I felt inadequate. Suddenly, I was expected to be more knowledgeable than the hundreds of artisans working on the job. But I knew I wasn't. In engineering, I had hardly scratched the surface, and when I jumped in as a bricklayer I was still a boot, and I never became anything more. Brickwork is an art form, and to be an expert you have to do what is necessary to become good in anything—work hard and practice. Occasional summer forays in bricklaying would never make me a bricklayer.

It is no wonder that there is a camaraderie of pride among bricklayers and other tradesmen, too. I am talking about real bricklayers, not some of those you see today who slap up cinder blocks in a house cellar. Brick must be laid to a level line, the walls must be brought up truly vertical, and the cross joints should be the same size, just as bed joints should be. The mortar should be spread cleanly between the bricks, not just smeared over the surface. The joints should be filled with mortar across the whole depth, not just with a layer that is visible on the surface. The horizontal bond must be consistent, with the vertical joints breaking at the same point over the brick below.

The corner-men, especially, have to bring up their corners with a certain number of courses within the prescribed heights. The critical heights, as you proceed, are sill-high, window-high, and story-high. Each corner has to be the same as the other corner men's. Once the foreman has marked these three heights, the corner men are on their own. When a line is strung from corner to corner, the less expert bricklayers lay the brick between the corners. Their concerns are still many, but they are reduced in number.

The wall also has thickness, so that backing up is required. Other brick, block, or both, have to be tied in, or bonded, to the front ones. This is where the boots come in. Our work is usually not exposed to view.

Horizontal bonding with the backup is accomplished in several ways. The ancient way, which uses headers, is still the most common. A header is a brick whose long axis is turned into the wall, resulting in what appears to be a half brick. Depending on the facing bond being used and the height of the brick being used, these headers recur in unvarying series of courses, including the use of fake headers (half bricks). Frequently different kinds of metal ties are used to bond the backup to the front.

The bond of the walls are many and can be intricate. A running bond or straight bond is just a series of stretchers with no headers appearing. This is sometimes called an American bond because Americans have developed the simple veneer, or skin, type of construction, where the structure is supported by a means other than masonry, and a veneer is simply applied as an exterior wearing surface.

But other bonds, such as the English, Flemish, double Flemish, Roman, and garden bonds, are more interesting. John Mulligan, in his comprehensive book, *Brickwork*, cites over twenty bonds. (I later came to know John, a delightful man, when for years we sat together on union labor negotiations.) These bonds are combinations of stretchers, headers, soldiers, rowlocks, and chinks (pieces), which, when properly laid, create a repetitive design in the wall. My father had a penchant for the diamond bond, a variation of the double Flemish (two stretchers and a header).

If you stand in the street you can see the subtle but obvious diamond pattern repeating itself, both horizontally and vertically. Step back sometime and look for these designs, especially in older buildings.

Naturally, these more intricate bonds are more expensive to build than simpler bonds. When I was a young boy, I asked my father whether the diamond bond had been specified on a certain job. We were on Southern Boulevard (near Arthur Avenue) in the Bronx, where he was building a new home for Judge Delaghi, whose first name I cannot remember. My father's simple answer was, "No! It looks nicer." Neither he nor I had ever heard of aesthetics, but I was proud of him for the selection he made for the judge. Truly, man does not live by bread alone. I always look at that building when I go to Little Italy.

But let's get back to Allentown, for some important events happened there. For one, I came to know Gaetano Vallese and Tommy Napoli. These two men became like fathers to me after my father died, and I loved them. I had met them both in 1937, when my father, Uncle Joe, and Uncle Dominick were doing the masonry work for a large housing project known as Garden Bay Manor, which covered many acres near La Guardia Airport. The builders were Norman K. Winston and Arde Bulova, whose Bulova Watch Factory was just across Grand Central Parkway from the job. Our country was just rising from the Great Depression, and hundreds were employed by my father, Uncle Joe, and Uncle Dominick. It is simply not possible to make readers understand the desperation for work that obsessed the sleeping and waking moments of my father's and uncles' employees. *La famiglia* was dependent on that one weekly wage. And *la famiglia* included not only your immediate family, but your relatives' families, too.

It was only natural that whole neighborhoods clung together as ethnic entities. It was common interdependence. When a parent, or a *paesano* (from *paese*, meaning town), emigrated from Italy to America, he was drawn by *la calamita* (the magnet) of hopeful security and protection from the expected onslaughts of a perilous life. These people gravitated toward the neighborhoods they knew would receive them, where those they had known had preceded them. The newcomer usually came first alone, to work, scrimp, and save, ultimately sending for his wife and children. My mother's father lived alone for six years in the Throggs Neck section of the Bronx before he had saved enough to send for his wife, my mother, and Uncle Fred. Later, my grandfather had a makeshift barn in a tumble-down, wooden shack behind the tenements on 204th Street in the Bronx. I was lucky to have seen this "barn" before it collapsed. The two horses he kept there provided his livelihood. This former vegetable farmer from Cicciano, which is near Naples, and later coffee farmhand from Brazil was a mild, lovable human being and the person, aside from my parents, who exerted the greatest influence on my philosophy of life. So softly did he influence my ways that I was not aware for over forty years that he had done so. I'll tell more about him later.

Back in Allentown, the day was ripe for brickwork. The air was dry and sunny, and it was not too hot. Uncle Joe was to give me my first lesson in production, and it started with the cornermen. What a crew we had! The *comparillo* system was earning its salt that day. I remember Jimmy Funicello, Vinny Lombardi, Curly DeRoberts, Patsy Dellamonica, my brother-in-law Jimmy Lionelli, his brother Sparky, my cousin Morris (Mauriello), Dizzy Dean (Curly's brother), "Slash" Minieri, George Birmbaum, Dario Quilici, Ettore Pasquini, Carlo Piccin, Guido Dal Pino, Al Dal Pino, Tommy Finnegan and his son, Aniello Lunedi, Tony Lunedi, and their father, Mezzo-Culo (which means half-assed). All of these people were superb bricklayers, and naturally all corner men. The walls would grow that day.

Mezzo-Culo, a spidery bundle of nerves, veins, and muscles, was a legend. He was as dark as a Moor, wore a handlebar mustache, and always had a "guinea stinker" (black cheroot) in his mouth. This bundle of a man didn't weigh more than one hundred pounds, and the only thing that concerned him was sex. He had been recently widowed—but even more recently he had married a young woman fifty years his junior! At lunchtime, he regaled the men with stories of his sexual prowess. His sons, Aniello and Tony, accepted their father's preoccupation with quiet assent. Mezzo-Culo swore that his sex drive was so strong that his young wife had to be ready to receive him as soon as he walked in the house from work! He even claimed he had no time to disrobe or bathe, so urgent was his need! Hi sons nodded in agreement, knowing their father's story to be true, since their father's new bride confirmed his claim to the whole family. I did not permit myself to conjecture how Mezzo-Culo handled his problem when he was working in Allentown, which is almost three hours away from the Bronx!

There were many other masons on the job In Allentown besides these corner men, as well as all the *manuali* and *scaffaioli* who tended them. You will come to know them.

By this time, Guy (Gaetano) Vallese, who was now the head labor foreman, had prepared every minute detail necessary to coordinate the laying of brick. The scaffolds around the outside and inside of the buildings had been erected the night before. The brick, stacked in neat piles, and the metal mortar pans were placed within easy reach of the masons, who would be spaced around the perimeter of the buildings. The mortar had been mixed an hour before the bricklayers' 8:00 A.M. starting time. The mortar was delivered by wheelbarrows up the plank ramps to the floors and then passed by shovels into the mortar pans. Eagle-eye Gaetano had already located the copper-clad flashings, which would be unfurled beneath the window sills and over the heads of the windows, as well as the cast stone sills. Also needed to avoid delay were window frames, door frames, louvers, built-in brackets, and the carpenters to install them.

Guy would take no chances; no delay could be tolerated, and he knew the jockeying would begin early. The carpenter contractor would delay sending his men in time to set the window frames atop the sills, and the iron contractor would send his load of steel lintels to the site with just the driver and no help. Thus, if we wanted to avoid delays, we would have to unload the truck ourselves. We would also have to sort out the different sizes and shapes of steel lintels and set them as well as the windows.

By 8:30 A.M., the brick were flying. In self-defense, Guy's men became the steel men, the carpenters, the waterproofers, and the masontenders. When I protested the unfairness of it all to Guy, his response was, *'Così è fatto il mondo'* (That is the way the world is made).

How secure these old-timers were in being able to cull out only those things in life which are really worthy of distress!

Guy called up to Uncle Joe, who was overseeing the progress on four different buildings and said, *'Sono pronto'* (They are ready), referring to the three corners ready for masons.

I could see the other walls were getting close to topping out scaffold-high. Where would he put the men? I ran up to the floor in question. "Why aren't you moving the corner men?" I asked Uncle Joe.

"Because I'm putting them in a hole," he said. "When they go too early, they drag it out. You just watch them shake their asses when I send them. Besides, the other building is running behind. They have to be able to compare with this crew. Competition, *figlio mio* (my son)," Uncle Joe said, assuming an Italianate posture.

American born and only twelve years older than I, he was never as interested in things Italian as I increasingly became. I saw this in my father, too. For several years, and thankfully only temporarily, I too almost succumbed to the siren call of Americanism.

This Americanization was not uncommon, though. The younger children of immigrants were driven to become American in their manners, speech, and dress, even to the extent that they often tried to reject *la famiglia's* way of life. Their behavior certainly was understandable, you will agree. From their vantage point, what did these children see? They saw their people maligned as "guineas" and "dagos," living in near penury and struggling constantly to overcome the onslaughts of an alien society, with little apparent success. Here's what Italian children, as well as their parents, often heard:

Guinea! Guinea! Guinea, guinea, goo,
Shine my shoes!
Fifteen cents for yellow, yellow shoes!
Dago! Dago!
Arrived a day ago.

Another sobriquet reserved for Italians besides guinea and dago was "wop." The original meaning of the word was not malicious, though. It stood for "without official papers" and was an acronym used by U.S. immigration officers at Ellis Island and other ports of entry. But the WOP abbreviation soon turned into another derisive blow reserved exclusively for the Italians, even though many other poor immigrants entered "without official papers."

What did these children not see? They did not see the desperation and *la miseria* (poverty) of the "old country" that had forced their parents to come here. They did not see the circumstances that forced *la famiglia* to start at the very lowest rung of the ladder. But most of all, they did not see the strength of character which centuries of oppression and deprivation had forged, a fortitude which afforded *la famiglia* the patient strength to rise from the ashes. Thus, many Italian children rejected their heritage.

Happily, the opposite happened to me. I was now of the third generation in America, and more secure. I too railed at the calumnies directed at my people (and still do), but I was far enough away from fear to start observing the beauty and strength of my forefathers in addition to the utter sincerity and philosophical simplicity with which they conducted their daily lives. Fortunately for me there was no need for conflict. I love my marvelous United States of America, and I love my Italian heritage.

I looked up and saw Uncle Joe finally shifting the corner men. He picked out Jim Lionelli, my brother-in-law, Vinny Lombardi, and Jimmy Funicello, three of the best. They were all "pick and dippers." When you saw a pick and dipper, you knew you were looking at a real bricklayer.

Most masons, and good ones, too, lay brick by spreading the mortar for the next course in a long, furrowed bed joint, sufficient for six, seven, or even eight brick. As the mason lays the brick to the line, his only concern is the cross joint between the brick, the mortar for which becomes available after compressing the brick with hand pressure. This method appears logical and easy, and it is most appealing to any beginner, as well as to many practiced masons. But this is not so.

The more expert pick and dipper picks up, at each bending, one brick and the exact amount of mortar needed for one brick only. In one deft movement, the trowel hand deposits the mortar; the same hand in a continuous and opposite motion swipes the bed-joint mortar flush with the brick course below, butters the cross joint against the previously laid brick with the same mortar on his trowel, and the free hand then presses the brick to the line, thus completing the process. A pick and dipper is poetry in motion. The wall is clean, the joints are neat, and there is no cacophony of banging trowels.

The better bricklayers always had clean shoes. Before one started, he cleaned off the scaffold planks of accumulated mortar, brick chips, and the straw that separated the bricks. For the day, the spot where that mason worked was his home, and he was going to keep it clean. The men also knew that untidiness led to accidents. Twisted feet and legs and banged heads were not only painful, but led to lost time. The bricklayers respected their bodies because they were the source of *la famiglia's* livelihood. Today you see phony construction workers shod in sneakers or what look like dancing slippers; such is their lack of respect for their own well-being. The compelling need to remain healthy is gone, sadly.

The three Jims (for some reason Vincenzo is commonly but mistakenly translated to Jimmy) were now in place. Each had the superior air of an artisan who relishes his expertise and the confidence that comes with it. I jumped up on a scaffold to watch these expert pick and dippers put on their show. Each was aware there was not much time—the gang would be down upon them in short order. Uncle Joe had really "put them in a hole."

I saw each of them check the coursing rod that Tommy Napoli, the bricklayers' foreman, had nailed at the corners. A good bricklayer will not take for granted that the foreman is without error. So many courses at so many inches per course to sill-high, so many more courses to window-high, and so many more to story-high could easily be miscalculated. Errors led to unequal sizes in joints, which were unsightly, or worse, to walls that were not level. Miscalculations could also lead to a disastrous "hog" in the wall, which I will explain.

In all of brickwork, there is no sin more cardinal than putting a "hog" in the wall. This occurs when one corner is laid up with, say, twenty courses of brick within a prescribed height, and the other corner has nineteen or twenty-one within the same height. The error does not become apparent in the first six or eight courses because the differential on each is not that pronounced. But the difference multiplies with each number of courses laid, and at a certain point the line is no longer level. The joints get fatter and fatter, or thinner and thinner, depending on which corner is nearer. Ultimately, if allowed to continue, there is no course left to raise the line to. As workers proceed from each end toward the middle, one side will come to a dead end with no vertical room to fit the brick.

To the contractor, this imbalance means having to demolish the wall. The attendant loss of money is considerable. The embarrassment is worse for the corner man, the crew, and the company. "Hog in the wall!" The "oink-oink" remarks go on for days, and bottles of pigs' feet appear overnight at the masons' shanties. Expressions of gleeful regrets are made known from other jobs all over town. The plumbers and iron men, especially, are unmerciful. I think this is because they are frequently of Irish persuasion, an ethnic group that took the brunt of derision before the Italians came on the scene. Since we were now the "low men on the totem pole," they made fun of us.

Jim, Vinny (James), and Jimmy were not going to let a "hog" in the wall happen. They affirmed the coursing in their heads. Four courses at 11 inches for standard-sized brick are easier to "feel" than one course at 2 3/4 inches, and four courses at 13 inches for jumbo-sized brick are easier to "feel" than one course of 3 1/4 inches.

There are two main ways to erect a corner. One way is to run out the two legs of the corner in decreasing lengths so that in profile two Mexican-type pyramids at right angles to each other are erected; the corner looks like two stairways. This pyramid method requires a lot of brick, and naturally more time. The other, faster way is to tooth out the wall, concentrating on height rather than width. This means introducing temporary supports for the toothing, because often the corner man has not yet laid the stairway which would support the brick above. All three opted for the latter; they had no choice since they were "in a hole."

I couldn't tell who was ahead. All three were in a furious race, yet all three were so competent that their graceful pick and dipping did not appear strained. In between header courses, the wall had to be backed up, that is, the inner wall had to be erected and tied in. Bricklayers back up a wall every seven courses on a standard-sized brick job such as this. First one Jim and then the other two flew to the interior scaffold. The pace was intense, and on each face a confident smile belied the pressure.

The contest continued as the interior men were shifted to the now-ready new walls. Mason lines were strung from corner to corner, and the excitement possessed the others. Teams were chosen by the accident of position; now it was a whole team on one wall opposed to the team on the other wall.

The foreman balanced the difference in the lengths of wall by the number of bricklayers in a line. The men were aware of what the foreman was doing and silently calculated whether their team was put at a disadvantage. If so, each had to lay another part of a brick to make up the difference—even more speed would be needed. Thus, the mason lines hummed with the activity.

The raising of a line to the next course is a ritual in itself. Union rules are very strict on this: No line can be raised before all men are "out." This means that every brick in that course must be laid. The two corner men who tie the line are essential players. A desultory player holds up the whole line; conversely, an avid corner man can make money for the boss.

The unfortunate bricklayer laying that last brick is hounded by every other eye in the line. Once the last brick is laid, one corner man rings out, "Yo!" or "Put it up!" to the corner man at the other end. This corner man then raises the line by inserting a nail or pin, which he has knotted to the line, into the top of the next brick course he erected. To prevent the pin from being pulled out of the wall, the corner man wraps the mason line around the corner. Then he yells, "Tie away!" to the first corner man, who then ties the line around his mason pin. After he has secured his pin, he signals completion by crying out some encouragement like, "Lay brick!" or "Fly away!" and the brick-layers lay the next course.

Uncle Joe was on the adjoining building. He had gone through the same movements with that gang. And from there he could observe the two foundation gangs. He smiled over them, sated with pleasure. It did not matter which of the three Jims had won the race; the end had been accomplished. Now he had not only two teams on the same building competing with each other, but he had two buildings competing with each other!

The excitement extended even to the laborers, for now they were part of their team. Sandy Jackson was on one building making certain that every sill, lintel, window frame, waterproofing flashing, and multitudes of other built-ins were ready. Dominick Vitolo was on the other building, doing the same. If the second team was to lose, it would not be because their *manuali* had let them down.

The walls were flying up and the other tradesmen marveled at this frenzy of *pazzi* (crazies) from New York—via Napoli. Uncle Louis, another of my father's brothers, was Tommy Napoli's counterpart as bricklayer foreman on the second team, but after the day's work ended, it was Tommy Napoli, by presence and experience, who was head man.

It was near noon, and the day was an assured success. Uncle Joe called down to Tommy, who was on the floor and said, "After lunch take that local guy off the twiggen."

I failed to tell you about the "twiggen." Just like a tennis net sags in the middle, so does the mason line. If the wall is long enough, there is a considerable sag. In order to overcome this, an intermediate means of support is needed. This is inaccurately called a "twiggen," a "triggen," and a few other things. Its original and proper name is twig. This name probably derived from the twigs of straw that for centuries accompanied the making of brick. Straw placed between the bricks prevents them from fusing together after they are removed, still hot, from the kiln.

A twig is folded around the mason line, and then supported on the brick laid by the "triggen" man. The twig is held in place by a temporary second brick. This is important because another strict union rule is that no bricklayer in the line can lay brick before the "triggen" is set. So, you see, there is one more step required after the two corner men raise the line before bricklaying can proceed. This "triggen" man must also lay his brick in course heights which correspond to the corners. When the wall is very long, say sixty feet, more than one "triggen" is needed.

Uncle Joe was telling Tommy to get one of the family or a *comparillo* on that twig. Tommy was a *furbachione* (wise old codger), and he had a purpose. He was giving a sop to the local bricklayers, so as to prevent a division of the men along local and imported lines. Joe agreed that Tommy should wait until the wall was topped out.

Andrea Acierno caught my eye. I told you earlier about that perfectly muscled little man who had been with my father since 1927. He was mixing the mortar for the second team. I approached him as he prepared to eat his lunch before the others. Mortar men always started and stopped before the others.

Andrea was still taking care of me. He said, '*Stasera mangi con noi*' (Tonight you eat with us). By us he meant the *scaffaioli*—the scaffold men and mortar men. Each group of *operai* (workers) tended to gravitate together. In this case, the *scaffaioli* had rented a whole house. Though virtually devoid of furnishings, it contained the three essentials: beds, a kitchen, and a bathroom. From Monday night through Friday morning, the *scaffaioli* lived together and did their own cooking and cleaning. Their wants were few.

On Friday afternoons, as soon as work was over, with a short stop at the house and a few ablutions sufficient to keep them until a proper bath at home, they piled into their cars and flew off to the Bronx. Their dirty laundry went with them. By 7:00 P.M., they were in the bosom of their families in their neighborhood enclaves. On Mondays, they started back to Allentown at 4:00 A.M., arrived at the job site by 7:00 A.M., and were completely ready for their mason by the 8:00 A.M. starting time. No part of Sunday was to be sacrificed away from *la famiglia* just to sleep in Allentown.

The *manuali* and *scaffaioli* were usually about half a generation older than most masons. This was not the only factor separating the groups. The bricklayers earned more money, were usually better educated, and were inclined to speak English. Most of the *comparilli* belonged in this latter group. Because the *comparilli* made more money, they did not eat as well. Andrea's invitation to me was in consideration that I was being forced to eat too much restaurant food, which by definition *ti fa male* (does you harm). Because my nightly duties included taking care of weekly payrolls, as well as keeping records of bills and inventories of ordered materials, I needed working space. A small-town hotel room provided the necessary facilities. This tended to separate me from the men in the evenings, but tonight I was going to get a proper meal.

Before I went to the house the *scaffaioli* had rented, I knew I would find certain foods: *una zuppa di minestra*, a soup essentially made of greens, mostly cabbage, with a prosciutto bone to lend flavor (my African-American friends would know this dish as collard greens and ham hock); a huge dish of oversized pasta made with bottled tomato sauce imported from the Bronx and scented with fresh basil and *pecorino romano* (sheep's milk cheese); and a delicious mixed salad containing home-grown tomatoes, arugula, escarole, and several kinds of lettuce and onions. The dressing would be pure olive oil and vinegar from Andrea's own wines. The essential accoutrements would be gallons of these same wines and huge round loaves of bread, again all transported from home. Dessert would be fresh fruit and possibly a piece of provolone cheese. In addition, dried figs and roasted nuts (almonds and filberts) would be available all evening.

The coffee served would be the Italian black, double-roasted bean, freshly ground each night and morning and made in a *maginetta*. A *maginetta* is a filter-type, tiny pot, similar in principle to a percolator, but it doesn't give coffee a parboiled taste. I loved the coffee grinder. It was a small box made of wood, with an outsized round wheel that had a tiny barbell handle attached to rotate the wheel. The ground coffee fell into a pull-out drawer below. The aroma was better than chocolate.

Dinner was early. Quitting time was usually 4:30 P.M. The *zuppa* had stewed for two hours in the morning. After a quick shower, the assigned chefs for that evening had the food on the table by 5:30 P.M. At home, the wives would have caught hell if dinner was not ready and waiting at 5:00 P.M.!

Before starting for the job in the morning, each man made his own lunch. This was a large and important part of the day—both the preparation and the eating. Aside from the community provisions for break-fast and dinner, each man transported his *cibo* (food) for his daily *colazione*. I told you about "o lunch" before.

Today, I had not only an invitation from Andrea for dinner, but he had insisted earlier that I share part of his lunch. Prices are far different today, but when I was young I was sent out for bread hundreds of times. The brick oven was in the basement of "la shoemaker's" tenement house across the street. So I have a clear recollection of prices, which were stable for many years, say from 1928 through 1941. The *paniellos* (round loaves) came in three sizes, and they still do. The small loaves cost a nickel and were as big around as a soup dish. The ten-cent size was as large around as a good-sized dinner plate, and the twenty-five-cent size was as large around as a basketball hoop. The height was in proportion. The huge one costs three dollars today, more than ten times as much as it used to. Twenty-five cents is not so much when you consider a subway ride used to cost a nickel!

Andrea had made his lunch on the "biggie." These *paniellos* were so large and crusty that housewives would have to nestle the loaves against their bosoms in order to slice them. Before slicing machines came along, an artist could paint a picture which would be universal among my people. It would show a housewife with a loaf nestled in her bosom and a huge bladed knife pointed toward her. In Andrea's case, the loaf had been sliced clean through the platter middle. It did not seem possible that one man alone could consume that huge delight, but I saw it done every day.

Today was a banner day, for Andrea still had leftovers from his wife's weekend magic. When I sank my teeth into my massive share, I tasted veal cutlets, sautéed broccoli, and *insalata mista* (mixed salad greens). Together with a bottle of Andrea's home-made wine, my lunch was fit for a king. Actually, there were very few kings who would eat as well that day!

I first met Andrea when I was a boy of about nine. That was around 1930. It was in Orchard Beach in the Bronx, which at that time was a summer colony of double canvas-topped bunga-lows. This community of about nine hundred temporary homes, all similar in size and design, existed on city-owned land. It was only seven miles from Bedford Park, where we lived and where my parents had grown up.

For each summer of my early youth, we actually moved to Orchard Beach. The open-to-the-sky bungalows survived the winters because the wooden floors were laid with open joints. The rain and snow simply melted through the spaces to the sandy soil below. The reinstallation of the two huge canvasses each spring was the hardest part of the new season's prepara-tions, but my father's *operai* made the job easy.

Orchard Beach was a politically plumb community—Demo-cratic party members only need apply. I do not recall exactly when my father moved into politics, but I do know that in 1921 he was still a bricklayer when I was born on the kitchen table in Bedford Park. But by 1930, I remember seeing him in a newspa-per photograph at a dinner in his honor with the Democratic biggies Ed Flynn, Congressman Charles Buckley, Judge Delaghi, Tom Fitzpatrick, and others. I tell you this because I never actu-ally saw my father lay brick, though I was told he was a pick and dipper, and one of the best.

Most of the tenants of Orchard Beach were policemen, fire-men, and Bronx municipal employees—all Democrats. Mayor Fiorello Henry La Guardia and his Parks Commissioner, Robert Moses, however, put an end to our idyllic summers when La Guardia was elected. The destruction of Orchard Beach was priority one. I have no recollection of those summers continuing after I was about thirteen years old.

Back to Andrea. Nearer to the water from my family's bunga-low was the LaRocca family's bungalow. Apparently, the LaRoc-cas wanted new sidewalks around their home, and they asked my father to build them as a favor.

In the morning *gli operai* (the workers) arrived. There was Zio Antonio o'Lungo (Uncle Stretch), Zi Giuan, Zio Antonio o'Lofaro, Andrea Acierno, Caggy (Achille) Mosca, Ralph Mosca (o'Lungo's son), and two burly men whose names I do not remember.

Zio Antonio o'Lofaro (dialect for the Loud One) and his wife had eighteen children, and they all lived on Villa Avenue behind Saint Philip Neri Church. Later o'Lofaro would buy a farm outside of Bound Brook, New Jersey. Such a move meant separating from the *paese* life style, but there was no other way to solve the problem of survival. O'Lofaro was a Mosca, an uncle to my brother-in-law-to-be, and all came originally from Afragola, where my own father was born. Two days later, after the concrete was mixed for the LaRocca's sidewalk, I saw o'Lofaro collecting the discarded linen cement sacks, which were stiff with hardened cement. I will tell you why later.

The first job was to demolish the existing cracked sidewalks. This looked like a monstrous task to me as a boy, for in those days there were no jackhammers, and the sidewalks went around two sides of the long bungalow as well as the front. Now I would see Andrea at work.

Two tools were elementary: a sixteen-pound sledge hammer and muscle. Andrea started on the rear of the house. The pounding thuds became incessant—when did this man stop? After a while the concrete began to surrender its integrity to the relentless poundings. Not only were broken chunks strewn about, but telltale cracks farther up the sidewalk preceded the actual blows. Andrea was on top of his project and getting more and more out in front. There was no holding him back now. What had appeared to my young eyes as a two-week project would be over in a day. No wonder Zi Antonio o'Lungo hadn't given him any help. The joy evident on Andrea's face was as irrepressible as the sweat coming through his rolling biceps.

Only two years later I would learn a similar lesson which would reinforce the first; it is one I will never forget, and I want to share it with you now. I was coming home from school, Public School 56 on 207th Street and Decatur Avenue, and I knew my father was building a home for a man named Shainess, not far from Nonno's house on Reservoir Oval. The jobs were always a magnet for me, and I would not miss the opportunity to pass by, especially if I could show off in front of a few chums.

Shainess's Clothing Store was on Fordham Road near Rogers Department Store, the pride of the Bronx, and across from the Corn Exchange Bank, my father's business bank. Shainess's was the foremost men's store in the entire borough, and this Jewish man was the confidant as well as custom tailor to all the Bronx judges, businessmen, and *politicos*.

Permit me to digress. It is sickening to go there today and see the deterioration and devastation caused by Rent Control, which destroyed first the thousands of well-built apartments, then the moral fiber of the community as whole groups of ethnic peoples were forced to abandon their churches, synagogues, and specialty food stores. While the sinks and plumbing were being ripped out, the drugs moved in.

The anarchy which now reigns is the result of "so-called" social justice. The politicians could count then (Rent Control was "temporary" they said over forty-five years ago.) You see, there are more tenants than owners, hundreds more for each one. Thus, to give a few dollars more to the landlord to keep up his property and maybe put flowers in the lobby on Friday nights was unconscionable. "Society must be protected against the landlord, who is always rich, always greedy, always thieving," Rent Control agents said.

Well, politicians can still count votes today. So Rent Control goes on, destroying up to fifty thousand housing units every year. But the mischief done to human dignity is incalculable. Society pays, but society is not real people, they tell us. Instead, it's a sort of shadowy magma, which, like quicksilver, is very difficult to get a handle on. Did you ever see Rent Control and those thousands of administrative people build even one apartment?

But let's get back to the Bronx and Shainess's house. By this time the first floor was on, and when I peeked into the basement I saw something which amazed me. Someone had left two large boulders, as big as small cars, in the cellar. How? Why?

I spoke to Caggy (Achille), and he very casually answered, "We'll get them out." I could not see how, but I got my answer several weeks later.

Again, on an after-school visit to the job, there was activity in the cellar. The two huge boulders were remnants of the terminal moraine, the debris left behind when the glaciers of the Ice Age began to melt. On the job, and universally in the construction industry, these huge, rounded boulders, some as big as houses, were known by the unsavory title "niggerheads."

I think it good to be confronted by some of the ugly, shocking things people say about or do to people. To see the words in print helps us all to realize that insensitivity to fellow humans must cease. We are all guilty, to a lesser or greater degree, but being guilty only to a lesser degree still does not absolve one of guilt.

The boulders were ringed by sawn tree trunks which had been soaked with heavy transmission oil. The wood had already been lighted and was burning slowly. The logs had been added for about three days, until the stones were red hot. I made sure I was present for stage two. Zi Antonio o'Lungo assured me he would wait for me: '*Ti faccio vedere come si fa*' (I will show you how it's done).

Fifty-five gallon drums, filled with water, were already placed around the cellar and a half-dozen five-gallon buckets stood by. The fires had already been stoked with quick-burning lumber to add a last burst of heat.

Someone yelled, '*Comincia!*' (Start!)

Together, five men flung whole buckets of water on top of the hot stones. Immediately, spalling occurred on the surface, but that was not what was really wanted. It took a good ten minutes before a muffled grunt emanated from the bowels of the boulders: the cleavage was done.

Next, the men wedged long crowbars into the cracks, and the stones rolled onto their rounded halves. In the meantime, Zio Antonio o'Lofaro and Andrea started pounding the still-hot stone with those sixteen-pound sledge hammers. More chunks flailed off. The fires were then respread around these main halves and kept burning through the night, and the breaking process was repeated the next day. Eventually, all the stone was reduced to excellent fill upon which the new concrete floor would rest. But not before one last interesting process took place.

The men attacked some of the larger pieces that remained in relays. They used three sledge hammers and one heavy-pointed chisel, which was strategically placed at the point of weakness in each stone. This vulnerable spot was obvious to the men, but not to me. It surprised me to see the long chisel was hand-held, a measure of the men's confidence in one another and a source of cringing discomfort to me.

Caggy held the chisel while Andrea, Zio Antonio o'Lofaro, and Zi Antonio o'Lungo ringed around him. Each started in turn with a light tap, then another a littler harder, and then, as they gained confidence in their footing and spacing, they stepped up the pace. Round and round they went, one after the other, rhythmically hitting the head of the chisel with a measured increase in ringing frequency; the men hammered the chisel harder and harder until the mass surrendered and shattered. I saw this rhythmic process repeated on stone walls many times.

Determination, intelligence, and muscle, all God-given gifts, can thus reduce nature to man's will.

Chapter III

Grandpa

Though my mother's father was not a bricklayer, he belongs in this book, and you will soon see why. I wondered as I approached this project why it seemed so difficult to draw a clear picture of this man, for I have already admitted that his influence on me was second only to that of my mother and father.

Some of the words that describe him are retiring, uncomplicated, resigned, and constant. How could such a simple man stand out from the hundreds of the powerful and ambitious doers and the shakers of the political, financial, religious, and builders' worlds I have known? This placid man was not a lecturer or a taskmaster, but I suspect that, had I been trained in the field of education, one thing I would have learned is that we really do learn by example.

Grandpa was not my dear friend for many years, probably not until I was well into adulthood. By this time, the illiterate farmer from Cicciano, which lies near Nola in the shadows of Mount Vesuvius, had learned to read and write English as well as Italian; both self-taught. He was still learning many years later when he proudly displayed a brand-new driver's license issued by the State of New York. This accomplishment, which he openly and gleefully savored, impelled my widowed mother to get her license, too. And when she did so, my wife, Emily, determined to do likewise.

Grandpa was unmarried when he immigrated to Brazil with some of his family. Since they were farmers, they were naturally cut out for the burgeoning coffee plantations that were increasingly being carved out of the Brazilian jungles. Here Grandpa met my grandmother, Rosina Napolitano, whose family surprisingly had emigrated from the same little *paese* in Italy. Since the families did not even know each other, I suspect that some kind of recruiting agent had been at work gathering peasants for rich Brazilian landowners across the sea. My grandparents' status did not improve much in Brazil, though. As my grandfather later told me, his family had worked a *masseria*, (small plot of ground) as tenant farmers when they lived in Cicciano. They did the same in Brazil, only with a different kind of crop.

My grandfather's name was Ruotolo, which loosely means a cubic measure and approximates a peck in English. My grandmother's family name was Napolitano, which is not surprising because Napoli itself is less than fifteen miles from Cicciano, both families' hometowns.

You will forgive me if I digress, because late in life I found out a little more about how my grandparents met. The source of my information is Joseph Napolitano, an eighty-four-year-old man who lives in California. In 1992, he wrote a letter to my dear Uncle Nick. Joseph is a cousin to my Uncle Nick and a nephew to my grandmother, Rosina Ruotolo, whose maiden name was Napolitano.

My mother always said she had been born in Sao Paolo, Brazil. We were pleased to find out that actually she had been born in Rancho San Francisco, a coffee plantation about fifteen miles from Rio Au Prieta, about thirty miles from Sao Paolo.

"In those days said town [Rancho San Francisco] consisted of one store and a few scattered shacks." From Joseph's letter I further quote: "Once my mother got a breast infection so my father went on their horse to Rio Au Prieta. It took all night through the forest, and he returned the next day with word that the doctor would come in two days. He did—Mother almost died from the pains. The world moves on." I wonder what our modern welfare recipients would have to say about those survival conditions?

Now I will get back to my grandparents' livelihood. As I noted, a *masseria* is a plot of ground, one among many, carved out of great estates, tenanted and worked but never owned by a family. Since tenant farmers lived in the towns nearby, each day my grandparents' family went forth to work the land, the *masseria* stone shack offering a storage place for farm tools, a shelter against inclement weather, a home for several goats, and relief from the noonday sun. Grandpa told me that they worked from sunup to sundown, with a siesta at noon, lunch consisting of a piece of bread, some onions or tomatoes, and occasionally some nuggets of cheese. A bottle of homemade wine was always available.

When I questioned how young bodies could survive on this menial fare, Grandpa told me to listen and he would tell me *nu fatto* (a story), which I will pass on to you.

One day a father and three sons started out for *la masseria*, as usual right after sunup. The young boys had already consumed the breakfast piece of bread and the hot "coffee" made from chicory leaves. They had put their hands to work as soon as they had arrived. As the sun rose higher, the boys could think only of the food yet to come.

'*Quando mangiamo, Papà?*' (When do we eat, Papà?)

'*Quando viene il companaggio!*'[3] (When the accompaniment comes!) The boys worked with renewed hope. Their father had implied that today the bread would be accompanied by some delight—salami, perhaps, or sausage. By 11:00 A.M., the boys had toiled half the day.

'*Quando mangiamo, Papà?*' the boys repeated.

'*Quando arriva il companaggio!*'

At noon, the boys asked the same question—and got the same answer. Now they were well into their siesta surcease from the sun. When was *il companaggio* coming, and who was bringing it?

Finally, at 2:00 P.M., the boys writhed and pleaded, '*Papà, non possiamo stare più!*' (We can't stand it any longer!)

'*Allora* (therefore) *è arrivata il companaggio*,' said the father. The boys looked about. No one had come. Where was the accompaniment?

'*Il companaggio è la fama*' (Hunger is the accompaniment), their father explained to them. The boys then devoured the plain bread and onions without further protest.

---

3. *Companaggio* is the Neapolitan equivalent of *accompagnamento*.

I have not studied why immigrants from so many other countries came to the United States and to South America. In the case of the Southern Italians, it was not only hunger, but the hopelessness of ever seeing any improvement. Italy was unified from 1861 to 1870. We know of the unification efforts of Giuseppe Garibaldi, Camillo Benso di Cavour, and Giuseppe Mazzini. Why then did a massive evacuation begin so shortly after Italy was unified? There was good reason. After more than thirteen hundred years of oppression, these souls decided it was hopeless to expect anything would ever change.

Southern Italy, including Sicily, was the scene of continual invasion and subjugation, beginning with the enslavement of tribes and whole communities by the early Romans. After the fall of Rome, the Saracens, beginning in the sixth century, A.D., invaded and pillaged Italy. These invaders were fundamentally Arabs from what are now the Palestinian and Syrian parts of Africa. Their influence is evident today all over Southern Italy in architecture, art, decoration, and everyday life. Many restaurants record this influence, bearing names like Il Saraceno or I Saraceni (plural).

That brilliant British writer, H.V. Morton in his book, *A Traveller in Southern Italy*, details the progression of invaders and oppressors, beginning after the Saracens with the Norman knights in the eleventh century, of whom the d'Hautevilles were the most oppressive. The twelve sons of Tancred (1030), including William, Drogo, Humphrey, Robert Guiscard (the Wise), and Roger (Ruggero) ruled. Their magnificent tombs can be seen in the cathedrals of Monreale and Palermo. At Monreale and La Cappella Palatina (the Palatine Chapel) you will see the incredible mosaics depicting the life of Christ, judged to be even finer than those of Saint Mark's in Venice and those of Ravenna. There is not a square inch of the walls not covered by mosaics. The ceilings are all intricately carved stalactited wood.

The lineage of Norman Kings continued with Roger (son of Roger), then William the Bad, then William the Good (his wife was Joan of England and sister of Richard the Lion-Hearted), and then another Tancred.

When William III, infant son of Tancred, was murdered in 1194, Henry of Hohenstaufen, Holy Roman Emporer and son of

Emperor Barbarossa (Red-beard), took over. The Hohenstaufens ruled until 1266, when an internecine war divided the spoils between two sets of scavengers, the House of Aragon in Sicily and the House of Anjou in Naples.

I will not bore you with minute details. Ten kings of Aragon ruled Sicily until 1410, then Spanish viceroys ruled from Madrid until 1458. Meanwhile, in Naples, the House of Anjou produced eight rulers. These reigned until 1442 when the Spanish defeated the French and Alfonso V created what later was to be the Kingdom of the Two Sicilies. Between 1501 and 1713, for more than two hundred years, foreign viceroys from Spain again ruled. Still no relief for the Italians!

Then the Austrians ruled in Naples, thankfully only until 1734. The House of Bourbon was then formed after some minor wars in that same year. This Kingdom of the Two Sicilies endured another 127 years until it became part of United Italy in 1861. After thirteen hundred years of continuous occupation and oppression, the cruelest blow of all was yet to come.

The modern story of the uprisings of the Italian peasants against the Bourbons, and later against the newly formed United Italian Monarchy (the Savoy dynasty), is a study in itself. I will not divert you further for I am getting too far away from bricks and people. If you wish to pursue this history, I heartily refer you to Queens College Professor Richard Gambino's book, *Blood of My Blood*.

The root of the peasants' problem was the *macinato*, the grain tax (from *macina*, meaning ground grain). This oppressive tax on the source of the two foods left for the *contadini* (peasant farmers) to feed their families, was the last straw. Of the invaders, it had been expected and endured for centuries. But when the Northern Italians, completely ignorant of and unwilling to learn of the desperation of their brothers in the south, cruelly sent in armies to quell the protestations of the people and then increased the *macinato* to support those very troops, the *contadini* quickly returned to their cynical distrust and hatred of government—all governments. So once again they reverted to *la via vecchia* (the old way) and to the security of *la famiglia*. "*Tutto nuovo, niente nuovo*" (All new, nothing new).

There was only one course left—to flee. Thus, in 1861,

Naples, the largest city in Italy and the fourth largest in Europe after London, Paris, and Saint Petersburg, was ready to disgorge its millions. The same was true for Southern Italy, including Sicily.

It is amazing to me to have observed, over the course of six decades, how many hard-working, clean-living, and easily satisfied Italian immigrants I have known. I would have expected to see a seething anger, brought about by the frustrations of centuries, leaving permanent scars of their collective psyche. But that is not the case. Italians are universally admired for being kind, compassionate, and friendly neighbors.

A word about the Mafia, that unholy alliance of vultures. Though the Mafia has caused smearing, undying harm, the American media has greatly exaggerated the ill the Mafia has done because sensationalism makes good copy. How many don't know Robert Stack and his television portrayal of Elliott Ness? Ask the young people of America if they know as well the all-American Pretty-boy Floyd, Ma Barker, Bugsy Siegel, or John Dillinger. Of course they don't. To be sure there are criminal elements in every ethnic society. The Irish had the Madden, Farrell, Connolly, O'Bannion, Moran, and O'Donnell gangs. The Jews countered with Arnold Rothstein, Louis "Lepke" Buchalter, and Meyer Lansky, in addition to Shapiro, Kastel, Bugsy Siegel, and Weiss. The Germans had Dutch Schultz, "Longy" Zwillman, and "Legs" Diamond.

In 1955 Albert Q. Maisel wrote an article published in *Reader's Digest* entitled "The Italians Among Us." He writes, "Studies have shown that our citizens of Italian origin do *not* have a peculiar propensity for racketeering, mayhem and murder. Arrests and convictions of Italians are no more frequent, per hundred thousand in the same age and sex brackets, than for any other immigrant group, and they are slightly *less* than for our citizens of native stock."

The Mafia in Sicily originated as far back as the fourteenth century during the occupation by the French, the most hated invaders of all. The original purpose of the Mafia was not criminal, as we know crimes against society to be. The word Mafia is derived from the first letters of the battle cry '*Morte ai Francesi Italia anelato*' (Death to the French Italy eagerly awaits). The original Mafia was what is called a partisan army, just like the American Revolutionaries, who were considered traitors to the British.

In the Mafia's sometimes successful routing of the French from the countryside, no system of jurisprudence or administration remained in the void. The strong leaders of the Mafia naturally assumed governmental positions and entrenched the system. As the decades passed, the Mafia was corrupted by the power it had acquired. When there were no more French or Bourbons to fight, the *corpus politico* was reluctant to surrender its authority. Moreover, the Mafia's authority had been prostituted by a vicious melding with the *latifondi* (baronial landowners), and the oppressed thus became the oppressors.

The peasants were left, once again, to get the short end of the stick. The Mafia in Sicily and its counterpart, the Camorra in Naples, feasted on the flesh of the downtrodden. And the same happened in the United States. How vividly I remember references to *La Mano Nera* (The Black Hand), the despised American version of the Camorra. Such were the fears of both sets of my grandparents, my parents, my in-laws, and others in the family that they made only hushed references to *La Mano Nera*.

It is a pity that these simple, industrious, God-loving people should have been—and still are—tarred with the same broad brush properly applied to their murderers. But 'Così è fatto il mondo' (that is the way the world is made), to requote Guy Vallese. Bewildered by a world seemingly over which they could find no control, these good people drew again on the only sources of their strength: their faith in a good God, *la famiglia*, and their willingness to work hard.

In 1876, when Grandma and Grandpa were born in the little town of Cicciano, a unified Italy had been in existence for only six years. As previously noted, that unification had done nothing to improve the lot of the peasants. In fact, it had exacerbated their hopelessness. Thus, after my grandparents crossed the sea as teenagers, separately and unknown to each other, and met on a coffee plantation in Brazil, they were not filled with hope, only with the hopelessness they had known in Cicciano, and they were fearful of an uncertain future.

But Grandma had another reason for feeling hopeless, at least initially. Fifty years later she privately unwrapped for me a tiny gold ring, the thinnest gold I have ever seen. An admirer had given it to her as a going-away present and as an admission that they would never see each other again. She begged me not to mention it to Grandpa *'perche e ùn buon uomo'* (because he is a good man). She never told me, but my mother later said that Grandma also had a tiny scar to the side of her eye where her admirer had nicked her, *'così non mi puoi mai scordare'* (so you can never forget me). She probably had never even held her "lover," but the memory lasted a lifetime.

The privations my grandparents endured crossing the sea on wood-masted schooners were, in my grandma's words, *'non puoi credere'* (you can't believe). She told me that passengers had to get their drinking water from a goatskin nailed to the mast of the ship. Can you imagine the indignities a young girl suffered in the hold of a wooden ship?

La masciata (the marriage compact) was made, and my grandparents were married. Love was an ingredient yet to come. Mutual respect was sufficient for the purposes at hand.

This interesting word, *masciata*, deserves some attention. It took me over thirty years to understand its root, for the word does not exist in the Italian language. I came to understand that many dialectal words were only approximations of proper words. Illiteracy was the norm, and some words we used everyday had as their dim beginnings the approximations of what somebody thought was understood.

To complicate matters, many words had roots in invaders' languages, Spanish in particular. For instance, as a boy I never used *un dollaro* (a dollar). The Neapolitan word was *scudo*, of course, from the Spanish *escudo*. Likewise, the Italian for hidden is *nascosto*. We never knew it. We grew up using *innoccuato*, a word we picked up from our grandparents. Its root I have yet to find, but again that is not too far removed from the English word innocuous, isn't it? My mother-in-law called her husband *'un cardillo'* when he was all spiffed up. We suspected she meant some kind of proud bird, but there is no such thing. I have become convinced she meant *'El Caudillo'*, the nickname for Francisco Franco of Spain, a dictator.

In Naples and the surrounding area, you still hear many

words pronounced with an initial "b" sound which are spelled with a "v": *vongole* (clams) is pronounced *'bongole.'* For the command *va* (go), you will hear, *'ba.'* These are Spanish influences. Also, the "sh" sound begins many nouns in place of the written "f," like I will use later when discussing zucchini flowers, which are properly spelled *fiorilli* but are pronounced *'sciurilli.'* Likewise, the word *fiume* (stream) is pronounced *'sciume.'*

To add some spice, many words beginning with "r," such as *ricordare* (remember), are pronounced with an initial "l" sound, hence *'licordare.'* To add further mystery, the "h" or *haeca* sound sometimes displaces the simple "a." This pronunciation is strong in Venice, too. If it were not for the fascination I have for the language, my efforts to unravel these derivations and pronunciations would be just too much.

But a long time passed before I found an explanation for *masciata*. As I explained earlier, every *compare-comparillo* arrangement began with subtle inquiries made in advance by go-betweens. So did marriage arrangements. There is a dialectal expression for these marriage arrangers, or ambassadors. It is, *'Porta le cassette rosse'* (She wears red stockings), a symbol of the well-intentioned emissary.

Years later in Rome, I was doing *la passeggiata* (the evening stroll) with Emily and our two children when I noticed a large sign across the street: L'Ambasciatore Hotel. Of course, the Ambassadors! *'L'* (or *'la'*), the definite article before nouns beginning with vowels plus *"ambasciata'* was very similar to *la masciata*. Once again, the unschooled peasant ear had found the right root, approximate though it might be. In this case, only the "b" intruded. That experience taught me a lesson, to have faith in the peasant use of many initially strange-sounding words or expressions. There is always a reason, and a good one, albeit well hidden.

The arranged marriage took place. My mother was born outside Sao Paolo in 1900. Disillusionment had set in earlier. Life was hard, my grandparents' lot was little improved, and they missed the security of family, a proper church, and the little Italian town's way of life. The admission that they had fruitlessly misplaced five years of their lives was hard to accept. Then something happened that forced a decision.

My grandmother was working in the fields. An anaconda, a

boa constrictor native to South America, was lying in the furrows of the tilled soil. My grandmother almost stepped on the huge serpent, which coiled to engulf her. She never could stop reliving the horror; I have heard the story time after time. We know she fled, remembering what she had been taught—to run across the furrows, not in them.

My mother was not yet three when the little family returned to Italy, their meager savings gone. But Grandma and Grandpa had a purpose. Grandma who was now pregnant with Uncle Fred, would stay with *la famiglia*, and Grandpa would immigrate to the United States to try once again to save enough to send for his wife and children. He did so eventually, but it took him six years of living alone in the Bronx to do it. He worked as a day laborer, boarded in the house of a family who took in immigrants as a means of earning a living, and saved enough to buy a team of horses.

Eastchester, which is south of Pelham Bay, was dotted with family farms. In all the years I knew Grandpa, my mother's father, not once do I recall him being without a plot of land to farm. He would get permission from people to make gardens in their unused backyards and then share his produce with them.

There was magic in his green fingers. He showed me how important it was not only to have rich soil, but to have stones and gravel among it for minerals, aeration, and most importantly, drainage. He explained how the roots of plants drown in rich soil unless the essential water is permitted to drain away.

Talk about recycling! Every meal was followed by cleanup. The scraps, including bones, juices, and fats were collected into small packages. In the evening he would walk, sometimes several miles, to set the scraps around the roots of the plants he was growing. Then he would tend the garden, weeding and tilling, enjoying the fading sun and cool of the evening. Whatever land he touched, he left improved.

At the top of Bainbridge Avenue between Public School 80 and Reservoir Oval still stands a handsome Revolutionary War farmhouse. In an unusual arrangement, a Jewish gentleman leased this historic stone house from the City of New York. This Jewish gentleman, in turn, had given Grandpa the right to make a garden. The plot was large, and the adjoining apartment building served as a convenient fence to what became an oasis for area residents. He used to take me there with him, and eventually the whole rear yard became a manicured pocket farm. He knew he was an expert, and he had found his simple peace.

One of Grandpa's many expressions was, 'Tutto il mondo è paese' (The whole world is a little town). He was talking about getting along with your fellow man, though today we have fancier words for it. I was particularly pleased in Naples one day, years later, when an espresso waiter uttered the phrase to himself. He made this observation when a flamboyant homosexual couple passed by. He shrugged his shoulders in casual acceptance and repeated the saying. His interpretation was a little different from Grandpa's: "There is nothing new, and we are all in this world together."

As far as I know, Grandpa only had three jobs over the span of sixty years he spent in America. He worked as a day laborer; then he drove a team of horses to pull a dirt wagon, which he contracted out with himself as the driver; and finally, he became a New York City Parks Department worker.

How many of you remember those forerunners of excavators' trucks? These wagons were made completely of stout wood, with two halves of a bottom that clamshell-opened for unloading. The horses pulled the wagons to where they were loaded with rocks and dirt. Grandpa was a private person, and those two horses were his only companions for over five years.

When my grandfather saw his family again, my mother was ten years old. Little Uncle Fred, who was seven years of age, did not remember his father. Later, when Grandpa would ride with me to different jobs, he would tell me stories. One had to do with Uncle Fred kicking him in the shins, resenting the *straniero* (stranger). But all things had to be endured—there was no choice. *Aspetta* (wait)!

It is not very difficult to understand the respect the Italian immigrants had for education. It was the way out, the solution to centuries of bondage. Whole families labored to afford an education for the one chosen to be the salvation of *la famiglia*.

The Italian people I knew were great citizens of these United States. They could hardly believe their good fortune, that finally there was an opportunity for even one of them to go forward, and they remained eternally grateful to this country. What a travesty that some of today's young, two or three generations later, should become merely spectators in the educational process so dearly purchased for them by their sacrificial progenitors.

If only the whole story of Italian immigration were peaches and cream. It was not. I will not gloss over the vicious reception my forefathers sometimes received in this country, but neither do I wish to dwell on it. The unjustified execution of Sacco and Vanzetti is only an isolated case among many episodes of unbelievable cruelty against my people.

In addition, Woodrow Wilson's attorney general of the United States, Alexander Mitchell Palmer, was a bigot of incredible stature. This man, supposedly selected to be the first bulwark of defense against injustice, organized the "Palmer Raids," a tactic whereby teams of federal agents descended on whole families or neighborhoods in the middle of the night, arresting indiscriminately, charging subversion, and holding many incommunicado until deportation. Years later, as Gambino points out in his book, *Blood of My Blood*, inquiries failed to find any link between subversion and deportation.[4]

But before Palmer, President Theodore Roosevelt had said the 1891 mob lynching of eleven Sicilians in New Orleans was "a rather good thing!" And these men had already been acquitted or had charges against them dropped! He even went on to boast that he had proclaimed the same at a party where there were "present various dago diplomats." The hero of the Rough Riders also said, "There is no such thing as a hyphenated-American who is a good American."

There were lynchings of Italians in 1891 in West Virginia, murders in Denver in 1893, and six lynchings in Colorado in 1895. In the same year, six were torn from jail in Hahneville, Louisiana; they were all severely beaten, and three were lynched. In Tallulah, Louisiana in 1899, five were lynched for permitting blacks equal status with whites in their shops. There were more: July 1901 in Mississippi; 1906 in West Virginia; 1910 in Florida and Illinois; and 1911 in Illinois.

---

4. Gambino, Doubleday, Garden City, NY, pp. 117–120.

The elder Senator Henry Cabot Lodge of Massachusetts ('the Cabots speak only to the Lodges, and the Lodges speak only to God'[5]) spoke often of his hatred for Italian-Americans. It is delicious justice, I say, that his grandchildren and great-grandchildren, children of the second Senator Cabot Lodge—augmented by the contribution of his Italian wife—had Italian blood in them. If the elder one had looked further (and maybe he did), he would have found that the family name Cabot was actually a shortened form of the Italian surname Caboto. John Cabot, an explorer for England who discovered the North American mainland in 1497, was actually Giovanni Caboto, and he was born in Genoa, Italy, as was his famous son, Sebastiano.

The litany of cruelties did not dissuade the great majority of my people from their gratitude and loyalty to America. Their sharply honed instincts told them that at least in these United States there was a system to redress wrongs, and ultimately justice would triumph. The ingredient born of centuries of trial was still needed: *pazienza* (patience)!

I find it difficult to comprehend the efforts to diminish the credit due Italians in the discovery and explorations of the New World. Christopher Columbus, Amerigo Vespucci, Giovanni and Sebastiano Caboto, and Giovanni Verrazano were all Italian, and the first to come. Ponce de Leon did not come on the scene until 1513, Ferdinand Magellan went to Brazil in 1520, and Hernando De Soto didn't appear on the scene until 1539. Sir Walter Raleigh was almost a hundred years after Columbus, and Henry Hudson did not appear in New York Bay until almost eighty years after Verrazano.

Many Americans have forgotten, but the second Continental Congress, even before we had a unified nation, authorized the construction of the first five ships of a fledgling navy, and three of those five were named after Italians: the *Christopher Columbus*, the *John Cabot*, and the *Andrea Doria*, which was named after an admiral of the Italian navy.

America, a good Italian name!

---

5. Gambino, ibid.

But back to Grandpa. In his way, he was a philosopher. We all spout proverbs, but do we live by them? Grandpa did. It seems logical to me that in the society of his youth, where the norm was illiteracy, small lessons and observations of how to conduct one's life took on more value in their scarcity. Today we are bombarded with so much casual information, much of which we have learned to mistrust, that we have become cynical that anything is precisely or accurately so. Our proverbs and mottoes have become clever prattlings to be taken out of closets filled with mothballs when conversation pieces are needed.

Some five years after Grandpa retired from the New York City Parks Department, I started taking him out to the jobs with me. He and Grandma still had a basement apartment in Uncle Fred's home on 201st Street, within sight of Saint Philip Neri Church. My mother and younger sister, Rosemary, lived doors away, nearer to the Grand Concourse.

Grandpa still rose early in the morning; he went to daily mass and was home by 6:30 A.M. What started out as a single invitation to keep him occupied became a joyous practice. Most of our masonry contracts were in New Jersey, though we lived and our offices were in Bronxville, New York. Two or three times a week I would pick him up in the Bronx before heading for the George Washington Bridge.

I had had a picture in my mind of my grandfather as a rather quiet, simple man, but he seemed to blossom as the months went by; I was an audience that became increasingly fascinated by the depth of his readings. Whole sections of the Old Testament became a guide for daily living. Grandpa presented the stories of Joseph, the prodigal son, and others so personally that for the first time I understood them. Joseph's advice to the king to prepare for the upcoming seven years of *magre* (meager) crops must have appealed to this farmer.

On the other hand, Grandpa was fascinated by the energy and complexity of our operation as he and I flew from job to job. His interest was a source of much gratification to me. How different his days were that he spent with me as opposed to those years he spent alone with his two horses.

And every day Grandpa had a lesson, a valid observation he had reduced to a proverb. You probably can understand why so many lessons identified with farm animals, especially *l'asino* (jackass), *il ciuco* (donkey—*ciuccio* in dialect), or *il mulo* (mule). For example, when an innocent bystander became the victim of the personal intrigue of others, Grandpa's comment was, *'I ciucci si appicicciono, ma le barrile si scassono'* (The donkeys fight, but it is the barrels that get broken). If he saw a neighbor or relative engaged in a fruitless endeavor, out would come, *'Chi fa la barba al asino perde il sapone'* (He who attempts to shave his jackass loses his soap).

Another time we arrived on a housing project in Plainfield, New Jersey. Uncle Louis was the bricklayer foreman, Uncle Johnny was his deputy, and Ralph Belloise was labor foreman. The "foreign legion" was the forty- or fifty-man corps that departed to outlying jobs from the Grand Concourse every morning at 5:30 A.M. After the loaded cars took off, it was coffee time at Bickford's, which was next to Loew's Paradise Theatre. Grandpa had known my father's brothers from their youth, forty years before. (My mother and her family had lived on 204th Street, my father's family on 203rd Street.)

Uncle Louis was better schooled than Uncle Johnny and good at the technology of laying out jobs and following blueprints. Uncle Johnny, on the other hand, was a good pusher and popular with the men. I can still hear Uncle Johnny saying, "Knob it up and go home," a comment he used to incite his men to reach a set goal and leave the job early. Both talents are needed to get a job done economically.

Uncle Louis, though, did not particularly enjoy the reputation of being a hard worker, a judgment which Grandpa had harbored for years. After observing Uncle Louis's apologetic reasoning to me for things which were not quite right in the progress of the job, yet seeing that Uncle Louis was qualified, Grandpa noted as he and I got back in the car, *'Pure il ciuccio, dopo un poco, si impara la via'* (Even the donkey, after awhile, learns the road).

This is a good time to tell you about Ralph Belloise and the Belloise boys. Ralph had all the qualifications of a successful labor foreman. He was intelligent, knew how to keep his men happy, was always prepared, and, besides being pleasant, was a hard worker. His jobs were happy jobs, and our rapport was always excellent. Ralph was part of the new breed, the born-in-America boys, and I could see he was fashioning himself after Guy Vallese, as well as extracting from Vince Basciano the street smarts necessary to survive. Ralph was a potent combination.

You may remember the Belloise family. Mike, a will-o'-the-wisp boxer, was recognized as Featherweight Champion of the World in 1936. The first of nine children born to Salvatore and Julia Belloise in the Villa Avenue section of the Bronx, Mike began a long, difficult road to stardom in the mid 1920's. All told, Mike fought over two hundred amateur fights, including pre-Olympic tours in 1928 and 1931 for the United States Boxing Team, during which he took home medals from all over Europe. In 1932 Mike had paid his dues and was ready to begin a pro career.

Seasoned well beyond his twenty-one years, Mike quickly gained recognition as a comer. Fighting as often as three times a month, Mike roared through his first eleven matches undefeated until he lost a decision to Lew Feldman in January of 1934. In June of that same year, Mike avenged the loss, turning the tables on Feldman, winning a ten-round decision on his way to an elimination bout the following month with Baby Arizmendi for the vacated World Featherweight title. In a grueling struggle, Mike lost a fifteen-round decision, and his title chances were temporarily shelved.

It took nearly two years, but by 1936, with a record of 35-4-3, Mike had earned another title shot. Determined not to let his chance get away, he fulfilled a lifelong dream by knocking out Everett Rightmire in the fourteenth round to become Featherweight Champion of the World! In that same year, Mike fought perhaps his greatest bout, which, ironically, was a loss. He went ten rounds with the immortal Henry Armstrong and even knocked down the ring legend. Armstrong, however, escaped with the split decision. Years later, Mike, whose charismatic personality had made him a crowd favorite even in distant California, gave an account to the *New York Post* of the tumultuous scene that ensued after this unpopular decision: "Of course, I wasn't happy with the outcome, but what I remember seeing is Mae West at ringside giving the referee hell and I couldn't help but get a kick out of it!"

When Mike passed away in 1969, at the much too early age of fifty-eight, he left behind a legacy of guile, character, and courage. He was idolized by those who watched from afar, worshipped by his peers, and loved by the ones who knew him best.

What I wouldn't do to go back in time and spend just one Friday night in the late 1930's, ringside at the Bronx Arena, watching Steve Belloise, Mike's younger brother, take apart his foe with savage right-hand counters on his way to stardom, then witness Mike Belloise, still ringwise, still master of the square circle, landing countless jabs and slipping punches, frustrating yet another opponent into hopeless resignation. Sadly, none of us will ever see a night like that again, except perhaps in the mind's eye of an old-time boxing aficionado who still remembers the Belloise brothers and their place in boxing lore.

The following is a letter about the "uncrowned" middleweight champion, Steve Belloise, written by his own son, Steve, Jr., who sent me a copy after it was printed in the *New York Post*.

Steve was a middleweight, reaching the very top with a devastating punch. People were attracted to my father's honesty, humor, talent, and great sportsmanship. He was a true gentleman, in and out of the ring. He touched people's lives, always willing to give of himself. His personality was charming and magnetic. Those who came in contact with him left with a smile on their faces and a good feeling in their hearts. To this day, some thirty years later, I can very proudly say I've always heard and read great things about my father. Steve Belloise, born in the Bronx, New York, on December 16, 1918, was the middle one of five brothers and four sisters. Steve's older brother, Mike Belloise, amateur, Olympic, and professional featherweight champion, was a great inspiration to him and very instrumental in teaching him the finer points of the fight game. Steve was able to get on Mike's fight cards right away, and on August 24, 1938, Steve began his professional ring career.

From 1938 through 1940, Steve fought thirty-five times. He scored sixteen KO's in thirty-one wins, beating guys like Eddie Dunne, Vic Dellicurti, Wicky Harkins, Sammy Luftspring, and Ceferino Garcia. It was the win over Garcia that earned him a title fight with Ken Overlin at Madison Square Garden. On November 1, 1940, at just twenty-one years old, Steve Belloise was fighting for the middleweight championship. Steve lost to Ken Overlin twice, in world title fights, both times being very close fifteen-round decisions. Then the war came and Steve was a star in legendary Gene Tunney's group of physical training instructors. He served for four years.

From 1945 through 1948, Steve fought forty times, winning thirty-six, twenty-seven by KO. Testimony to his power was proven on May 27, 1946, in a fight with Coley Welch at Madison Square Garden. It was so impressive, it was in *Ripley's Believe It or Not*. In the second round Welch dropped his left hand after a jab and Belloise countered with a right smack on the chin. Welch went down, took the count of nine, got up, staggered across the ring and fell down again, took the eight count, got up again, staggered across the ring, and went right back down again for the KO. Belloise knocked down Welch three times with one punch . . . that was power.

In 1949 Steve received a telegram to fight champion Marcel Cerdan for the title, but he was moved out of the fight by Jake LaMotta—the hero of the movie *Raging Bull*. Then came a nontitle fight in welterweight class with the legendary Sugar Ray Robinson. In August of 1949, this author watched Steve at Yankee Stadium lose to Sugar Ray, pound for pound considered the greatest fighter of all time.

Steve Belloise retired from the ring in 1950 with an honest, respectable, and brilliant career that spanned twelve years. He fought 110 bouts, winning ninety-five, fifty-nine by KO. He had thirteen losses and two draws.

My father, Steve Belloise, spoke highly of all his competitors and refused to squawk over decisions that went against him. He did feel, though, that he had beat Overlin twice back in 1940. His only regret was not getting another title shot during all those glorious years of being a top middleweight contender. He felt he deserved one. . . .

Steve Belloise, my unforgettable father and hero, loved and admired by all his fans, friends, and family, was a dedicated, loving father, a superior fighter with real class, and a true champion.

Rest in Peace, Dad—I Love You, Steve, Jr.

This author goes along with all of that.

The Belloise boys had fashioned a crude boxing ring in the basement of their home, and makeshift matches were always being made. If you were present, you had to go three rounds with somebody. I had no stomach for this activity, but I couldn't "let people talk," could I?

I never could keep the two expressions straight, but more than once I had both my clock fixed and my bell rung in that basement. Young Sal Belloise went on to become still another fighter, and even my cousin Mike Palmieri gave it a go as a "Simon Pure" amateur in the Friday-night fights in the basement of Our Lady of Refuge Church on 196th Street and Valentine Avenue. I never told my father about these basement activities, because if he had known how poorly I fared, I would have gotten a worse beating—just for losing.

On the day Grandpa and I went to Plainfield, all three Belloise brothers were on the job. Mike had become a timekeeper for us, and Steve had become a bricklayer. This comedown from the lofty heights must have filled him with chagrin. Steve's end was sad; he was a victim of Alzheimer's disease at a young age. Whether the ring pounding contributed to his state is an unanswered question. I now own and operate a nursing home with my son, and Alzheimer's disease is still far from understood. Mike's end was sad, too. Ultimately, he became a postman, but for years before he was in poor health.

But on the day we hit their job, all three brothers were razor sharp. The Belloise wit was well known, and at lunchtime the repartee was fast and furious, like Mike's dancing around the ring. The two boxers had even developed a light night club act and used it to pick up some spending money and entertain the men.

Mike would have to spend time with me in his capacity as timekeeper. Grandpa watched. Mike had a little routine about the old-fashioned Italian weddings that took place on second-floor dance halls, with the kids tossing cartons of premade sandwiches to outstretched hands, mimicking the broken English of some of the guests: "Hey, throw me a cream-pump!"

The Belloise family lived—as did their mama, who lived to be over 103 years old—on the corner of 204th Street and Valentine Avenue, right alongside the tunnel that goes under the Grand Concourse to Villa Avenue. Grandpa had watched them all grow up (there were nine children in all), and he knew their antics from years before. His comment that day in Plainfield as he watched their compulsive performance was, *'Chi è nato quadrato, rotondo non può morire'* (He who is born square cannot die round).

One time I was part of the Employers Contracting Group bargaining collectively for a new three-year pact with the mason tenders' and laborers' unions in New York City. Local unions from five boroughs were all represented. The meetings took place in the Port of New York Authority Building on Ninth Avenue and 15th Street in Manhattan, and between our representatives and their groups, there must have been forty men stretched along huge tables. John Mulligan was there.

After some days of negotiating, we had reached an impasse on several working conditions, including walking time (important on high-rise buildings), wash-up time, and permission to pay by check instead of cash. This latter was important to us, for too many stickups were occurring, and the danger of being shot was very real to us and to our paymasters, Lew Porter, and office manager, Russ Lando.

The laborers' unions were always easier to negotiate with than the bricklayers' because the latter's work ethic was so high, but the delegates for the laborers were under a lot of pressure from their men to get conditions similar to those enjoyed by the masons. Emotions started running high—an unhappy situation because that is when reasoning goes out the window and emotion storms in. Silence descended. Five minutes of petulant silence in a room of forty grown men seems like an hour.

Suddenly, I had an inspiration. I started with, "I want to tell you a story my grandfather told me," and I told these men the story about the drunken farmer, which I will share with you.

One day a *contadino* (farmer) came down the mountain on his *mulo* and went straight to the wine shop. These delightful shops are an Italian town's equivalent of a pub where the men gather to drink the *padrone's* (owner's) wines, play cards, and exchange stories.

This day the farmer started drinking white wine, then switched to red wine, a practice frowned upon supposedly because the mixing of the two leads to drunkenness, a state which is not freely accepted in Italy. In any event the farmer got drunk, and when he eventually stumbled out to his *mulo*, his friends had to help him mount. As he slowly ascended the mountain in a stupor, he rolled off his beast and ended up in a drainage ditch on the side of the dirt road.

After a bit, with stars spinning round his head and his *mulo* patiently waiting nearby, he managed to address the two wines in an expression appropriate to the moment: *'Se ne vi accordate tutti due, ci ne andiamo tutti tre, ma se non vi accordate, qui stiamo tutti la nottata'* (If you two can get together, all three of us will go home, but if you two can't agree, all of us will spend the night here).

The resultant laughter broke the tension (fortunately, I was able to tell the story in Italian because most of the laborers' delegates in New York were Italian), and negotiations proceeded to a compromise solution. When I told Grandpa of this episode, he was ecstatic, smilingly insisting that I repeat the story for weeks thereafter. He was extremely pleased with his part in helping to solve a problem which, in the magnification of his mind, had represented a threat to the entire construction industry of New York City. I did not disabuse him of his joy. Besides, it was true, and one of those tiny incidents in life which makes the difference between existence and dignity.

At one point, I was sitting on the employers' negotiating committees for both masons and laborers in Westchester County, New York, Bergen County and Hudson County in New Jersey, as well as in New York City. This eight-part chore became too much, demanding too many evenings, and eventually I had to cut back. The reason I mention this is to show you that behind the obvious facade of an industry—or the fence around a foundation hole—exists an apparatus that is essential to coordinate man's talents and produce for the common good exciting designs of habitat and commerce. I became an admirer of the democracy at work in this apparatus, the collective bargaining process. To be sure, it is far from perfect, and we are still learning how to use it (observe foreign competition), but it is still the only game in town.

Money was another subject that received a lot of attention in the peasant guidelines. You would think that a people who for centuries lived every day desperate with privation would have a high regard for the accumulation of wealth. The opposite was true. To be sure, hard work was expected for the security of *la famiglia* and the opportunities for education and advancement. But excessive wealth was viewed with considerable alarm, for it was a potential threat to the well-being of a family. Judicious use of money was essential, often brutally taught; ostentation, though, resulted in some rough handling.

My grandmother, who brooked no patience with ethereal ambiguity (I suppose you never do after being chased by a huge snake), often said, *'Chi fa vedere i soldi fa vedere il culo, e chi fa vedere il culo è un finocchio'* (Who lets you see his money lets you see his ass, and who lets you see his ass is a homosexual).[6]

A dear friend, Ed Perry, taught me an expression in English that I wish could have stemmed from Italian. Nonetheless, it will make it easier for you to understand how *la famiglia* felt about the accumulation of too much wealth: "If you want to see what God thinks of money, look at the people He gave it to."

One time I was at lunch in Newark with Grandpa and two lawyers. We were in the Roost Restaurant, at that time a rather fashionable meeting place for businessmen. Grandpa and I had just come from two nearby schools, the Kinney Street School and the McKinley Street High School. We were building these schools for the Arthur Venneri Company, General Contractors of Westfield, New Jersey. Our company was involved in a nasty

---

6. The word *finocchio*, which literally means the herb fennel, is also a vernacular expression for a homosexual, like the word faggot is in English.

arbitration procedure having to do with final payments from a general contractor for contracts on the Westfield Junior High School, the Union Junior High School, and a public housing project in Elizabeth.

Grandpa was beginning to enjoy these breaks from routine. He was quite natty in his dress and was an entertaining conversationalist. Whenever his English failed, I would jump in to help. So after the lawyers and I discussed our legal strategy, Grandpa told us the story of the hard-working farmer who had amassed considerable wealth and his spendthrift son. The father watched unhappily as his son squandered money on parties and shallow friends. As old age neared, the father became increasingly apprehensive and finally one day took his son into the barn to show him a haltered noose hanging from a hayloft girder. The father then said, "When I am gone, my son, when you have thrown away all your money, when your fair-weather friends are gone, and when your depression is unbearable, I want you to come here and hang yourself, for surely that day will come."

And, of course, the day came. In his friendless despair, hounded by creditors, the son decided he had no alternative but to do what his father had predicted. So he stood on a barrel and slipped the noose around his neck. As he jumped off the barrel and the noose tightened around his neck, the hayloft collapsed. His father had sawn through most of the wood girder and had camouflaged the weakened beam with hanging straw. Gold coins and hay together then showered down upon the son. As his head emerged from the mixed mountain of both, he cried out and admonished himself for his foolhardy actions, thereby acknowledging to his deceased father: '*Mi avete fatto fesso una volta, ma mai più*' (You made a fool of me once, but not ever again). The son had learned his lesson.

When I told this story to my own son on a beach in Spring Lake, New Jersey, in the presence of his father-in-law, he wondered why I had waited so many years to tell him. Gratefully, there had never been a need. But the danger is always there.

I will now tell you the story of "How Many Parts to a Chicken?" This was not Grandpa's tale, but it illustrates the constant need for diligence. Anthony Mazzucca and I were riding along the east shore of Lake Champlain, headed for the SAC Air

Force Base in Plattsburgh, New York. Tony was chief engineer and head man for the Venneri Company. It was the beginning of the B-52 program, our nuclear defense shield for many years, and the Venneri Company had sublet to me and my uncle the masonry work on an Air Force hospital and some thirty other buildings.

Tony and I had decided to combine business with pleasure on our trip. So the night before we had stayed over at the Basin Harbor Club, a Vermont resort on the shores of the lake. Well rested, we eased into a philosophical discussion as we motored toward the ferry on Grand Island. Our conversation turned to concern for our children and the bad influence money often had upon them. This phenomenon was one I had observed as quite common among second and third generation Americans of Italian origin. It is truly astounding to observe the changes the security indices had made upon the attitudes of my parents and their generation as compared to that of their grandchildren. My father, who had come to the United States as an immigrant boy of six, was desperately concerned—even obsessed—with survival. My mother, who had emigrated from Italy to America on a masted schooner as a child of ten, was also.

After my father died in 1947, Uncle Joe and I remained as partners in the masonry business, and together we continued to operate one of the more successful masonry firms in the New York metropolitan area, employing more than five hundred bricklayers and laborers, including a host of ancillary support workers. Though our success was not so overwhelming that suddenly all of life's anxieties were allayed, the contrast between the family's fortunes in the early 1900's and half a century later were astounding, even incomprehensible.

From Plattsburgh, Tony and I were going on to Buffalo, where we were building nine high-rise buildings for the Buffalo Housing Authority. Monetary success for each of us could not be denied, yet economic security was still nebulous. A beneath-the-skin awareness we would carry all our lives told us that now was no time to relax. This undercurrent warned us that without continued diligence the whole house of cards could collapse. Diligence had been drummed into both Tony and me: *'L'occhio del padrone ingrassa il cavallo'* (The eye of the owner will fatten the horse). And without the eye of the owner watching, *magre* (lean) years were sure to follow.

And then, of course, we couldn't "let people talk." But it was even more than that. Tony and I both knew that failure for the family brought with it shame and derision, a thoroughly unacceptable state of affairs. There was no compromise with poverty. How many times I remember my grandmother, my mother's mother, brutally warning, '*Meglio che dicono che lo possono uccidere che Dio l'aiutolo*' (Better for people to say out of jealousy, "They should massacre him" than "God help him.") The objective is to be envied, not popular. Luigi Barzini in his book, *The Italians*, develops this theme more completely.[7]

Both Tony and I feared the effects largesse could have on our children. We were being tugged in two directions; a delicate balancing act was now required. To whom could we turn in this dilemma? Governments and society could not be trusted to avert disaster. The vigilance of the family was required, maybe even more so than before. And we were right. Look at the drug scene which is now upon us. Has largesse, due to lack of diligence and earnestness, inspired this tragedy? To a great degree it has, I think.

Tony's circumstances as an infant and child were considerably more severe than mine, perhaps even worse than my parents'. His mother had died when he was a young child, and he had been raised by his grandmother and his father. They had to leave Argentina to come here. Tony's father persevered in his daily work, and the three scrimped and saved enough to put the scion through engineering school at Cooper Union in New York. The efforts of three generations were needed to accomplish that.

Tony and I bemoaned in concert as we rode: "Two families could live off the waste in our house." "We were not allowed to discard even a morsel from the table without making the sign of the cross over it." "The lights were never left on in unoccupied rooms." And on and on.

Finally, Tony said, "My six kids think there is only one part to a chicken—the breast. Do you know how many parts there are to a chicken?"

---

7. Barzini, Luigi, *The Italians* (Atheneum Press, 1964).

Now we were all revved up, and I wanted to hear Tony's version. "Tell me," I said, and he related the following.

"The president of Argentina asked my grandmother to take charge of the palace kitchen around 1895. This job was manna from heaven for my family because the family was assured of daily bread. My mother was born in the palace, and soon the little family's good fortunes exceeded by far that of their countrymen. Even parts of a chicken that are not edible were useful. The chicken droppings in the gardens fertilized the arbor and nourished the grapevines. The fine feathers of the chickens were plucked and used to stuff soft pillows and mattresses, while the large feathers were used to make headdresses for the children, who would simulate the Indians who still lived nearby.

"My grandmother killed several chickens at one time and collected the blood, which was made into a blood pudding called *sanguinaccio*. This looks and tastes very much like chocolate. The bone marrow was extracted and made into a pâtè, which was used as an open sandwich spread, and the gelatinous part of the feet were cut away and used to make an aspic.

"In addition, the chicken livers, kidneys, and heart were used to make a fine sweetbread dish, which my grandmother usually made for the president's breakfast. The long intestines were also used. They were cut open, cleaned, salted, and used as a webbed wrapping for a combination of sausage, prosciutto, and eggs. This was called *migliatella*, a type of Calabrian *braciola* (*rollatina*).

"At last, the main body of the chicken was presented as a roast on Sunday, with a stuffing made of bread, cheese, and more eggs. Any chicken meat left over from Sunday was stripped from the bones and made into a chicken salad. Thus, everything but the carcass, skin, and bones was eaten, including all the parts, except the breast. That was saved for my children," Tony added wryly.

"But these remaining parts had two more important functions," Tony went on. "First, they were added to the neck, feet, gizzards, breast bones, and head and used to make chicken soup. Whatever was still edible was eaten with bread dunked in the soup. Second, and finally, the bones, carcass, skin, and remains from the soup were ground up and fed to the pigs. Only the waste from the cleaned-out intestines was discarded—nothing else.

"How many parts to a chicken? You tell me, Frank."

My people were never very far from reality. There were lessons to be learned having to do with every facet of coping with life. The warnings I received through parables and stories were not intended to be cynical observations, only realistic appraisals of the world the way it is.

When Grandpa said, *'I soldi degli altri si contano con la palletta; I nostri si contano uno, due, tre,'* (Other people's money is counted with a coal shovel; our own is counted one, two, three), he was advising how foolish an enterprise it was to waste time exaggerating other people's wealth. You have seen this easy game played many times, sometimes directed at you.

On one occasion we were in Scarsdale, New York, an affluent suburb north of New York City. This time we were working on four apartment buildings, two at a time. Uncle Joe was still using his technique of "competition, *figlio mio.*" Though his technique was still bearing dividends, we needed to invest in a forest of lumber for scaffolding. The buildings were each a quarter of a mile around, and the erected scaffolding for six stories was impressive.

Grandpa digested this display of affluence as I consulted with a half-dozen foremen and uncles. When Grandpa saw Patsy Mosca (son of Zi Giuan), Louis Mancuso, and Strawberry (Harvey Paffenroth) arriving with even more truckloads of scaffolding, he must have calculated in his mind the probable expenditure required. As we drove away, Grandpa's peasant instincts compelled him to warn me: *'Ricordati, figlio mio, la gelosia è nata prima di Gesù'* (Remember, my son, jealousy was born before Jesus Christ).

Vince Basciano, who died in 1982, used to worry about me. We were doing an apartment building on the northeast corner of 78th Street and Second Avenue in New York City. New York is a tough place to work. Vince was concerned because petty bribery, in self-defense, ran rampant in the system—just to keep peace.

I might as well talk about the bribery problem here because it is utterly stupid to throw the contractors into the same guilt pot with the petty extortioners (as the mayor and other politicians do). The takers, not the givers, initiated these payoffs. It should clearly be a matter of intent: Is a father or mother of a kidnapped child guilty for having paid ransom? Certainly not.

If a contractor is trying to get his job done, and police, firemen, safety inspectors, building department inspectors, highway inspectors, and sanitation inspectors come cruising along and want to make it tough for you, there is no way contractors can get their job done. I am not talking about gross violations endangering the safety of workers or people. I am talking about being subject to so many petty rules and regulations that one's head swims! Maneuvering delivery trucks for unloading, debris strewn in the street, even temporarily, an errantly placed extinguisher, and a hydrant temporarily blocked by a truck that is backing equipment into the building are all potential causes for issuing summonses. You can see why the bribery started in the first place.

New York City has been in the midst of much larger scandals and convulsions brought about by almost every city department. Every day we read about the parking violations mess; the different borough presidents' convictions; the nine school inspectors on trial for conspiracy to organize bribe-taking; a $290 million plan to modernize schools announced in 1984, though "Little equipment will function" in 1987; and those on trial for bribe-taking and conspiracy in different boroughs' cable television franchises. The list goes on and on.

The whole city system is a closed club, and to be a member you have to play ball with the boys at the top. Plans are constantly being "lost" in the city's building department, where they are processed for construction approval. The problem is that after each inspection the plans have to be retrieved and delivered to the next subdepartment, and at each stop a fee has to be paid'on a separate line. The approval face sheets are constantly "falling behind filing cabinets" or getting "lost" in the confusion as they go from planning, to plumbing, to electrical, to elevators, to asbestos, to structural, to fire, and on to at least ten other stops.

The way the whole system is designed has made it so cumbersome that a new "corps" of experts has emerged—professionals who spend their whole lives as "expediters," people who are paid well to "walk" their plans through the departments. Builders simply cannot afford to lose many months while their plans vegetate in hidden recesses. How do you rescue them? I know you don't like to hear about this, but you already know the answer. The shakedowns are going on right now as you read these pages.

When Vince would tell me about these cash expenditures—petty bribes—he did so with trepidation, because he knew they were a source of irritation to me. This particular day he felt again I was being naive.

"Buy me a coffee," he said, a ritual that always preceded one of his lectures on the ways of the world. When we sat down, he said without further preamble, '*Senza i soldi la Messa non si canta*' (Without money the High Mass is not sung).

This acerbic observation of life is unfortunately pretty accurate, a fact I recognized but was unwilling to concede to Vince, mostly to keep him off balance. It was important to let Vince know I would not accept the premise that every situation must have a cynically considered solution, for that would foreclose the possibility of a better one. Vince was constantly trying to protect me from myself. He sincerely felt my perceived naiveté represented a threat to *la famiglia's* success. Remember, he was a *comparillo*.

But it is important to note what the expression about the High Mass also hints at. Later I want to talk about the relationship of the Italian man to his church. Vince believed these petty extortioners represented *il governo*, and you did not place your faith in government. Actually, the petty extortioners were antagonists to be warily jousted. Thus, contractors assuaged the mammon of iniquity with a little peace offering—sufficient only to permit them to get through the day. Tomorrow would bring tomorrow's problems, and they would be con-fronted—tomorrow. I agreed with Vince much more than he thought.

My people had an expression for these petty extortioners. They were called *mangia-franchi* (the verb *mangiare*, meaning to eat, combined with the word franked, meaning free—as in politicians' mail). We have a similar word in English for these eat-for-nothing people. We call them freeloaders.

Grandpa recognized the *mangia-franchi*, and as usual he had a proverb: '*I mangia-franchi, vivono accorcita e portata pure*' (The freeloaders survive by shortcut, without responsibility, and they are carried, too.) Remember, if you think the disdain is too severe, bureaucrats are a relatively new phenomenon in America, but in Italy the downtrodden contended with them for centuries.

In fact, the term *mangia-franchi* became part of the language. If you look up the words *ufficiale esattoriale* in *Cassell's Italian-English Dictionary*, you will find three English translations: the first two are tax collector and excise officer; interestingly, the third is extortioner.[8]

Welfare was looked upon with shame by these industrious people. You simply did not admit to your neighbors how desperate were your circumstances. It was considered a loss of dignity to be on public dole, a shame upon the whole family. This was not acceptable and was the antithesis of *fare la bella figura* (to project a fine image). It was more important to do things with *garbo* (with a flair, panache, or éclat). How then could the family create and maintain that image if it were known that public assistance was the source of revenue?

Women, especially widows, slaved mightily to send their children out looking clean and apparently wanting for nothing. Was the perception the reality? Only if you did not sacrifice your dignity. Do you remember, *'Chi fa vedere il culo è un finocchio'* (Who lets you see his ass is a homosexual)?

We have an overworked expression here in America: "The perception becomes the reality." That would never do in Italy or among Italians. Barzini in *The Italians* exquisitely leads the reader through a maze of ambiguity. I am paraphrasing him here, not quoting. He points out that in Italy the perception frequently coincides precisely with the reality. Then again, it may bear absolutely no resemblance to reality. And then again, it may be somewhere in between.[9]

It is up to you, the player, to arm yourself with what you can see, feel, touch, and smell. Then you will be ready to select how much of each element you wish to accept. To be realistic is to be *furba*, not only to see things with clarity but, for the sake of human relations, to choose not to divulge your awareness that all

8. *Cassell's Italian-English Dictionary* (Funk & Wagnalls, 1964).
9. Barzini, *The Italians*.

is not exactly as it is presented to you. That trait was shipped over in our blood.

The antithesis of *furba* is *fesso*. One is *fesso* when he permits himself to be made a fool. It is a low state, the subject of complete derision, unadmirable in every respect. The word also can mean simple-minded and of inferior intelligence, but it is rarely used in this obvious manner, nor is it discussed here in that context.

It is more expected that one should possess enough dignity to warrant membership in the human race and to conduct himself accordingly. One frequently hears the word, *mafioso*, to describe a man of outstanding quality. This use is completely unconnected to the popular American use of that word. Three British professors have just completed *A History of Sicily*, surely one of the most comprehensive studies ever attempted. Sir Moses Finely of Cambridge and Denis Mack Smith and Christopher Duggan, both of Oxford, say as follows: Though *mafiosi* existed, "the mafia" almost certainly did not. The issue is complex, but there is very little to suggest that there was ever a criminal organization of the kind described by the authorities. Yet in the confusion of the 1860's the idea of such an entity was undoubtedly attractive to northern bureaucrats faced with an alien culture and recalcitrant population. . . . In local parlance, the word mafia had denoted qualities of beauty, independence, and assertiveness. It now began to take root in the public imagination as a catchall for what was least acceptable to the new dispensation in this strange society.[10]

To Italians, though, if a man possesses and exhibits admirable qualities of dignity, bravery, and kindness and is *furba*, taking responsibility for all his actions, he can be adjudged *mafioso*, a concept that undoubtedly goes back to the origin of the word.

There could be no male chauvinism present in the assessment of a man dubbed *mafioso*. In my eyes that was the glaring weakness in *Godfather II*, the ersatz movie which followed the truly exciting *Godfather I* and was designed only to make many more millions. When Michael Corleone actually struck his wife, the whole movie fell apart. No *mafioso* man would stoop to do that,

---

10. Finley, Sir Moses, Smith, Denis Mack, and Duggan, Christopher, *A History of Sicily* (Viking Press, 1987).

even one that was *Mafioso* rather than *mafioso*. Women enjoy a special place, and when a man violates their comparative physical weakness, he exposes himself as a weakling, totally bereft of dignity. That man is a *fesso*.

I remember an interesting episode that took place on Nonna's porch on Reservoir Oval. My father was talking to his mother in the late afternoon, and I was nearby. They were conversing in Italian, which I understood, and my father was expressing concern that my older sister was becoming interested in boys. I saw the conflict of cultures at work. The old way was for girls to be constantly chaperoned, but my fourteen-year-old sister was not.

Nonna nodded toward me and said, "And what about him?"

'*Chillo* (he or that one in dialect) *è un fesso*,' responded my father. He did not mean this comment as a complete condemnation of me, but rather as a specific criticism for not recognizing by instinct what he perceived as a younger brother's responsibility. I remember my two reactions. The first was, "I'll show you," and the second was almost instinctive. I betrayed no emotion, or even awareness, that I understood. Had my father been aware, he would have had to deny his own careless appraisal, for I was being *furba*, by definition. He had trained me better than he thought.

Today, in a skilled nursing facility such as the one I own with my son, we teach and practice "reality orientation" in handling our patients. By avoiding "soft-soaping" our very ill charges and by encouraging patients constantly to be aware of their surroundings and state of health, we permit them to gather the dignity needed to carry on. I see a connection between that and being *furba*.

The denigration of Italians in America did not begin until after the Civil War. Up until that time, the culture and impact of Italy on civilization was freely recognized and admired. For example, William Paca, who would later be governor of Maryland and chief justice of the Maryland Court of Appeals, signed the Declaration of Independence. You will find his name just below that of John Hancock. His father, Aquila (Eagle), had been high sheriff and a member of the House of Burgesses. His grandfather, Robert Paca (whose original name was Pacci), was granted land in Anne Arundel County in 1651. The Pacas imported silks and gowns from Italy for the wealthy members of the Colonies.

Philip Mazzei, Virginian, was a dear friend to Thomas Jefferson, who, proficient in Italian, constantly translated Mazzei's writings into English. Mazzei was more comfortable writing in his native Italian, though he had spent sixteen years in London. President John F. Kennedy wrote in his book, *A Nation of Immigrants*: "The Great Doctrine, All Men are Created Equal, incorporated in the Declaration by Thomas Jefferson, was paraphrased from the writings of Philip Mazzei."[11]

Mazzei was confidant to George Washington, Marquis de Lafayette, James Monroe, James Madison, and Patrick Henry "to whom he presented himself for enlistment after the shot heard round the world. At that same spot he met Carlo Bellini, professor of romance languages at the College of William and Mary, Williamsburg, later to be Secretary for Foreign Affairs for Virginia."[12]

When Mazzei sailed to Europe as Virginia's special envoy seeking funds, Jefferson wrote to Richard Henry Lee: "I have been led the more to think of this from frequent conversations with Mazzei, whom you know well and who is well acquainted with all those countries. . . . His connections in Tuscany are good, his acquaintances with capital men there, in Rome, and Naples great. . . ."[13]

Moreover, there are many "Palladiums" throughout the world. These theaters, dance halls, night clubs, and places of elegant assembly (my father did ballroom dancing at the Palladium on 149th Street in the Bronx) all derived their names from Andrea Palladio (1508–1580), master architect from the Veneto region in Italy. If you travel to the areas around Vicenza and Padua, you will find the most significant collection of grand homes extant in this world. And in Venice you cannot miss his two churches on the Grand Canal, Santa Maria Della Salute and

---

11. Kennedy, John F., *A Nation of Immigrants* (Harper, 1964).
12. Musmanno, Michael A., *The Story of the Italians in America* (Doubleday, 1965).
13. Musmanno, p. 13.

the lovely complex of San Giorgio Maggiore on the tiny island as you look out from Saint Mark's Square.

This architects' influence was great outside of his native land: "Palladio's *Four Books on Architecture* (1570) was a significant work of Renaissance architectural theory. Palladian design influenced the work of Inigo Jones in England during the 1600's and the Georgian style of architecture in England during the 1700's."[14]

Thomas Jefferson studied and possessed Palladio's books of masterpieces. From these books came the design of Monticello, Jefferson's home, which is known to us all, as well as the impressive main building at the University of Virginia in Charlottesville, the Rotunda, which Jefferson designed and modeled after the Pantheon in Rome.

Do you know Francis Vigo? There is a statue of him in Vigo County, Indiana. Giuseppe Maria Francesco Vigo was born in Mondovi, Italy, in 1747. He came to the United States in 1774, became a fur trapper in the Northwest Territory, and went on to become not only a scout for American general, George Rogers Clark, but a spy against the British. But Vigo did more for our country. When General Clark was stymied by lack of guns and equipment to attack British general, Sir Ian Hamilton, at Fort Vincennes, Vigo offered General Clark his entire estate, to be paid through his bankers in Saint Louis. Those funds helped equip the American forces.

The expedition against Fort Vincennes was completely successful, and the entire Northwest Territory was freed: "On February 25, 1779, Hamilton surrendered, the pestiferous bear was pulled off the Continental's back, and Yorktown was assured."[15]

However, Vigo, who became a United States citizen, was made a colonel in the Indiana militia, and was honored by Washington's summons for advice in 1789; ironically died penniless. There was not twenty dollars to pay for his funeral! In 1876, though, almost a hundred years later, the Supreme Court of the United States awarded to Vigo's heirs the sum of $49,898.60 from the Federal Treasury for money put forth by him in

---

14. *World Book Encyclopedia*, World Book, Inc. Vol. 15 p. 107.
15. Musmanno, p. 17.

behalf of the United States.

Another Italian man who helped make our country a better place is Father Kino. If you visit our capital, specifically the Hall of Commons in the House of Representatives, you will find a statue dedicated to him. He was really Father Eusabio Chino,[16] a missionary out of Trento, Italy. One hundred years before the Revolutionary War, Father Chino was performing missionary work among the Indians in what is now northern Mexico and southern Arizona.

While Chino built chapels and houses for the Indians, he also taught them advanced agriculture and animal husbandry, as well as carpentry and masonry. If you read Musmanno's *The Story of the Italians in America*, you will find that Professor H.E. Bolton of the University of California eulogized Chino as "the cattle king of his day and region." Bolton explains that Chino raised and herded a large number of cattle for the Indians, "not a single one of which was possessed by him."[17]

Father Chino himself was preceded by Fra Marco da Nizza, an Italian who had established missions all the way from Mexico to Phoenix, Arizona. That was ninety years before the pilgrims at Plymouth Rock.

Suppose you knew a man who was both a recipient of the Congressional Medal of Honor and then director of the Metropolitan Museum of Art in New York. That would be quite a fellow, and so he was. Colonel Louis di Cesnola, later a brigadier general, was born in Piedmont, Italy in 1833. In 1860 he came to the United States, organized a private school of cavalry, enlisted in the New York cavalry when the Civil War broke out, and received a commission as major. At the Battle of Aldie in June 1863, the United States honored di Cesnola with the highest award for heroism granted by our country. He was also appointed by President Lincoln to be an American consul to Cyprus. Di Cesnola became an archaeologist and discovered nine ancient cities and thousands of artifacts. The French art historian Perrot wrote, "The name of General di Cesnola has been written

---

16. "Ch" in Italian followed by "e" or "i" gives a "k" sound.
17. Musmanno, p. 5.

in the history of archaeology, [and] the discoveries of Cyprus were an event without parallel.[18]

In May 1879, by unanimous vote, the trustees of the Metropolitan Museum of Art in New York appointed General di Cesnola as its director. He supervised the museum's move from 14th Street to the magnificent building on upper Fifth Avenue, and he remained director for twenty-five years.

This former Italian military academy cadet, archeologist, and museum director died in 1904. J.P. Morgan was an honorary pallbearer, and Archbishop Farley officiated at the funeral. The little girls from the Italian Orphanage of West Park sang di Cesnola's proud farewell. You can read more about di Cesnola in his biography by George H. Story.

But so many Americans are entranced with fiction, not history. Once again, I refer to Robert Stack and his selectively fictional portrayal of Elliot Ness, an FBI agent chasing down exclusively Italian criminals. Americans have been trained to associate Italians with the Mafia. Why is it so difficult to admit that the very person who created the bureau that pursues the Mafia, among others, was an Italian? How well-kept is the secret!

Now here is the true story, and ironic it is. The FBI was created by an Italian! He was Charles Joseph Bonaparte (his family name in Tuscany was Buonaparte), and he was the attorney general of the United States in the cabinet of Theodore Roosevelt and a former secretary of the navy.

Prior to his appointment as secretary of the navy in 1905, Bonaparte was valedictorian of the 1872 graduating class at Harvard, where he stayed on to get a degree from the Harvard Law School. Next, he was appointed a member of the Board of Indian Commissioners, whose job it was to investigate conditions in Indian territory. Then from Baltimore, where Bonaparte practiced law, Theodore Roosevelt assigned him to investigate fraud in the post office department.

Once Bonaparte became attorney general and began to pursue the robber barons and monopolies, he became known as "Charlie the Crook Chaser." He personally handled these cases

---

18. Lepis, Louis A., *Italian Heroes of American History* (New York: Italians of American Descent, Inc., 1976), p. 59.

before the Supreme Court, and it was here that he realized the government needed an organized investigative force. Bonaparte persuaded President Roosevelt in 1908 to issue the directive creating the Federal Bureau of Investigation.

Incidentally, though Bonaparte was a grandnephew of Emperor Napoleon of France, he boasted that he did not have "a drop of French blood in his veins."[19] The Italian family on Corsica from whom "Nabulione" issued were immediate descendants of the Buonapartes of Tuscany and the Ramolinos of Genoa.

It should be noted that once a year, under the aegis of John LaCorte, founder of the Italian Historical Society of America, there is a ceremony in the Great Hall of the Rotunda of the Department of Justice Building in Washington. This ceremony is to honor Bonaparte as founder of the FBI. Each year the director of the FBI addresses the public at the spot where a bronze plaque records that history. As New Jersey director of the Italian Historical Society of America, I attend that ceremony.

In the nineteenth century, while America tortured itself with where Italy and Italians were to be fitted in, England was having a love affair with Italy. To begin, Elizabeth and Robert Browning left England and lived in the villa of Casa Guidi in Florence. For sixteen years until her death in 1861, while the prolific Robert wrote authoritatively on artists Fra Lippo Lippi and Andrea Del Sarto and was host to the literati of Europe, Elizabeth composed her own poetry, among which is the immortal line, "How do I love thee? Let me count the ways" from her poem "Sonnets from the Portuguese." You can visit her grave in the Cimitero Inglese in Florence. Robert Browning died in Venice, but that was only after he had returned to London subsequent to Elizabeth's death. He wrote in *Andrea Del Sarto*, a dramatic monologue, "Ah, but a man's reach should exceed his grasp, or what's a heaven for?"

Percy Bysshe Shelley, he of the stormy career, lived permanently in Italy from 1818 until his death in 1822. He visited Lord Byron's villa frequently in the Euganean Hills of Este, which is an hour from Padua. Tragically, Shelley drowned in a sailing

---

19. Lepis, p. 91.

accident near Livorno (Leghorn) in 1822. His famous *Prometheus Unbound* and *A Defense of Poetry* are among at least nine works he wrote in Italy.

John Keats lived mainly in Rome and was buried there in 1821, but not before he was able to write, "Open my heart, and you will find inscribed upon it Italy." Who among us does not also remember his "A thing of beauty is a joy forever?"

The volcanic Lord Byron spent much of his time in Venice, where he wrote most of *Don Juan*. For years he occupied the Palazzo Mocenigo, the scene of one of the most tempestuous affairs in history. Byron's mistress was Margherita Cogni, an illiterate peasant girl of twenty-two who abandoned her husband and attached herself to Byron. He referred to his lover as an "untameable" but "fine animal." Margherita was a tyrant in the household and eventually had the more than a dozen servants shape up the previously cobwebbed and ominous palazzo.

Byron's letter to John Murray is considered one of the best he ever wrote, and in it he tells about this tigress of a woman and what happened on the stormy day he almost foundered on a foolish trip to the Lido of Venice. "On seeing me safe, she did not wait to greet me, as might be expected, but calling out to me, '*Ah!, can' della Madonna, e esto il tempo per andar' al' Lido?*' (Ah, dog of the Virgin, is this the time to go to Lido?)[20]

The text of Ludovico Ariosto's *Orlando Furioso*, an epic poem, was well-known and studied in England. As early as 1591, Sir John Harrington translated the Italian. The original script was, and is, in the library of the City of Ferrara, Italy. Many British, Scottish, and Irish made pilgrimages to Ferrara to study Ariosto's text, along with Torquato Tasso's *Gerusalemme Liberata (Jerusalem Unchained)*.

Edmund Spencer modeled *The Faerie Queen* on *Orlando Furioso*. Thomas Macauley took it on a ship to India, while Keats learned Italian from it. Moreover, Robert Southey, poet laureate from 1813–1843, read it when he was a child; Sir Walter Scott said often he loved it; and Byron knew it in the original. William

---

20. Morton, H.V., *A Traveller in Italy* (Dodd, Mead & Co., 1964), p. 362.

Wordsworth, poet laureate from 1843–1850, took it on an Alpine walking tour in 1790.

Italy also inspired Macauley, historian and poet, to write his voluminous *Lays of Ancient Rome*, with the famous "Horatius" (at the bridge).

Others came, besides the British, to refresh their souls in Italy. German composer Richard Wagner wrote his last opera, *Parsifal*, in the Ruffolo Gardens of Ravello, overlooking Amalfi. He wrote most of *Othello* in Venice.

Stendahl (Marie Henri Beyle), novelist and Frenchman, wrote the travel guide of Italy that for over a century was the ultimate authority for those taking the grand tour. In 1839, he wrote *The Charterhouse of Parma*, a story of political intrigue, in Italy.

Henry Wadsworth Longfellow, who taught Italian at Bowdoin College in Maine and translated Dante's *Divine Comedy* into English, Nathaniel Hawthorne, and Samuel Clemens (Mark Twain) also tried to awaken their American brothers to the joys and treasures of travel in Italy.

And then there is William Shakespeare, the greatest of all. Opinions differ on whether he ever visited Italy, but if he did not, the effects that country had upon him were profound, like no other. Let us look at the masterpieces he wrote with settings in Italy: *Romeo and Juliet, Anthony and Cleopatra, Julius Caesar, The Taming of the Shrew, Titus Andronicus, Much Ado About Nothing, The Winter's Tale, The Rape of Lucrece, The Tempest, The Two Gentlemen of Verona*, and *The Merchant of Venice*.

"Open my heart, and you will find inscribed upon it Italy."

Grandpa was not yet through with his *lezioni* (lessons). One day he accompanied me to New Rochelle. We were trying to finish a small apartment building Uncle Joe and I owned. Even though it was for only forty-eight families, finishing a building requires constant, repetitive attention to hosts of little corrections and omissions. If you have ever built a home, or redone a kitchen, you know what I am talking about. You need a little paint here or a few missing tile there; there are chipped walls, unstained or unsanded oak floors, hinges missing or screws loose; or, perhaps there is unglued, resilient tile, a loose toilet seat, or a bent medicine-cabinet door. In the construction business, there are also items that "walk away" from one day to the next. This petty stealing really wreaks havoc with builders. Every time you send a tradesman to fix or replace something, the open apartment becomes vulnerable to the pilfering of hardware, electric switches, stove handles, light bulbs, and so on.

Charlie Platt, who was a great find on this job, was surprisingly sent to us as a laborers' union shop steward, and he became a loyal company man for years thereafter. He was a willing jack-of-all-trades, and he tried, along with Russ Lando, our office manager and temporary "punch-list" organizer, to get the job done. The punch list is the list of all those things needing attention. It requires constant follow-up with electricians, plumbers, roofers, carpenters, waterproofers, painters, and other tradesmen. The ever-willing Russ had been pressed into service, temporarily separated from his office for parts of the day.

Grandpa silently observed all, making his own inspections along with them and noting the need for my involvement. I was not to be disappointed—he was ready to pull a lesson out of the past.

'La coda è difficile a scorticcare' (The tail is difficult to skin), he uttered as we drove away.

He was right. To wrap up any venture is harder than when it is ongoing. When Grandpa's family farmed the countryside outside Caserta, Italy, they always butchered their own meats—usually pigs for prosciuttos, salamis, and sausages, but frequently lambs and sheep, and more rarely, as a community effort, cattle. Grandpa explained that after cuts are made around the neck and the tops of the legs and a long slash is made on the underbelly, it is quite simple to tear the hide away from the flesh. Two strong men can do it in short time—that is, until they get to the tail. Then it is very difficult to separate the hide and flesh. It takes longer to skin the tail, especially around the prized tuft, than the whole carcass!

Grandpa's recollections like these were always a joy to hear, especially the way they brought me back after a strenuous session.

Many proverbs were composed in the essential singsong, and considerable poetic license was taken to make these adages rhyme. I would not say that making proverbs rhyme is a uniquely Italian trait, but the singsong was commonly heard and important to the peasant ear. Of course, there is an advantage in Italian, for almost all words end in rhyming sounds. Richard Armour, that gifted American, would have had so much easier a life if he could have composed his priceless ditties in Italian!

I remember, too, Grandpa's appropriate singsong when he observed a husband and wife arguing at family gatherings:

'Tra moglia e marito non mettere il dito.' (Between husband and wife you don't put your finger.)

This proverb is still a good piece of advice.

My other grandfather, Nonno, would say the following singsong on a rainy morning as he bewailed the apparent loss of work for the whole day:

'Quando piove cappelletta, piove tutta la giornaletta.' (When it rains little priests' hats, it rains the whole day.)

I am certain you have seen those little bubbles gently floating away atop the curb water.

The *comparilli* developed their own, more hopeful petition on rainy mornings as they were forced to crowd the bricklayers' shanty:

"Rain before seven, stop before eleven."

There are singsongs for every facet of life. This one was lightly used, both by the critic and by the all-too-ready "victim" as he or she succumbed to the temptation of devouring the last tasty morsel on a platter:

'Più vicino i denti che i parenti.' (Nearer to the teeth than to the relatives.)

These are for the one person who "never eats" but just "wants to pick":

'Chi non ha volete diciasette se ne fottete.' (Who didn't want any—seventeen were devoured.)

'Chi fa da se, fa per tre.' (Who does for himself does for three.)

Here's one that teaches us that appearance isn't everything:

'Non è l'abito che fa il monaco.' (It is not the habit he wears that makes the monk.)

This one resigns us to the reality that everyone's life is difficult:

'Ogni casetta c'ha la sua crocetta.' (Every house carries its own little cross.)

This is one for the poor bargainer:

'Quello cambia l'occhio per coda.' (He trades an eye for a tail.)

These two singsongs rebuke the fellow who waxes on incessantly but accomplishes little:

'La cera si struda, ma la processione non commincia.' (The candle burns down, but the procession never begins.)

'Troppo fumo, ma niente arrosto.' (Too much smoke, but no roast in the oven.)

"There's many a slip "twixt the cup and the lip" is similar to this time-honored singsong:

'Dal dire al fare c' è mezzo d'un mare.' (From saying to doing lies half an ocean.)

Here are two favorites:

'Chi la dura la vince.' (Who sticks it out wins.)

'La buona donnetta in cucina sembra a tutti una regina.' (The good woman in the kitchen appears to all like a queen.)

For the exaggerator:

'Tre figge, (dialect) la fa nove ruotole.' (Three figs, he makes it nine pecks.)

Everyone can benefit, especially our children, from this proverb:

'O tiene'o scortica la trippa.' (You've got to do something in life—you either stick to it, or you scrape tripe.)

The following singsongs are taught in all Italian humanities classes and are a part of every grade school curriculum. The author is unknown.

Il potere intossica l'anima
quand il vino le gran' menti.
Nessuno e' così buono o così sapiente
un uomo, da essergli affidata
una potenza illimitata.
(Power intoxicates the soul
as wine does great heads.
No man is wise enough, or good enough,
to be trusted with unlimited power.)

Appenna che si mettere a parlare
si commincia gia' a sbagliare.
(As soon as you start to speak,
already you have begun to err.)

La lingue batta
dove il dente duole.
(The tongue seeks out
where the tooth hurts—in other words, pay
attention to what you know
needs attention.)

Il diavolo fa le pentole,
ma non le coperte.

(The devil makes the pots
but not the covers.)

Senza le castagne,
Non si fanno le lesse.
(Without chestnuts, you can't
make chestnut porridge. What this really means is,
without effort, nothing ever gets done.)

Corruptio, otime pessima (Latin).
(When the best become corrupt,
they are the worst.)
(Taught by Father Joe McNamara, deceased)

The rule of the three C's for espresso, in Italian:
La regola delle tre ce:
Caldo, Carrico, Commido
(Hot, full-bodied, comforting)

Also, the rule of the three C's for espresso, in Neapolitan:
Cazze! Come Cocce!
(Balls! How searing hot!)

Acerbic relatives say the following to young ladies in their
family:
Guardalo bene'guardalo tutto!
L'uomo senza' denari,
o'quanto e' brutto!
(Study him well—look him over completely!
A man without money,
gad! How ugly he is!)

Per ogni lacrima di bambino che si asciuga,
si accene una stella in cielo.
(For every tear that is wiped from
the eye of a child,
a star is lighted in the sky.)
(Monsignore Carroll Abbing of
Boys' Towns of Italy)

Per morire e pagare,
c'e' sempre tempo.
(To pay and to die, there is always time.)

This is often spoken on the way home from a picnic:
Che bella vita, se durasse.
Mangia, bera, e stare a spassa.
(What a wonderful life, if only it could last.
Eat and drink and have nothing to do.)

La gallina ruspante ci ha la gozza piena.
(The soil-scratching chicken
has a full gullet.)

Pensando tristessa ècome seduta
nella sedia-a-dondolo.
Lo puoi fare tutta la giornata
ma non vai nessuna partè.
(Worrying is like sitting in a rocking chair.
You can do it all day long,
but it won't get you anywhere.)

Marzo è pazzo.
Guardi o'sole
e cerchi l'ombrello.
(March is crazy.
Observe the sun and seek your umbrella.)

Grandpa had a delightful sense of humor which he mostly kept well-hidden around the house, and he possessed the stand-up comic's ability to laugh at himself or, better yet, to laugh at the foibles and the failures of the people who inhabit this earth. One of his favorite characters, through whom he vicariously exposed his own wry humor, was named Bittordo. Years later I was to find that his real name was Bertoldo. I was in Little Italy on Mulberry Street in Manhattan and chanced upon an illustrated comic-like book entitled *Bertoldo, Bertoldino, and Caccaseno.*

Imagine my joy when I found that this compilation of 200-year-old stories was the precise source of Grandpa's Bittordo episodes. I was certain that all of Grandpa's sources were the hand-me-down type, and now I had further proof.

This Bittordo was what Grandpa described as a *spassatempo* (time-passer). The king kept Bittordo around for laughs (in English Bittordo would be called a court jester). There always was a battle of wits going on between Bittordo and the king, with the king constantly sentencing Bittordo to punishment for insolence. Bittordo, in turn, constantly thwarted the king's directions by outwitting those the king assigned to punish him.

But each story about Bittordo and the king contained a lesson, mostly about the frailties in human nature. To illustrate, one time Bittordo displeased the king, and his punishment was to be chained and paraded before the populace, then whipped and abused by the people. Bittordo pleaded that he be permitted to carry a sign exempting his head from abuse, for otherwise he would be brain-damaged. The king agreed. So Bittordo made up a large sign that he would carry at the head of the parade.

Word had spread of the retinue issuing from the castle, and as the drums alerted the people, a crowd flocked to the streets. What the people saw was Bittordo carrying a sign which said, '*Salvativi il capo, e il resto battate con tutta forza*' (Spare the head, and the rest batter with all your strength). Naturally, the people interpreted this sign to mean, "Save the head of the parade and beat the rest of the participants with abandon'! Again, Bittordo went unscathed as the crowd pelted and whipped the king's men, who were behind the *spassatempo*.

Another time Bittordo irritated the king, and his punishment was to be locked outside the castle gates at night.

"But I shall freeze," protested Bittordo. "How shall I keep warm?"

'*Riscaldati dai calori del Vesuvio*' (Warm yourself with the heat of the fires of Vesuvius), replied the king.

Of course this suggestion was ridiculous, for Mount Vesuvius was twenty miles away.

When Bittordo was cast out into the night, he observed hundreds of clay pots and amphorae piled up on the loggia. To keep warm, he started moving them, one at a time, from one side of the loggia to the other. When he had finished one side, he started moving them back again.

The soldiers came for Bittordo in the morning expecting to find him frozen; instead, they found him *'tutta sudato'* (all perspired).

The king then summoned Bittordo and asked him, "How did you survive the cold?"

'Mi sono riscaldato dai fuochi del Vesuvio' (I warmed myself with the fires of Vesuvius), he answered.

That his very own words should be used infuriated the king, and he warned Bittordo, "I will give you an impossible task, and if you do not succeed, you will have to admit your cowardice before the assembled court. You are to be locked out again and required to scale the ramparts of the castle during the night."

Bittordo realized as he gazed at the sheer walls that he was going to have to admit defeat. But he was to have the last word.

When in the morning the soldiers hauled the half-frozen jester before the king, he castigated Bittordo thus: "You are a man totally without courage, admit it!"

In a response precisely appealing to a pragmatic society designed for survival, Bittordo answered, *'O' corragio ci sta; quell' è la paura che mi fotta'* (The courage is there; it is the fear that damns me).

On a Saturday afternoon, late in August of 1960, I was dressing in the locker room of Leewood Golf Club. Grandpa was in Misericordia Hospital, only fifteen minutes down the Bronx River Parkway. I decided to go see him; I found him alone and resigned, but still in distress. He complained of the pains in his back and shoulders. The signs were ominous.

I spoke to him in Italian as I held his hand. "Grandpa, I am going to give you a little rubdown."

He brightened, and it was then that I, and I think he, realized that I had never seen this private man's body below the neck. The floor nurse provided me with everything I needed, including the small towels to protect his modesty. When I removed his upper pajama, I was in for a surprise. Grandpa had always jokingly told me that he and I were *'della razza dei neri'* (of the race of blacks). Since he was a farmer, his face had been exposed to the warm sun for eighty-four years and was much darker than mine. But his body was milk white, completely free of marks, blotches, or hair follicles—just like a baby's! I reflected how we foolish moderns in our sophisticated world are no longer aware of the devastation caused by cooking our flesh in the searing sun. The old-timers never did, and they didn't have an ozone problem.

Carefully, I kneaded his lower spine and buttocks, then his neck and shoulders. His contented sighs of submission were my reward. The best was yet to come. After I had him refreshed with rubbing alcohol, dusted with talc, and pillowed with fresh linens and pajamas, he seemed to revive.

'*Vieni vicino. Ti voglio benedicare*' (Come closer. I wish to bless you). He reached up and gently touched my cheek. '*Che ti possi cambare cent'anni. La Madonna ti accompagna*' (May you live a hundred years. The Virgin walk with you).

Several days later he was dead. There was no need to cry. It could not have been any better.

Leonardo da Vinci said, '*Mentre mi imparai di vivere, mi imparai di morire*' (While I was learning to live, I was learning to die).

O simple yet noble Ulysses, your odyssey is complete.

Epilogue

Several hundred miles south of where my grandparents were born, the toes of Italy's mainland boot end, only three and a half miles from the football of Sicily. The mountains forming the toes fall almost straight down into the sea. That area is denoted La Sila on the maps of Italy. This forest supplied the huge pine masts for the ships of ancient mariners. The boot of Italy, together with Sicily, intrudes like a pointed finger into the Mediterranean Sea.

Much history is written here.

Before air travel, no commerce or contact between east and west was possible without being intercepted by Italy. There are only two sea lanes open: the sixty miles between Sicily and Africa, and the three and a half miles between the boot and football. This latter is the historically treacherous stretch of water now known as the Strait of Messina. These dangerous waters, however, were known in Greek mythology as the waters between

Scylla and Charybdis. The Greek poet Homer wrote about them in *The Odyssey*, an epic poem which relates the story of the travels of Ulysses (Odysseus in Greek), King of Ithaca.

Scylla was a beautiful nymph, but when she refused to return the love of the sea god, Glaucus, he appealed to Circe, a sorceress. She, in turn, wanted Glaucus to love her instead, and when he would not, Circe in a rage turned the innocent Scylla into a ferocious sea monster fated to inhabit those waters. The once-captivating nymph became part woman and part fish, with heads of dogs growing out of her waist. Scylla went to live in a cave in the mountains across from Charybdis, who was a whirlpool personified. Those mountains, and the plateau above, are the La Sila of today. All sea travelers, therefore, had no choice but to steer a middle course between the two frightening evils. And so eventually did Ulysses. This has come down to us as the commonly used expression "between Scylla and Charybdis," which means having to make a choice between two evils. Our young people today inelegantly say "between a rock and a hard place."

These stories of the classics were not unknown to the peasants. Though there was a considerable lack of formal education, daily exposure to the ruins of Greek and Roman temples, architecture, sculptures, frescoes, and paintings contributed to a culture alive with the sense of history.

If you visit the island of Capri, which is only twenty miles from Cicciano, on an isolated flower-bedecked path close by the tennis courts you will find a restaurant named Glauco. It takes its name from the sea god, Glaucus, mentioned above.

Back on the mainland, visible across the bay, hangs the multi-colored town of Positano, which today is a magnet and mecca for devotees of the arts, theater, and dance. Each summer these patrons come from all over the world to climb up and down the ancient stairways that also serve as the alleys and paths of this bewitching town stuck onto the face of the mountains. The gaily colored houses sit like boxes piled one atop the other, slightly set back so that the roof of one becomes the courtyard for its neighbor above.

The concept of condominiums, with common ownership of essential land, halls, paths, gardens, and entrances, is a postwar phenomenon in the United States. The physical topography of the mountain-scarred land of the Italian boot, however, forced the concept of condominium ownership to exist for over two thousand years.

If you go to Positano, among other records of the past, you will find Le Sirenuse, a luxurious small hotel of seven set-back levels. This hotel's dialectal name refers to the Sirens, the beautiful sea nymphs who called out to Ulysses and all other sailors passing by. From their homeland on the island of Capri, these treacherous but irresistible nymphs caused mariners and their ships to founder on the rocks. The sailors, intoxicated by the beautiful voices of the nymphs, would forget their home and friends and eventually starve to death.

Unnecessary to the point I am making, but interesting nonetheless, is the story of how Ulysses resisted the beckoning calls of the Sirens (known in modern parlance as the siren song). First, he sealed the ears of his sailors—but not his own—with molten wax, and then he had them tie him to the mast of the ship. The sailors could not hear the calls of the Sirens, but Ulysses could, though he was unable to free himself to go to them. Only in this manner was the ever-curious Ulysses able to sail his men past the temptations of the Sirens but still be able to hear their enchanting voices.

Interesting also, and to complete the story, is Homer's lesson on human nature. The Sirens had their own selfish motives for their determination to tempt the sailors. A condition of their survival was that the Sirens would die if someone sailed by unmoved by their songs. Positano and Capri still bewitch passersby, while nearby Sorrento forever calls out to its sons and daughters in that hauntingly tearful song "Torn A Sorrento" (Come Back to Sorrento).

I would like to add here one more piece of information about Ulysses. During his travels, he wore the armor of Achilles, which was given to him by the Greeks in recognition of his heroism in the Trojan War. You will remember Zi Giuan's son, Achille, was named after that hero.

You will also find in Capri or Positano, and in every other town, other recordings of the past, such as the Hotel Poseidon (named after the god of the sea) and Cove dei Saraceni (Cove of the Saracens), as well as the restaurant Buca di Bacco (Cave of

Bacchus, the god of wine).

Pompeii, the ancient city destroyed by the eruption of Mount Vesuvius in A.D. 79, lay only twelve miles from Cicciano, my family's hometown.

This constant exposure to ancient history and a culture that values its past is reflected in the heroic names given to countless Italian children, and does so to this day.

For example, the street urchin Orazio is named after the Roman poet, Horace. From the heroes of the Trojan War come your headwaiters, Ettore (Hector) and Achille (Achilles). From the Punic Wars between Rome and Carthage come the school-boys, Annibale (Hannibal) and Ammilcare (Hamilcar, Hannibal's father). You will remember Hannibal as the general who brought the elephants over the Alps and almost defeated Rome on its own turf.

Then there are the everyday Romans sporting the street names of former emperors and generals: Ottavio (Octavius), Cesare (Caesar), Marcello (Marcellus), Augustus, Claudio (Claudius), Adriano (Hadrian), and Massimo (Maximus, which means the greatest).

Your barbers are Romolo (Romulus) and Remo (Remus), to whom the aforementioned restaurant owner on Capri, Glauco (Glaucus), goes for hair trimming. Moreover, schools are full of Dantes and Virgilios (Virgil), as well as the occasional Petrarca (Petrarch).

Other restaurant owners are Omero (Homer), Ercole (Hercules), and Dario (King Darius of Persia), joined by the biblical Ennio (Ennaus) and Sansone (Samson). My people's children would not be left without a legacy.

Also on Capri the dogs, all of whom are of one black strain, are named Tiberio after Tiberius, the tyrant emperor, the remnants of whose villa you can still visit today. You can stand at the spot, which is about a thousand feet above the sea, where he had his slaves thrown to the rocks below simply for enjoyment!

But before the reign of Tiberius, his stepfather, Caesar Augustus, had built his villa on the highest point of the island, almost three thousand feet above the sea, and the remains are there for you to enjoy as you sip your ever-present espresso. The chair lift takes you above the steep hills over which Augustus was pulled in a sled driven over felled trees by relays of hundreds of slaves. Most of the pavements upon which pagan gods were depicted in mosaics have been removed to the National Museum in Naples across the bay. The people lived every day with these presents.

We see a parallel today in our own country. The black mother, adrift in a mostly matriarchal society, often devoid of material riches with which to endow her newborn, creates unique and tortured spellings of names. This singular effort is an attempt to distinguish that child from all the rest, and hopefully to bestow an individual sense of pride and security. That is their legacy.

I saw in Grandpa every day a conscious attempt to link himself with tradition, with the past. He strove constantly to educate himself and to leave a legacy greater than that with which he entered this world. He did.

Chapter IV

New York, New York

It was the winter of 1950. Uncle Joe and I were coming down the elevator in the Fuller Building at Madison Avenue and 57th Street, and his eyes caught mine.

"I know why you did it," he said.

We had just closed the contract with the George A. Fuller Company, one of the leading general contractors in the country, to do the masonry work on the Lever Brothers Building. The building, only then in foundation stage, had excited people in the construction scene like no other postwar building. Having received much notoriety, accolades for the building's design had come forth from all directions.

How I thirsted to get that building! I could see in my mind's eye our family name on Park Avenue. Now I can look back and smile at myself. As success comes, naiveté is replaced by blasé, if I can make a noun out of that.

It is interesting to reflect that the more exciting memories in our lives are those we knew when we were struggling toward success. Success, once attained, has an unfortunate way of diluting that excitement. The answer, I suppose, is to find new challenges—possibly in altruistic pursuits.

Uncle Joe was right; I had signed the contract for my father. He had died three years before, a young man of fifty. You see, I had lowered our price over two hundred thousand dollars in order to get that masonry contract because I knew before we went in that the Fuller Company was reluctant to break its pattern of subletting only to Anglo-Saxon, Irish contractors. I had to make them an offer they couldn't refuse, and I did. We had beat out the John B. Kelly's of Philadelphia—or had we beat ourselves?

When Uncle Joe and I stepped out of that elevator, two things were certain: we would have to move like hell not to lose our shirts, and we were happy. Two hundred thousand dollars was big money in those days, not to mention the year of effort we would invest. But on the other hand, we were going to work on a building that was famous before it was even completed!

Within a day, our men knew about the contract. Vince Basciano, one of my father's *comparilli* and now second in command only to Guy Vallese among our labor foremen, came up to me in New Rochelle, a waterfront suburb of New York City. We were doing the brickwork on Harbour House, a cluster of seven apartment buildings overlooking Long Island Sound. The builder was Aaron Diamond, a sterling man who was brilliant when it came to construction financing. Aaron had become my mentor in real-estate analyses. He had invited us to participate in syndication ownership of several apartment buildings in New York City. That was the beginning of a long and happy relationship which lasted until Aaron's death in 1984.

"Take me for coffee," said Vince. "I want to talk to you."

Vince loved these one-on-one confabs away from the job. It was a perk he had earned with dedication, and I recognized his need. When we sat down in the Howard Johnson's on Boston Post Road, Vince asked me if I remembered what he had said to me as we embraced at Gate of Heaven Cemetery immediately after my father's burial. I did. He had said, "Don't let people talk."

I no longer resented this old story. My ego had been considerably satisfied over these past three years, yet I knew emotional maturity was a continually satisfying goal still to be attained. Vince wanted me to know that my father had been 'un uomo rispetatto' (a man of respect), and further, that I still had an obligation to carry forward for my family and for that little Italian neighborhood known as Villa Avenue in the Bronx. I know it is difficult for you, my reader, to understand this. Villa Avenue was connected to 204th Street by a tunnel under the Grand Concourse. When you spoke of one, you spoke of both, including Saint Philip Neri Church.

"I know about the price," he said. "Don't worry. You give me Dominick Vitolo and his father, Giuseppe, as well as Dominick Carrozza with Sandy Jackson and Andy, and Ralph Belloise on the bells, and we'll make that hoist fly. The men are all primed—they're rarin' to go." (The hoist is the construction elevator that delivers the material to the floors in high-rise buildings. Its operation is a pulse of the job. Split-second timing is essential.)

Italian men are forever embracing, and frequently I see others looking askance, especially at those walking arm in arm. But our embrace at that moment was instinctive and sincere, and very satisfying. Vince was a bear of a man, and we must have been a sight—he was wearing his sheepskin coat and rubber, knee-length boots! Loyalty like that can't be bought for money, nor can money buy such memories.

And the job was a success, in all ways, because of the determination of our men. We also got a few breaks. Someone said, "It seems the harder I work, the luckier I get."

Behind the facade of what was a mostly green exterior, a brand-new material—foam-glass insulation—was to be installed against the entire concrete structure and exterior walls. Only the line of actual see-through windows was exempt. Joe Orefice and Louis Jodice, our two in-house engineers, and I had researched this new material. It was jet-black spun glass, sharp as a razor, and formed into two-inch-thick blocks that were two feet long and sixteen inches high.

A jurisdictional dispute among unions had ensued regarding this new insulation. The roofers, as well as the masons, had claimed this material. Fortunately, the matter was resolved before we had to start work. Since the use of a trowel was involved, the bricklayers had won out. Good for us! We would not have to engage strangers as installers.

Because we didn't know what to expect, I had decided on a

conservative, but competitive anticipated production per day per bricklayer. Half a year later, when it came time to start the work, I spoke to Uncle Joe about my concerns.

We decided to take the erstwhile apple farmer, Uncle Andrew, now a top-notch layout man, and develop a separate crew under his control. The decision was sound. Within a week, Andrew and his men had developed new techniques and their own tools for cutting and fitting this insulation. They soon discarded the heavy gloves, which we had thought would be needed to protect the hands against the ripping and tearing of the foam glass. They were too unyielding to permit easy handling. Plain, soft cotton gloves were the answer, so we ordered them by the gross. New ones were needed every few hours, but the results were instantaneous. Production soared! The men were doubling and tripling my estimates of output, and they did so for four months!

One of the reasons I wanted to get the masonry contract for the acclaimed Lever Brothers Building was to increase our company's visibility. But my endeavors to do so threatened to fail. In the six months between contracting for the job and its actual start, I had some attractive porcelain enamel signs made. These metal-backed signs in maroon and gray were dignified and read simply "F. & J. Puzio Const. Co. — Masonry, Westchester, N.Y." The sidewalk bridges lined three streets—the whole block front on Park Avenue, as well as East 53rd and 54th Streets between Park and Madison Avenues. Sidewalk bridges are the heavy-timbered walkway tunnels that permit pedestrians and workers to pass or work safely in front of construction projects. Atop these bridges we erected our signs, visible to thousands passing daily.

Within a week, the trouble started. Al Stola, our head foreman on the job, was instructed by the Fuller Company to remove the signs. This he refused to do without authorization from his office. That afternoon, I got Al's message when I stepped into our office in Bronxville, New York. I told him not to do anything until I got to the job in the morning. Well, the next morning the construction manager for the Fuller Company told me that Jim Murphy, the company's vice president, had given him the instructions to have us remove the signs. I refused to comply.

The next day we received a telegram at the office stating that we were "in violation of our contract." I was aware of the fine print the Fuller Company was talking about. I had signed the contract, knowing full well that buried among the reams of printed pages was the simple prohibition against displaying our name. The Fuller Company was not alone. Many general contractors like to make it appear as if they alone man every facet of the building's construction. Actually, corps of subcontractors in every trade engage the little men who give soul to a structure. I had chosen to disregard the clause at signing. I was prepared at that time neither to abandon the chance to do the building nor to pursue a fruitless confrontation. But by evading the sign issue during the contract negotiations, I would see the issue magnified later.

I would rely on my wits, like my ancestors, to deal with the Fuller Company and their insistence that we take down our signs. One of my mother-in-law's bywords must have been buzzing in my ears: '*Dice sempre sì, che non è mai peccato*' (Always say yes, for it is never a sin). In other words, there is no need to confront the issue prematurely.

I reached out for advice from my two adoptive fathers, Tommy Napoli and Guy Vallese. That night we met at the Mezza Luna (Half Moon) Pizzeria on 187th Street and Arthur Avenue in the Bronx. This pocket Italian neighborhood was—and is—the largest of the half-dozen or so Bronx enclaves that sheltered Italian immigrants as they arrived from overseas.

Interestingly, each of these neighborhoods developed into a rather homogeneous *paese* (hometown) representing the different Italian provinces. Arthur Avenue was home to those mainly from Bari (Baresi), Calabria (Calabresi), and Apuglia (Apugliesi). Our own area of Bedford Park, Villa Avenue, was almost exclusively Neapolitan. The Throggs Neck and Soundview areas supported the Genovesi (Genoans) and Abruzzesi (the Abruzzis). White Plains Avenue, North of Pelham Parkway, was peopled by an amalgam of those south and east of Naples. The Sicilian influence, however, was not strongly felt in the Bronx; it was much stronger in other boroughs, though.

The same divisions were noted elsewhere, too. East Harlem in Manhattan was home mainly to Siciliani (Sicilians) and some

Napolitani (Neapolitans) north of 112th Street. Mulberry Street (East Village) in South Manhattan was strongly Neapolitan. Greenwich Village (MacDougal Street) was mostly Alt' Italiani (North Italians). There was a logical reason why so few Alt' Italiani migrated to the United States. *La miseria* (poverty) was not so prevalent in those relatively affluent parts of Italy, so people from these areas had few reasons to leave. This is why you hardly ever meet immigrants from Tuscany, Piedmont, Veneto, or Bologna.

There was also an interesting division of skills among the workmen. The Tremont Avenue area supported many plasterers and tile layers. The East Bronx and Soundview areas, with the superb Genovese bricklayers, were replete with experts in marble, concrete work, and cement finishing. Our own area of Bedford Park was heavy in stonemasons, bricklayers, and construction laborers. The Sicilians in Harlem and Brooklyn were mainly into lathing and plastering as well as the garment industries. The seamstresses, garment cutters, and tailors became the backbone of the ILGWU, the International Ladies' Garment Workers' Union, one of the strongest unions in the United States.

But let's get back to Tommy Napoli and Guy Vallese. The Mezza Luna (Half Moon) Pizzeria still had the old-fashioned brick oven. To make the real Neapolitan pizza, only this behemoth of an oven with its ceramic stone floor suffices. These ovens derived from the Saracens, who had periodically invaded Southern Italy beginning in the sixth century. It is a pity to see these ovens go. I know of only two left in the Bronx and four in Manhattan. I have been told there are others in Brooklyn, but the only one I know is Totò's in Coney Island.

I opted for pizza and clams *oreganata*, both of which are made in the open coal-fired oven, and a salad. Guy and Tommy were from the older vegetarian school. Escarole and beans over a bed of broken chunks of hard Italian bread, with a side order of broccoli *di rape* sautéed with garlic and oil, was their choice. The homemade wine was served in carafes laden with fresh-cut fruits. What satisfaction!

Tommy and Guy knew my problem regarding the signs. "The first thing you do is stop fighting," said Tommy. "You give in, then *aspetta*" (Wait and see what happens).

Guy chimed in. "You leava that to me."

But this was not Guy's job. He was occupied at that time at the Danskammer Power Station, about sixty miles up the Hudson River north of Newburgh, New York. In addition to the construction of the Lever Brothers Building and work on other jobs, we were doing the brickwork on a new generating plant for Central Hudson Gas & Electric Corporation. (Walsh Construction Company was the general contractor for the generating plant.) But I knew that Vince would defer to Guy's intrusion on his job. Guy's quiet demeanor belied his authority. He was absolutely adored by his men. Vince would not challenge that.

The next morning the signs came down, and they remained down for several weeks. Upon my visit to the job site one day, though, I noticed one of our signs sticking out near the twelfth floor on East 54th Street, back from Park Avenue. The next day it was gone. A complaint call came in from the Fuller Company's construction supervisor—someone had seen a sign. By that time it was too late. Signs would appear and disappear on different streets, at different times, on different levels, and on different sides of different hoists. This cat-and-mouse game went on for months, and it was not only a success, but a source of fun for the men.

In the summer of 1951, President Truman sacked General MacArthur in Korea, but New York City honored MacArthur with a hero's welcome and a fabulous parade up Park Avenue, which passed right in front of our building. Nobody noticed or cared to object by parade time, but suddenly there appeared five of our signs, festooned with ribbons of red, white, and blue. The television cameras carried the scenes of hundreds of construction men, including ours, wildly greeting MacArthur. Naturally, our signs received prominent attention.

At our annual Christmas party that following winter, I found out exactly what had happened. The Saturday after my meeting with Guy and Tommy, Guy had visited the job site. Dominick Carrozza and Dominick Vitolo had been assigned the job and the strategy. I was not to be compromised with the Fuller Company. I learned that at coffee break each morning the whole crew of laborers decided where to place the signs, if any, that day. The whole affair became a morale booster, and after a while the

Fuller Company gave up the ghost. By the end of the job that winter, we had had enough exposure to satisfy even me.

Of such simple pleasures were the rewards of these hard-working men! *'Dice sempri sì, che non è mai peccato.'* She was right again.

A large part of the job we did on the Lever Brothers Building was installing the structural facing tile (SFT). All the stairwells and a cafeteria that spanned one whole floor were completely formed of SFT. This is not the flat tile you see in your bathroom. As the name describes, it is structural in nature, that is, it can support itself and other loads. The utility and beauty come in its surface. The ceramic glaze is integrally baked on in selected colors and can be either smooth- or sandy-grained. When sandy-grained in its natural buff biscuit color, it is called salt-glazed tile (SGT), a surface you will see in many public buildings, like Grand Central Terminal. I'm sure you have seen SGT in hundreds of public restrooms, too. Competently handling structural facing tile (sometimes called PG by the men for porcelain glaze) is probably the most satisfying work a brick mason can do.

Our top bricklayer foreman, Al Stola, had been assigned the Lever Brothers Building for several reasons. Al was a superb craftsman who was tall, rugged, and handsome; his very presence commanded respect. After a few days on the job, he could point out architectural inconsistencies or errors in the construction plans. He was always cooperative, quietly suggesting a solution to a problem. Al's attitude quickly earned the confidence of the foremen of other trades, and at job meetings, the architects' and builders' representatives sought out Al's suggestions. No matter how expert, designers cannot foresee all the problems which come up in actual construction. Professional people understand this and are anxious for the advice experts like Al can give.

Most SFT comes in twelve-by-five-inch blocks, with thicknesses ranging from two-inch (called soaps), four-inch, six-inch, eight-inch, and sometimes, on special order, twelve-inch, depending on the loads the walls must carry.

The beauty of SFT comes also in its utility. When the work is completed properly, the entire room can be washed down with a hose. There are no exposed pipes, ducts, electrical cables, baseboards, or trim. All built-ins, including doors, windows, closets, cabinets, and fixtures, are enclosed or supported on pedestals cleanly and completely built of SFT.

In order to complete a room with SFT, a multitude of special shapes of tile must be baked, some of which are extremely expensive because they require hand-molding. I will try not to confuse you, but I will ask you to use your ability to visualize. If you start out by remembering that you want to avoid all sharp corners and that hygiene is paramount, you will follow me.

At the bottom of any wall or partition you want the wall tile to meet the quarry-tile floor. This requires a cove base, which on the bottom has a curve which translates from wall to floor.

Around a window you first have a sill, which requires the installation of bullnose pieces, which have a rounded exterior angle along their length. On the side of the window you need bullnose jambs. These are regular stretchers with a bullnose return added on one end. To trim the other side of the window, you simply turn this piece over so that the bullnose end is on the left rather than the right. To form the head, or top, of the window you need bullnose lintel pieces, which are much like the sills.

The really interesting challenges come in where the jambs meet the heads and sills, requiring two curved pieces precisely cut to match against each other. To accomplish this cutting, large diamond-embedded electrical saw blades are needed. These rigs are not handsaws, but table benches installed with rigid saws. These sixteen-inch blades are precision-machined, with industrial diamond chips baked into the graphite steel edge.

The cutter for this job is a mason, selected because he has a particular talent for such precise work. Sometimes so much cutting is required that two or more saws have to be set up.

I wish not to confuse you, but I want you to appreciate some of the difficult work a bricklayer encounters when building a room out of SFT, such as when two intersecting walls both meet the cove base, or when the top of a dwarf wall (one that is not as high as the ceiling) not only is exposed on two sides and requires a double bullnose top, but also happens to be the right and left end of the wall and thus requires bullnose ends on the right and left, as well. Wow!

My description here is intended not only as a primer on

masonry, but as a reminder that brickwork is an art form: when a bricklayer puts on his overalls, you are watching an artisan at work. An understanding of the intricacies of a bricklayer's trade lends dignity to his work and life, a goal which is increasingly slipping away from us. I wish I could tell you lack of pride and dignity does not represent a threat to our country. It does. Witness the Japanese, younger people.

It took six months to complete the stairwells as well as the kitchen and cafeteria on the Lever Brothers Building. The take-off men, Joe Orefice and Louis Jodice, had to be precise in antic-ipating, estimating, and ordering all the special shapes needed. Sometimes as much as three months' lead time is needed for the factory to produce complicated specials. The real distress is when these packaged pieces finally arrive, only they are chipped or cracked. Frequently, too, they are lost in transit or handling among the thousands of shapes in inventory.

To see the finished product, however, is very gratifying to the men as well as to us: As Guy had said, '*Piano, piano è fatto il mondo*' (Little by little the world is made).

Some really funny things happen in new York Town. Sooner or later we should have expected something like the following to happen, and it did.

Most New Yorkers know the Sutton Theatre on East 57th Street, just east of Third Avenue. In 1960, there was a Schrafft's restaurant right on the corner of Third Avenue, immediately adjacent to its neighbor, the Sutton Theatre. Schrafft's was a chain of deluxe sandwich shops and ice-cream parlors. They are no more, and the quality of life in New York suffered with their demise. In those days, this particular one catered mightily to the extremely well-kept ladies and other well-to-do residents of the Sutton Place area, probably the most affluent part of the city.

On the other side of the Sutton Theatre, we were building Harridge House, a twenty-story apartment building which would run all the way through to 58th Street. Aaron Diamond was the builder. Uncle Joe and I were small partners.

Earlier I mentioned sidewalk bridges. Well, each lunch hour some of the men, especially the younger ones, repaired to a section of sidewalk bridge to watch the world go by. And an interesting world it was here near Schrafft's, with bejeweled dowagers, chauffeured shoppers, and cane-toting, derby-topped gentlemen.

If you were good at balancing yourself atop the one-inch edge of a one-by-six, you became one of the observers that lined both sides of the sidewalk bridge fencing. Actually, the observers were part of the show because they knew that their outrageously large *panini* and their affectedly rough demeanor were as much a source of interest to the hoi polloi as vice versa.

Among the observers one day, besides me, was Frankie Rocca, one of our younger bricklayers. This twenty-six-year-old carried his mischievously handsome head on a rugged six-foot-one body, all of which was perched this day atop the fencing. Even his black hair and bronzed face were covered with the white patina of mortar. Suddenly, all our eyes were drawn to a fascinating sight. Coming toward us from the East River precincts of Sutton Place was an extremely well-kept lady undulating in all the right places, her white-blonde hair perfectly coifed, with four white French poodles stretching the sleeves of her black, tightly-tailored suit. Fifty pairs of eyes drank in the scene as they followed her approach from the east. It was her day, and she was going to make the most of it.

As she paraded down the sidewalk bridge, we expressed our approval with unconscious murmurs and wide-open stares. As she passed Frankie Rocca, she must have noticed a picture much to her liking, for after several more steps she stopped, backed up to where he was seated atop the fence, looked up into his eyes, and said calmly but distinctly for us all to hear, "I'm going to fuck you."

Frankie jumped off his perch, bowed like a cavalier of old, and said, "Lady, you came to the right place." With that he offered her his arm, and off they strolled back toward Sutton Place, the snow-white giant and the sexy lady in black, with four confused poodles in tow.

Much to his credit, Frankie never volunteered a word about what happened after that on Sutton Place. He came back about half an hour before quitting time, the smug look on his face the same as that which would appear years later whenever anyone tried to bring up the subject.

Only in New York Town.

In all our years of construction, with thousands of men and hundreds of projects, as far west as Detroit and as far south as Norfolk, we never had a fatal accident. I cannot recall even an overnight hospital stay for one of our men. For this we can take some credit, but not much. It was simply ordained to be otherwise. By whom? I can only thank God that I never had to make that call on the wife and children of one of my men.

But one accident was so close, and could have been so massive, that after twenty-five years I still tremble at the thought of it. The incident happened on Sutton Place and 59th Street, overlooking the East River, with the most spectacular Queensboro Bridge alongside. The site was the most superb I ever worked on, and the present residents of this white-and-pink brick apartment building have no idea of the price that was almost paid to create their dwelling. The builder was Carl Morse of Diesel Construction, our bricklayer foreman was Al Stola, and our labor foreman was Vince Basciano.

If you have ever observed high-rise construction, you know that the reinforced concrete contractor (or structural steel erector) creates his frame of the building, then the masons follow behind and lay the brick to enclose the structure. It would be too expensive for the builder to allow the masons to wait until the structural frame itself is completed before starting the brickwork. Therefore, the practice of the masons installing temporary outriggers at intermediate floors to support their hanging scaffolding is used. We would usually start when the concrete men had gone past the tenth or twelfth floor. On the rest of the building, we would follow about eight floors behind.

This practice introduces serious safety hazards, however. Working below other tradesmen is dangerous enough, but when you examine the standard equipment of reinforced concrete contractors, you are justifiably concerned. Their mainstay rig is a huge crane with a swinging boom that rises thirty floors or more into the air. The wet concrete is hoisted in massive buckets by the boom and then dumped in a hopper.

On the floor where the concrete and mechanical contractors are working, heavy-duty, motorized buggies transport the concrete from the hopper to where it is needed. These buggies look like big golf carts, with gaping maws which tilt to disgorge up to half a cubic yard of concrete. The concrete alone weighs over a ton. The drivers of these buggies fly around on plywood "raceways" that are erected over the already-installed reinforcing bars. The drivers are an elite corps of "cowboys," exciting everybody by their speeding, twisting, turning, and braking reflexes. The opportunity for disaster increases, for at the edge of the deck there is nothing.

The concrete contractor was DIC-Underhill, a marriage of the two largest and most proficient operators in that business at the time. They were working around the twentieth floor, and we were around the eleventh. The exterior scaffolds in this type of construction are pumped up via cables in two stages per floor, once at "scaffold-high," an intermediate height at which brick are laid at head level, and above which efficient and quality work cannot be performed, and again at "story high."[21]

At scaffold-high, the entire crew of men must be shifted to new walls. A cycle of clockwise or counterclockwise coordination with the other tradesmen is established on each job, so that ultimately on each floor the entire perimeter of the building's walls are traversed twice. On this day, about twenty bricklayers and their ten *manuali* and *scaffaioli* were topping out walls on an interior courtyard facing both south and toward the East River.

Corner men were already bringing up their "leads" on walls facing Sutton Place. Al Stola sent word for Frank Mazzarulli to start shifting the men to him. Frank Mazzarulli was a deputy foreman to Al on this job, but he was awaiting the start of his own job on the Blue Cross-Blue Shield Building at 27th Street and Lexington Avenue. He started sending the men to Al, retaining a few for "pointing up" and "brushing down." A good foreman never leaves his work unfinished, and Frank was one of the best.

A good brick wall is just like a well-tailored suit: there is a reason for both, and the word is finish. In brickwork there are always malformed joints, especially at window jambs and where steel angles support the brick over openings. There are "snots," clumps of loose mortar that adhere to some of the brick, and

---

21. The scaffolds hang from cables which extend from structural beams embedded in the concrete many floors above the scaffolds. The men use winches to wind up the cables to raise the scaffolding.

these must be cleaned off. There are also open joints that need to be filled. Important, too, is the cleaning out of the weep holes, the system in cavity-wall construction (mostly used in high-rise buildings), whereby air is permitted to ventilate the backs of the bricks.

Five minutes before it happened, thirty men were working around the eleventh floor. Two minutes before it happened, seven men were there. The last to leave was Frank Mazzarulli.

On the twentieth floor, the drama was unfolding. A concrete buggy "cowboy" was flying east toward the edge of the courtyard. His fellow workers judged his daring by the coordination of his speed, his sideways-skidding stop, and the simultaneous dipping of his rig's maw to unload the wet cement. Something went wrong. The sideways skidding didn't stop the buggy. With lightning speed, the operator flew off his perch, rolled toward the edge of the building, and held on. The buggy flew over the edge of the building.

The men in the street tell me there were two noises—the sharp crack as the buggy's three tons demolished our scaffolds, followed by a dull thud that shook the building when the rig hit the courtyard. Our men on the whipping scaffolds grasped for cables, or anything else to hold onto, as caterpillar undulations circuited the building.

Aside from the fear, no one was hurt. Frank Mazzarulli, by a stroke of luck, had just turned the corner. The scaffold men had not yet returned to start pumping up the scaffolds, and the rest of our men had been able to hold on. In the courtyard below, not a man had been working or passing by.

The damage was considerable. A jumble of scaffolds, steel, and newly erected walls lay in the courtyard. Many steel outrigger beams, embedded in concrete, were grotesquely twisted.

There was no more work that day. There must have been some worried celebrating on Gun Hill Road that afternoon, for who among us controls his fate? We were fortunate to have a little cadre of faithful workers from that area of the Bronx. Together with Frank were his brother Joe Mazzarulli, buddy Joey Torrenti, and Joey's two sons—all bricklayers, or soon to be—and Frank D'Angelica, who I believe was a brother-in-law. Frank D'Angelica was becoming a top-notch labor foreman.

Destiny was not yet through with Frank Mazzarulli. This conscientious gentleman and avid fisherman had yet another date about eight years later, after Uncle Joe and I had parted. The site was New York City, the building again was a high-rise apartment, and the scenario was remarkably similar. But there was mourning on Gun Hill Road that night. The concrete man's wooden jack pole came straight down, passed through the overhead protection plank, and drove straight through Frank's body eighteen stories below. He never knew.

'La vita è come una cipolla; più si scortisce, più si piange' (Life is like an onion; the more you peel it, the more you cry).

This episode could be entitled "The Lady in the Window," and it happened at 310 East 70th Street in Manhattan, just east of Second Avenue, on the south side of the street. We were building two apartment buildings for Aaron Diamond, the larger one being across the street at 315 East 70th Street. Uncle Joe and I were minority partners. These buildings look like twins because the white-enameled face brick, with tiny, black, speckled iron spots (pyrites), was used on both. Go there and see.

Tommy Napoli was the foreman, with Uncle Louis as his deputy. Guy Vallese was the labor foreman. Al Stola was coming later to start the other building, which was running about six weeks behind this one. The latter was to have Frank D'Angelica as labor foreman, his first venture in that capacity. Guy would keep an eye on him by overseeing daily from across the street.

Young Frankie D'Angelica's enthusiasm was always a joy to watch. He possessed a healthy, happy ambition and was well schooled, which reflected in his keeping meticulous records of inventories, assignments, employees' time, and equipment installations. The record keeping was a new and welcome approach, for the old-timers had been forced to keep records in their heads (though they had considerable success, I might add).

The bricklayers' shanties were always put about three floors above the ground floor, for several reasons. Two obvious reasons were that, being above the ground level resulted in less morning commotion and easy access to the job site after climbing a few flights. The third reason tied in with production. Another union rule was that the men had to start out together from the shanties when (and not before) the shop steward blew his whistle. This means walking up (or down) whatever number of flights to and from their work stations, and that added up to four "walking-time" trips per day. When you are working on a building that is twelve, eighteen, or more stories high, saving those initial four floors can be a considerable factor. Today the unions require passenger elevators for building workers who must climb more than twelve stories. Not then.

But a discussion of walking time is not the reason for this story. Adjoining this modern apartment building on the west was an older, twelve-story building, where the so-called lot-line windows were permitted to be installed in slightly recessed walls, designated as "air shafts." When our building went up alongside, you could almost reach across to the recessed windows.

You can visualize that as our building progressed, the concrete floors above cut out most of the light to the adjoining buildings. In the early morning gloom, the occupants were forced to turn on the lights, and each of these lighted windows stood out like a beacon in the recess, isolated from its neighbors above and below, as well as cut off from the windows of the residents on the other side of our new building. The result, like the girls in Amsterdam who do their advertising in street-level window boxes, was the reason why putting our shanties on that floor was not such a good idea.

I knew nothing about what was going on until I visited Tommy Napoli on about the seventh floor early one morning. It was just before the 8:00 A.M. starting time, and I heard the shop steward's whistle as Tommy was laying out.

After waiting for what seemed like ten minutes for the men to climb the four flights, I asked Tommy, "What's going on?"

He said, "You'd better go down and shake them up. You'll see!"

I found Uncle Louis trying to break up the congregation at the far side of the building. The sight that greeted me was a tableau, a real stage setting. The lights were on in the kitchen opposite, the flimsy curtain pulled back, and clearly etched there was this very well-formed young woman standing before her kitchen range, attired in flimsy panties and nothing else. She forced herself to be completely oblivious to the twenty or so pairs of eyes ogling her from very nearby. Whether she was advertising or was the female version of a lecher, I do not know, but she sure was entitled to the attentions she was getting! My comments like, "Come on, let's get to work," were really unnecessary. My presence had already broken up the party, and the men were sheepishly trudging toward the stairs.

"It's like this every morning," said Uncle Louis. "She starts early. At least we don't have trouble getting the men to the job early."

Later I spoke to Tommy and Guy about what we should do. Guy said there was no sense in moving the shanties; the men would congregate on that floor anyway. I had Tommy inform the steward and the men that if they did not start out for work at the whistle, we would dock the laggards an hour and require them to start at 9:00 A.M. There really was no more trouble after that; the men simply took in the burlesque show earlier in the morning.

I can just hear the judge intoning, and my reader, too: "And you, Mr. Writer, did you return to the scene of the titillation for a few peeks?"

"Guilty, Your Honor, on all counts—several times!"

Once, again, only in New York Town!

Chapter V

Making the Wine

We all have our passions. For some it is fishing, for others golf or bowling. For my people it was making wine. You could feel the excitement building about the last week in August. On Reservoir Oval, Uncle Al was helping Nonno air out the barrels. My two cousins, Sonny and Jamesie (sons of Uncle Johnny), and I had already been told by Nonno that by September 15 we were expected to stomp the grapes.

Across Mosholu Park, Uncle Nick was already pressed into service by Granpa. Zi Giuan, only 500 feet away on Reservoir Oval, was trying to hide his operations from Nonno. But Nonno knew that Zi Giuan's obscured backyard already contained the barrels cleaned out by cousins Caggy (Achille), Louis, and Johnny Mosca.

Up in Williamsbridge, there was more activity. Zi Antonio o'Lungo and his two sons, Guy and Ralph, were devoting the entire weekend to preparations. Would they steal away to the West Farms New Haven Railroad to see when the grapes were expected in, or would they run the risk of meeting relatives in the New York Central Yards on Webster Avenue, just above Fordham Road? Nobody would admit anything, especially regarding what varieties of grapes and what combinations they were planning to use this year.

Over on Villa Avenue, the Lionellis were well prepared with Jimmy as well as sons Sparky and Louis, to help Zi Vicinze. On 204th Street, Uncle Dominick had plenty of help, too. Five sons, my cousins Tony, Morris, Mikey, JoJo, and Rudy, were pressed into service by Aunt Rae (Raffaela). Because she was an overwhelming and vocal force, all five sons toed a very straight line well into adulthood. Uncle Dominick, a different type, kept his own counsel and let Aunt Rae run the ship—only because he wanted it that way. Uncle Dominick would go and inspect the grapes when he was good and ready. Also on 204th Street, the Mennas, the Ardolinis, and the Monacos, all *famiglia*, were getting ready.

The cleaning of the barrels was an involved process. Sediment from the previous year's *orecchi* (ears), the dehydrated skins of the grape, would be encrusted along the entire interior lining. How did one get it off? A length of heavy chain was guided through the bunghole, the two-inch hole found at the top of the fattest circumference of the barrel. Whipping the chain about inside the sealed barrel was where the young arms came in. When Nonno was finally satisfied, after relays of whipping, he would declare the barrels ready for the next step.

Years of alternate filling and swelling, in addition to expansion and contraction from the fermentation process, had loosened the metal bands around the staves. But Nonno wanted the barrels airtight. Two special tools were needed. One was a T-shaped tool, and the other was a ball-peen hammer. The T-shaped tool had a blunt end with a flat flange on one side, into which was machined a groove designed to accept the edge of the metal band. This permitted the band to tighten the staves, as one could now easily pound down on the T-shaped tool with the ball-peen hammer.

Then the barrels were filled with water for two or three days. After the wood swelled, the rings were pounded down again. The barrels were still not ready. The next step involved sulfur sticks. The bunghole cork was inserted in the now air-dried barrel and loosened just enough to permit only enough oxygen to sustain the burning of the sulfur sticks to enter the barrel. Nonno said this burning process purified the wood and removed any extraneous odors of previous *orecchi*. When the sticks were consumed, the residue was removed; the remaining gas was left in for an hour or so, for the pungent odor from the *orecchi* was yet very distinct.

The most prized barrels were the used ones that had contained applejack or bourbon. (In Italy this was not a problem; chestnut was the premier wood of wine makers.) The oak staves would surrender their raw-wood taste to the previous alcohol. Every wine maker had his own ideas about which used barrels he would seek, all of which was part of the mystique of the "wine master."

All of the grapes came from California (although later some of the younger generation began to experiment with the New York State Finger Lakes varieties). About the first week in September, the grapes started arriving in boxcars at different railroad terminals around the metropolitan area. The commission agents had made their own deals with the California growers; these agents, in turn, would sell the grapes to us. Sometimes the orders were placed in advance by my grandfathers, but this assured only delivery, not the quality or selection desired. So even though they didn't want their choices known, it was inevitable that they would meet and casually try to ignore one another when at the sidings.

The most popular varieties of grapes were known as Granaccia, Alicante, Zinfandel, Malvasia, Gragnano, and Moscato. The mix or proportions depended a lot on the particular quality and variety of what had come in. Sometimes plans prepared as a result of previous years' experience had to be put aside due to the selection of grapes. The expertise of the wine makers in my family, based upon their having lived close to the soil, would be sorely tested. Successful vintages, the measure of which would not be known until the following year when the barrels were tapped, would be freely distributed—gratis. Unsuccessful years would be conveniently hidden—for home consumption only.

An abundance of separate chores attended the winemaking process. The boxes of grapes were stacked up outside on the walk going down to the cellar door. First on the list was grinding the grapes. The *macinillo*, the grinder (from *macinare*, meaning to grind), was a hand-operated, wheeled device which was installed on top of the barrel. The wide maw had V-shaped sides that first accepted the bunches of luscious fruit, then passed them down to the bottom as grinding proceeded. Here the *macinillo* mashed the fruit, stems, and juice and then passed all of this into the propped-up, temporary barrel, where the fermentation process began.

The boxes of grapes weighed thirty-six pounds each, and about six hundred fifty pounds of grapes would yield fifty to fifty-five gallons of wine.

After a minimum of four days, and up to a maximum of ten if the weather was cool, a half-barrel (one that was cut in half), which is called *o'cubillo*—a word whose origin I would love to know—was placed under the barrel and its cork removed. The fermented juice then ran out into *o'cubillo*, while *la vernaccia* (the must, or mash) remained in the whole barrel and acted as a filter. This juice was then carefully poured into a permanent barrel, which was braced to prevent any movement for up to half a year. After those minimum four days, *la vernaccia* was removed from the temporary barrel and put into the wine press.

'*Lavatevi i piedi*' (Go wash your feet), demanded Nonno.

Jamesie, Sonny, and I were all too ready to comply. This union with nature was exciting to us. It was Saturday morning, and these next two days promised to be unique. Today, we three grandsons of Mastro Mauriello were going to be *i scascianti* (the crushers). One of our functions was to walk around the inside of the wine press, atop the mountain of *la vernaccia*. Uncle Johnny, their father, was there to help, along with his younger brothers, Al and Joe.

Nonno's wine press was the biggest I have ever seen. Wine presses varied quite a bit in size, with the smallest unable to accommodate even a boy, all the way up to Nonno's three-boyer. And they all looked alike. The center core, where we stomped, was a circular stockade made up of vertical oak strips which were open-spaced to permit *il sugo* (the juice) to drain through. This juice ran down to a circular trough which completely encircled the stockade. A depression in this trough collected *il sugo* for distribution into the casks—in accordance with Nonno's predetermined varietal proportions.

In the center of our stockade was a huge worm screw that reached all the way to the cellar ceiling. This device did the real work of squeezing out the juice after we boys completed the stomping. The screw forced down two semi-circular boards, compacted the must far beyond the pressure of our feet, and forced it to surrender its lifeblood to eager Bacchus.

We three had our fun for over an hour at each pressing, delighting in our contribution and, of course, exaggerating our efforts by smearing purple grape juice over our faces and arms to impress our mothers and anyone else we ran into. The process was repeated three times and the effluent added to the permanent barrel. By the end, *la vernaccia* was an almost dry mass and had to be removed from the press. We used it as fertilizer and spread it over the garden. In some parts of Italy, especially in the Barolo wine areas, *la vernaccia* becomes the basis for the fiery grappa, a brandy-like restorative.

Then came the important part. In each home the wine maker would nurse his baby. Oxygen is the enemy of wine, and a premature marriage of the two will result in *aceto*, the proper word for vinegar, but in this case an unfair and humiliating characterization applied to wine by all-too-anxious critics.

The fermentation process, though greatly reduced, did not stop completely after the wine was put in the permanent barrels. As a result, gas continued to generate, and the resultant pressure had to be relieved. How did you release this pressure and keep out the oxygen? By installing a clever homemade device which has been in use for centuries. It is similar in principle to the water trap in a toilet. Many people mistakenly believe the U-bend trap in the bottom of a toilet bowl is to catch jewelry accidentally dropped into it. No so! The trap prevents rising sewer gases from entering the room by forcing them up the vent pipe, which extends above the roof.

Here I must interrupt and tell you that this ventilation device was not universally used anymore than any "secret" or "technique" was universal. This is where the variables in wine making entered the picture, and about which each "expert" was so vehement. Other wine makers would let the barrels swell up for months, until they were close to popping their corks, and then hurriedly draw off a glass or less.

Anyway, let me describe this ventilation procedure. As I described earlier, at the top of the barrel there is a bunghole. A cork was hammered into this opening to seal the barrel. Through the center of this cork was drilled a hole, which is less than half an inch across, and a piece of rubber hose (now plastic) was inserted. Molten wax sealed the cork around this intruder. The exposed end of this tiny hose was elevated so it was higher than the barrel. Then it was bent into a U shape and lowered into a shallow water wash. The level of this water was always higher than the end of the tube itself so air could not retreat into the tube. As time progressed, you would see tiny bubbles of compressed gas exiting the barrel and passing through the water wash. When the bubbles stopped after several weeks, the device was quickly removed and the bunghole sealed with a full cork.

The time for tapping the barrel took on an almost religious judgment. Premature tapping could be disastrous. It was not uncommon for some wine makers to wait half a year, then transfer the wine to a second barrel, where it remained for up to another six months. Others succumbed to the temptation much earlier, sometimes after only four months. Obviously, the longer the wait, the better the chance the sediment would have settled, resulting in a clearer wine.

Some vintners followed a different process. It is called "racking," or decanting, in English. Only cloudy recollections survive for the dialectal word. My brother-in-law uses the word *tramontare*, but he was mistaken; it turned out to be *tramutare*.[22] This was the transferring of the wine over a period of four months, in diminishing steps, from barrel to ten-gallon jugs, then to five-gallon jugs, then to demijohns, and finally to gallon jugs. But this process was done only when the moon was full, and only in clear weather. How much of this was superstition and how much

---

22. *Tramontare* means to wane, and *tramontana* from the mountain itself, is a north wind which refreshes Italy. My *Cassell's Italian-English Dictionary* tells me that *tramutare* is not only a dialectal word, but it is a proper Italian one, and the one identifying the racking process, meaning to decant.

was based on knowledge, I don't know, but the former is so much more intriguing. Of course, it made more sense to opt for the first, for, as Grandpa said, '*Meglio che fai affari col diavolo conosciuto che quello che non sai*' (Better you do business with the devil you know than the one you don't). The racking process, done very gently, resulted in increasingly sediment-free wine.

There was one other interesting process in which the whole family joined. Let me back up to that four-to-eight-day wait after the first fermenting. A gallon or two of the first draw-off had some sugar added to it and boiled. This produced *vino cotto* (cooked wine), which, when left to cool, produced a cake of jelly. This could be eaten with a spoon or used as a sandwich spread. The taste of this was our first hint of what ultimately would be the finished product. Nonno observed our reactions anxiously. He really wanted only measures of approbation. Most times he got them. Those wine-making days are remembered with satisfaction.

The compulsion to try our hand at wine-making has never really left us. Many grandchildren of Italian immigrants are returning to the presses in increasing numbers. I did this year in union with a friend from Trenton, New Jersey. Statistics also show that many have returned to growing their own grapes, surprisingly in parts of the East under difficult weather conditions; but they are persevering with considerable success. We never really leave our roots, and we should not have to. It is interesting to observe how Wednesday's grandchildren try to recapture *la via vecchia* (the old way), as opposed to Tuesday's children, who actively tried to reject the ways of *la famiglia*.

Writing about the railhead on Webster Avenue at the beginning of this chapter reminded me of a story my father told us about his early days as an immigrant boy. There was a huge coal yard farther up these same tracks from Fordham Road, and the long lines of coal cars would slowly wind their way for unloading. Here was an opportunity. My father, then about ten years old, and only four years in this country, would take two of his younger brothers, Louis, who was about eight, and Johnny, who was only about six, down to the sidings.

There were always crewmen riding atop the piled-up coal cars. The three boys would throw stones of railway ballast at the men. Naturally, the crewmen responded with the ammunition at hand—lumps of coal. After the trains passed, the boys would gather the pieces of coal into gunnysacks and carry them home to proud Nonna. These were an important addition to the family's supply of fodder for the central coal stove.

Ben Lucarelli told me a similar story. One of the joys of my later years was getting reacquainted with Ben, one of the more successful general contractors and builders in New Jersey. I never really got to know him well when I was doing brickwork for his company. We did schools in Hoboken and Elizabeth; public housing projects in Newark, Paterson, and Jersey City; high-rise apartment buildings all over New Jersey; and a considerable amount of construction work at Raritan Arsenal, Fort Dix, and McGuire Air Force Base. I didn't see Ben much, though, for the people I dealt with were his engineers—Joe Welch, Tony Salvador, Len Perna, and Ollie Johnson.

This sterling man, the son of immigrants, was an engineering student at Stevens Tech who was later honored by his alma mater. When Ben was around eleven years old, he, too, used to go down to the coal yard trestle, the one that runs along the beginnings of the Palisades between Jersey City and Hoboken. Sometimes he took a younger brother along with him.

Ben's technique for filching coal was a little different, for he knew as a resident of Jersey City that all trains entering Hoboken stopped atop that trestle, as required before entering the tunnel separating the two cities. The boys would climb up the trestle and then atop the peaks of coal in the cars. Supported on their backsides and arms, the boys used their legs to hurriedly kick off some of the black treasure, which would fall through the bridging to the ground below. Then they would climb down and gather their loot. Ben said it was always a close call with the railroad police, but he suspected that the police deliberately avoided collaring them so that their daredevil efforts would be rewarded.

One day the boys hit a bonanza. The year was 1918, and the train atop the trestle was filled with doughboys going off to the war in France. Ben and a younger brother climbed up the trestle, sensing the need of the soldiers to adopt them. Ben even went into the first car.

To the cheers of the soldiers, accompanied by warnings to return to the ground, the boys monkeyed down as money began raining down from the open windows. In a charitable farewell to America, the doughboys had decided there was no need for American coinage where they were going. The boys' pockets were soon stuffed with money. Just as my father had given the coal he pilfered to Nonna, Ben and his brother gave the money, every penny, to their mother.

Likewise, when I received my first pay envelope on Boscobel Avenue in 1933, it was delivered to my mother, unopened. No one ever told us to do that. We just knew.

Grandpa

Mom – 1917

1929 Cadillac (see Chapter VI "Dad")

Emily and Author – 1985

Dad 1918 – U.S. Soldier

Aerial View Linwood Park Apartment
(see Chapter VI "Dad")

Apartment Building – Sutton Place and East River
(see Chapter IV "New York, New York")

Author and Dad – 1923

310 EAST 70TH STREET
NEW YORK CITY

Apartment Building – East 70th Street
(see Chapter IV "New York, New York")

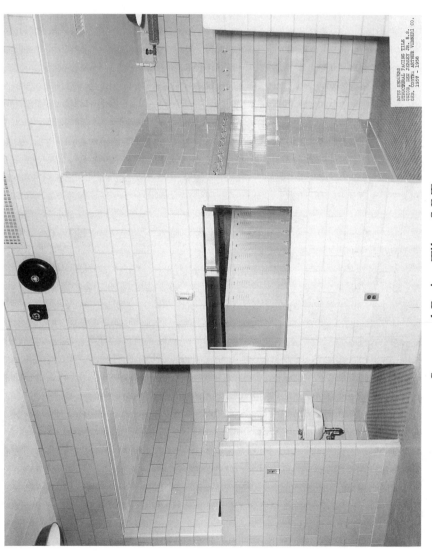

Structural Facing Tile – S.F.T.
(see Chapter IV "New York, New York")

Chapter VI

Dad

My father was an enigma. (Aren't we all?) He was powerful, in will and muscle, a combination which he fortunately zeroed in the right direction. There was violence in him. Had he become a criminal, he would certainly have been a terror of terrors. But he could also be gentle. There was no ambivalence there. He knew precisely what was needed for his family's honor; and you accepted his decisions and actions, on his terms.

Everyone about him, family and friends, his workers, immediate neighbors, and our Italian *paesani* (community members) was aware of his presence and influence. He was a leader—no doubt.

The thickening of age had already exacted its toll on the dad I knew; he was a bull of a man, with a barrel chest that ran from his neck down to his waist. But the photograph I have of him when he was in the army during World War I shows a different man. It shows him standing in a rowboat holding an oar, and he is brawn and bronze all over. His rippling muscles look more like those of "Bomba the Jungle Boy" than those of "Tarzan of the Apes." But either way the fierce power shows through. He died in 1947, a young man of fifty. The explosion within his chest was too powerful even for that superb body and will to contain.

Why should you know about him? Because if you want to

know about the immigrant movement in our country, you should have a clear picture of one of the typical players whose position was both son of an immigrant and boy immigrant. My father was in that first transitional generation from immigrant to American.

What were the secrets of his successes? What were the forces that destroyed him? What was the anger within him? What was his Achilles' heel? I have often thought, in retrospect, that his violent end really was inevitable; that what he was trying to accomplish for himself, for his family, and for his people was just too much, even for him.

There was a weakness within that seemingly impenetrable armor. The weakness was education, or rather the lack of it. Dad had only gone to sixth grade, and only that on a part-time basis. This realization dogged him all his life. What would have been acceptable to others, and was, and what he hid so assiduously from the world—because you could never tell by his speech or demeanor—was not acceptable to him. To this lack he privately attributed every frustration, every failure, every reason for not accomplishing the very heights of his ambitions. He hated to receive mail, for the simple receipt of a letter which might require a written reply would change his whole personality. "The pen is mightier than the sword." It stripped him of his armor.

In the meantime, he pursued his goals, powerfully, relentlessly. Hours of the day meant nothing to him except opportunity for work, for accomplishment. He no longer would accept being the barefoot boy who would wear no shoes from the end of school in June to the start again in September. Nothing and nobody could stand before this steamroller of ambition. That included his brothers, his sisters, his parents, his children, his workers and associates, and his *compari* in that little Italian neighborhood of Bedford Park.

He was employer, adviser, helper, and guide to the entire neighborhood. If you did not do things his way, you were cast aside. You had to accept your share of responsibility for improving the image of his people. Laziness was nauseating to him. Indolence was the ultimate crime, with "all there is to do." If he was aware, or even suspected, that a petitioner was not doing enough to help his own relatives still in Italy, he would scratch him off the list.

Evenings and weekends brought a stream of *paesani* to Reservoir Oval. Someone needed a job or wanted to apprentice a son; someone needed a union card, a mortgage, a co-signer, or a loan; someone needed a city permit or perhaps help with a building violation; or someone had a family problem with the church.

All of these appeals required follow-up. Oh, if only he could write! If only he could succinctly express himself!

Education was the only answer in his mind, and I cannot argue with my father. Of course there was validity to his expectations—so few of his *paesani* were literate at that time. But he gave too little credit to the common sense and willingness that effectively accomplishes the sort of thing he was doing. I am sure today he would be sick to his stomach at some of the products of our present educational opportunities.

How much of it was ego? A part, I guess. But if I stand back and review from the vantage point of over fifty years, I see a dedication and self-sacrifice that transcends ego satisfaction.

Going down the path to perdition was one of the fears he had for his children or siblings. The slightest transgression, like coming home late from school, brought a confrontation.

"Do you want to grow up like Lefty Louis, Dago Red, or Gyp the Blood? I'll kill you if you ever do anything wrong," Dad would rebuke.

I would love to know who these guys were, and if any one of my readers can shed some light, my sister Theresa and I would be most grateful. We used to look at each other when he threatened us, wondering who these mysterious characters were. We really didn't want to be like them at all.

And in the same breath he would talk about coke and dope and opium. I am amazed that cocaine was prevalent that long ago. We were going to be killed for that, too. You might not approve of his methods, but I am grateful to him. They certainly were effective. To this day, I have never even had a lighted cigarette in my mouth.

His seven brothers and sisters were subject to him, also. Word always got back to him about what they were doing, or whether they had been disrespectful, even momentarily, to their parents. The four unmarrieds paid, adult or no. More than once I saw Uncle Al and Uncle Joe bloodied—severely. My father once slapped even Aunt Florence, the rebel, and sent her reeling across the room. Aunt Mary, the one who later married Uncle Andrew, the apple farmer, was never much of a problem. I could see my father favored her, and she adored her older brother, violent though he could be.

Why did this man, who could be so gracious and gentle, act this way? I have given this much thought over many years, and I believe it was the immigrant experience. Sufficient evidence suggests this.

A set of situations and circumstances presented itself, a void which cried out for someone to fill. The *paesani* needed their champions, too, and he possessed all the necessary attributes. But enough generalizations. Let me tell you some of the things I saw and heard, and perhaps a more balanced view of my father will emerge. Dad deserves that consideration, for he was far from all bad—very, very far. Clearly, it was compulsion.

Nonno was a bricklayer from Naples who had worked in "Arabia." He spoke Arabic rapidly, but I suspect it was only the Libyan and Tripolitan parts of the Mediterranean that saw him. When the family came to the United States in 1902, it consisted of Father Mauro and Mother Teresa, who were my grandparents, and Grandmother Marossa (Mama Grossa), my great-grandmother. The children were Raffaella, who was eight years old; Francesco, my father, who was six years old; and Luigi, who was three years old. The other five children were born here, Uncle Johnny just making it under the wire. Two other babies had been buried in Italy.

My father's recollections of Ellis Island were dim, but not so of the Statue of Liberty, about which he spoke with much emotion. His more vivid recollections of that day were of his mother's admonition: *'Dobbiamo trovare lavoro'* (We must find work). This six-year-old was programmed at an early age.

He told us that when he was eight he went to work at 6:00 A.M. with the German baker on 204th Street. By the age of ten, he arose early enough to go to work with the milkman at 4:00 A.M.; at 6:00 A.M. he worked with the baker, and then at 9:00 A.M. he went to school. How do I know this is true? Because Mrs. Connolly told me.

In my youth, the bane of our lives was the Irish. Since it is my function to record history, not to create it, I cannot deviate from the truth. I will tell you more about this later. But for now you must also know that my life and my family's lives would have been immeasurably poorer without Mrs. Connolly, Joe McGinnis, and some others.

A happy thing happened to me when I got to eighth grade in Public School 80 on Mosholu Parkway in the Bronx. Of the six different classes, I was assigned to the one of Mrs. Connolly, who was my father's sixth-grade teacher twenty-five years before. She and he had maintained a unique friendship over all those years. Once or twice a year we would ride to her home in Larchmont, New York, for a Sunday visit. Larchmont looked very different from the Bronx. The elderly lady would relate to us how her predictions about my father's ultimate success were fulfilled. And the still obedient rogue bull-glowed in the love he felt. Things like that should never come to an end. Maybe they don't.

One day in my class Mrs. Connolly interrupted the subject at hand and said, "I want to tell you a story about Mauro's father." (I had foolishly changed my name at age eighteen from Mauro, my grandfather's, to Frank M.—a stupid condescension to an imagined more accepting society. Only three years later I regretted that immature move.) Mrs. Connolly continued, "One day Mauro's father was asleep in my class, and the children nearby were prodding him, 'Frank, Frank, wake up!' I stopped them and said, 'You let that boy sleep. He has been up since three o'clock this morning, working first with the milkman, and then delivering buns and rolls.' You should remember, my students, there is more to life than what you will gather here." She had confirmed what my father used to tell us, the accuracy of which we silently had felt was colored because we know how he felt about the importance of education.

Whenever we rode up the Boston Post Road to Larchmont or Playland in Rye, we would stop in Mamaroneck. These Sunday rides were my father's joy. He loved cars as much as he loved ham sandwiches and ice cream, all three of which where inimical to the peasant life style, and all three of which contributed to the buildup of cholesterol in his arteries.

On one of these Sunday drives, my father pointed out the corner at the end of the trolley line where a diner had stood. He had been a delivery boy for Railroad Express Agency, the fore-runner of today's United Parcel Service. Delivery from the Bronx took several hours, but the fine homes and estates to which my father made deliveries entranced him. He also looked forward to the tip, sometimes as much as a quarter. When he was finished with the deliveries, he would walk back to that diner, salivating for the ham and egg sandwich that was to be his reward. And there he swore that when he was old enough and rich enough he would have as many ham sandwiches as he wanted—and the fancy cars, too.

We had thinly sliced Polish ham sandwiches every Sunday night after these rides—for as long as I can remember. I have clear pictures, too, in my mind of the Jordan Straight Eight, an emerald green monster, with a searchlight, big enough for the *Queen Mary*, mounted on a gleaming pole, and the elegant café-au-lait Chandler touring car. These beauties preceded the stock market crash of 1929, so I must have been quite young, between five and eight. What is significant is that my father's rise must have been dramatic, for he was still a bricklayer when I was born on the kitchen table in our house on Webster Avenue in 1921.

But this succession of impressive rolling stock, including his 1929 Cadillac, clearly shown in a family photo, was soon to end. In the first chapter I told you that on the day I went to work in 1933 I was seated in my father's Model A Ford. The comedown for my father and so many others had arrived quickly. That was the year of bank closings, and the fourth year of the Great Depression.

If you want to know why I still pick up pennies on the street, I will tell you. The year was 1932. Marossa (Mama Grossa), my great-grandmother, who was close to ninety, had saved through-out her entire life the magnificent sum of slightly less than three hundred dollars, most of that from my father's generosity. She kept it in her mattress—where else? About a year before, my father had convinced her to put the money in the bank so it would earn interest. Complying with my father on this issue was traumatic for her. Were not the banks allied with the govern-ment and the *mangia-franchi*, oppressors to all? But she relied on her godlike grandson, and he had reassured her. Besides, it was the bank he used for his own personal financing. The bank was

"The Bank of the United States," unfortunately no kin to the United States of America.

Sometime earlier in 1932, my father was driving to lunch at Sormani's, an elegant, potted-palm restaurant on Pelham Parkway in the Bronx. In the car, on their way to the gracious Victorian home with the wraparound porches, were Democratic Party bigwigs Ed Flynn, a national power, Tom Fitzpatrick, leader of the Bronx, and Assemblyman John Devaney.

Suddenly Flynn said to my father, "Frank, do you have any money in The Bank of the United States?" When my father affirmed he had, Flynn added, "Well, you had better get it out!" He didn't do so.

Two weeks later the scene repeated itself.

"Frank, did you do what I told you?"

"No, not yet."

"Well, you guinea son of a bitch, you deserve to lose it all." Now my father couldn't wait to get away; he knew the drinking would go on all afternoon.

But he did get to the bank before closing time. He told the bank manager that he wanted to withdraw his whole savings, six thousand dollars.

"Sorry! We don't have all that much here. We will give you twelve hundred dollars today, and the rest in a few days."

The next day the bank was closed.

The next scene showed me in a line with my father, mother, and Marossa, whose sobbing was uncontrollable. We were four abreast, and the line snaked out of the corner entrance to the bank on 204th Street, up Perry Avenue toward Saint Brendan's Church, and wrapped around the apartment houses at the corner of 205th Street. We stood in that line for parts of three days, finally gaining admission. My parents got about two hundred eighty dollars more, and Marossa about thirty.

Through the years dribs and drabs were forthcoming, but never totaling more than 15 percent. Marossa was buried before all that was over, but my father made it good to her, and more.

Banks continued to fall, one by one. Finally, in November of 1933, Franklin Roosevelt declared a bank holiday, and a series of reforms were initiated. The scars remain to this day, but so do the lessons, beautiful lessons: *'Non tutti mali vengono per nuoci'* (Not all bad comes to do harm).

My people were equipped for survival. Are the *nouveau riche* prepared? Do you expect to forge character with doles and welfare? Do you believe "it can't happen here?"

I still have no patience with friends who insist on putting $1,000 down on the roll of a dice or who can't enjoy a game of golf without $500 at risk. Why? Do they throw money around to flaunt their disdain for the value of money, thereby implying unlimited wealth? Can it be that these people have no more important things to do with it, like relieving suffering somewhere? Grandpa used to say, *'Quando squaglia la neve si vedono i stronzi'* (Only when the snow is melted will you see the turds).

So, observe with understanding when you see me stooping for pennies.

Much earlier I told you about Zi Antonio o'Lofaro collecting the linen sacks in which the cement was originally delivered to the jobs. Everybody wanted them, and the cement companies set up a deposit system for them, just like those for glass bottles today. My father, as a boy, had treasured these himself, and when he became a contractor, he made no move to deprive his men of a little perquisite. These sacks had a valuable purpose, even though they were indelibly branded with the names of the cement companies. I remember Lone Star, Hercules, Lion, Saylors Portland, Lehigh, Century, Allentown, and others stamped in big, bold, black letters on these sacks.

Jim Lionelli told me he used to go around with his father, Zi Vicinze, on Saturdays in a horse-drawn carriage, visiting many jobs in the Bronx to gather any linen sacks left behind. They took these sacks home and hung them on lines in the backyard. For weeks they were alternately dried and whipped, until finally there was no trace of coagulated cement dust within them. Then the women laundered them—repeatedly. After a few weeks, the linen became luxuriously soft and pliable. The housewives would then fashion the sacks into sheets and pillowcases. All over the Bronx, and other boroughs, too, people put their heads down on these luxurious, linen-lined pillows. But no matter how many washings of the linen, those stamped black letters never came out. The ingenuity of man is endless, especially where survival is at risk.

My father never stopped getting a leg up, even when poverty was no longer a threat. Uncle Nick, who is only eight years older than I, told me about heading for work down the Grand Concourse early one morning with my father, his older brother-in-law. Uncle Nick had chosen my father for his *compare*, so he had a second claim to a summer job. My father was enjoying the luxurious feel of his new LaSalle. Suddenly his visage changed, the car bolted ahead, and within several blocks they swerved in front of a huge truck laden with cinders. My father jumped out, the driver and his helper started, expecting trouble. My father was a handsome, immaculately dressed, street savant; he usually dressed in knickers and Argyle socks, and his instincts taught him how to disarm the men who earned their bread with the sweat of their brows.

The driver asked, "What's the matter?"

Instead of answering the question, my father said, "Excuse me, sir, where are you going with those cinders?"

Years ago cinder trucks were every bit as prevalent as garbage trucks and looked just like them. Coal was the fuel of furnace, and cinders were the residue of burned coal. Every building had its army of cinder-filled garbage cans lined up on the sidewalk.

"We're going to the dump on the Harlem River."

"How would you like to make five dollars and get rid of them in five minutes?"

My father queried.

The driver and his helper could not refuse this offer. Five dollars was half a day's pay; besides, they would save at least an hour in driving time. The driver followed my father and Uncle Nick down the Grand Concourse, past Fordham Road to the Poe Garage, opposite Loew's Paradise Theatre.

Joe McGinnis and his taciturn partner, Mr. Sheridan, owned this mammoth, six-story garage. McGinnis was as warm as Sheridan was cold. My father did a lot of masonry work for them in that building, for through the years the value of commercial and retail space in that area multiplied geometrically. The huge ramps, large enough to accommodate even oversized trucks, made access easy to every floor.

The driver dumped the cinders right next to where they were needed. My father planned to use the cinders as a fill to support new concrete floors. Cinders are every bit as good an aggregate as gravel when mixed in concrete, and they are lighter in weight. My father's quick wit had saved at least a hundred dollars—of those days' dollars. Zi Giuan was pleased, too. He had better use for his men than transporting a whole load of cinders by wheelbarrow.

I worked on that job, too, through the years. Caggy (Achille) Mosca and Patsy, his younger brother, who was later to be a truckdriver for Uncle Joe and me, were there, too. It was at Poe's Garage where I saw Caggy's talents at work. I mentioned him in the first chapter, you will recall.

Zi Antonio was there, and of course, the ubiquitous Andrea Acierno, still singlehandedly demolishing twelve-inch brick walls with that sixteen-pound sledge hammer. If I have trouble remembering what year it was then, I can look up when Primo Carnera, the Italian heavyweight champ, was demolished by Max Baer. His loss cast a pall over the job for several days—it was so unexpected. How could such a gargantuan specimen, and Italian to boot, lose to a mere 220-pound fighter?

Joe McGinnis and Dad had become close friends through the years. They were both *compari*. Joe and Jenny, his wife, had been asked to baptize Rosemary, my younger sister. Joe was always a source of encouragement to me. I was aware of his admiration for me, too. And I needed the accolades Joe dispensed, for my father was so incredibly demanding that it was hard for me to distinguish when, if ever, he was pleased.

Moreover, Joe was a wise man who was way ahead of his time. When I was still a boy, I listened as he preached about how the peace of the Western world would never be secure without a "United States of Europe." His valid observation is still not a fact, even though a second World War has interceded. He was ahead of his time—and still is.

I also remember, years later, Dad telling me never to forget something Joe McGinnis had taught him: "If you can't say anything good about a man, don't say anything." This willingness to

acknowledge the source of a lesson taught to him was one re-
freshing facet of Dad's personality. Around the dinner table one
night he said, "Chick Meehan taught me something today. He
told me always to call a man by his first name. Remember that!"

"Chick" Meehan was the fabled football coach at New York
University. He and Dad had teamed up to do all the work for the
Thom McAn shoe stores and the Chock-Full-O-Nuts stores,
which at that time proliferated all over the city. Chick was the
contact man, and Dad's men did the work. I will tell you about
NYU football later in this book.

Even as I write this, I know that my statement about my father's dissatisfactions is not quite true. I was my father's companion at six-day bike races, midget car races, amateur fights at our
Lady of Refuge Church on 196th Street, football games for NYU
at Yankee Stadium and the Polo Grounds, and constant, constant
exposure to business from when I was only nine—nights included. I felt his love, and I came to understand that I was an
extension of his compulsive need to attain perfection.

Was it fear of criticism that drove him? Was it a sincere belief
that his combination of physical strength, sharp, native intelligence, and consummate will made him the only qualified ar-
biter of what was right for everybody around him? Or was it still,
despite all those accomplishments, that self-created monster of
restraint, "I am not educated enough."

Moreover, why was he so sensitive to the judgment of others?
He often scolded, "Don't let people talk!" Were those "people"
only the *'Americani,'* that is, all those who denigrated the *'Italiani'*?
Was society, he himself, or both, imposing impossible demands
upon him, like a dog tirelessly trying to catch his own tail? I
think so. This time the perception, or the delusion, had become
the reality.

The mischief that is caused by the vicious game of deriding
other ethnic peoples is far more serious than we admit. The
effects last for generations. We Italians grew up hearing "guinea
bastard" and "dirty wop," and we responded with "stinking Irish
Mick" and taunted with "potato eater, potato eater." The words
dilute with time; the anger stays hidden.

I would like to take you back to another scene. Uncle Louis,

Uncle Johnny, and Uncle Joe, three of Dad's brothers, told me this story, which took place on a small job. I do not know if I had been born yet. There was a pile of sand nearby, and Nonno was being abused by three burly plumbers. My three young uncles were nearby, but the plumbers' wrenches were momentarily forcing a standoff.

From the building came my father, with a disarmingly quiet, "Now, what's the problem?" In a flash, a right fist crushed into the face of the nearest plumber. Teeth and bone went flying as a left fist dug into the stomach of another, almost exiting his back. The third plumber threw his arms upward in abject surrender and fell backward onto the pile of sand. It was over in seconds. My uncles studied their brother in silent awe. Within moments, though, everyone was back at work.

"Every problem requires a solution!"

"You will learn to respect me—one way or another!"

The Irish, who were Monday's immigrants to us, Tuesday's Italians, were, in turn, Tuesday's immigrants to those who were here before them. The Irish also paid the price. Note what Bob Considine says in *It's the Irish*: "The Irish who came to America, eventually like a tidal wave, were unique in two respects. They were the first, really, to suffer segregation and discrimination. And of course they were the first to do something about a symbolic and neatly printed sign they read in the windows of Boston, New York, and elsewhere: "Man wanted. No Irish need apply."[23]

The "know-nothing party," less than sixty years after the signing of the Declaration of Independence, self-styled itself "The Native American Movement," . . . It called for the expulsion of the Irish Papists and proclaimed "America for Americans."[24]

Just before the turn of the century came the American Protestant Association. This was followed by the Ku Klux Klan, whose effective end is close, but not yet written, and already we are nearing the end of the twentieth century.

We cannot climb the ladder of success by standing on the shoulders of our fellow man, for pushing another down into the mire brings us closer to the muck ourselves.

23. Bob Considine, *It's the Irish*.
24. Musmanno, p. 97.

The simple lessons are obvious. If we Wednesday and Thursday immigrants wish to put an end, finally, to the cycle which distorts our people and makes emotional cripples out of generations of children, we must welcome all new Monday brothers, the Koreans, the Hispanics, the Orientals, the Afghans, and all the rest. There is a good, selfish reason, too. These are the people who will supply the energy and commitment for the next great steps forward. Besides, as Grandpa had said, *'Tutto il mondo è paese'* (The whole world is a little town).

There are many things wrong with our country, but there are many things right, too. It seems tiring sometimes to parade the genius of our founding fathers. But it was genius, truly, for time after time we are led out of the morass of hatred, bigotry, and calumny by the precepts they outlined for *us*.

Today, Americans appear to come out a poor second to the Japanese, Russians, Europeans, and others when we compare the dress, manners, deportment, and commitment of their children to ours. And it is critical we address these problems, for they are a fact.

But we have a secret weapon. That unique weapon is our Constitution, which guarantees opportunity and the liberty to pursue it, a written invitation to the boundless ingenuity of man, a magnet which has and will continue to draw ingenuity to these shores. It truly will be a great country when finally we get it built.

There is a significant story, about my father when he was involved in politics. He was driving Tom Fitzpatrick up the Grand Concourse, maybe just after the stockmarket crash of 1929. I was in the back seat. Fitzpatrick said, "Frank, where is the chauffeur's cap I bought you?" My father then reached under the driver's seat, pulled out a chauffeur's cap, and put it on his head.

I still feel the pain of that blow to my stomach. I could not believe that the hero of Bedford Park, the worshipped champion, could so degrade himself. Were my father's ambitions (or fears) so boundless that he had to sacrifice even his pride? Or was it still, *'Pazienza,* my son; all things must be endured. It is all part of the plan'?

I still draw satisfaction in recalling that I did not let the opportunity pass. I leaned my eight-year-old body over the back of the front seat and said to Fitzpatrick, "You know, I don't like you." I expected a massive swat from my father, but it never came, nor did he ever mention the incident to me again.

How righteous of me to express that satisfaction! The truth is, that right was purchased for me. You know by whom: by my father, by Grandpa, and by Nonno. I would not want my mistakes in life paraded before my eyes, and I am certain you would not, either. How easy it is to judge a parent, especially when we demand so little from ourselves! *'Quando hanno scoperto gli errori, si diventano subito dottori'* (As soon as they discover the errors, immediately they become the experts), as Rudy Marchesi's mother said. I will tell you about Rudy later.

I think it is important to note the statistics which show that in this twentieth century the three ethnic groups most avidly pursuing higher education, in order, are the Jews, the Irish, and the Italians. What did they all have in common? They all suffered from racial discrimination and prejudice. Two of them still do. May I again quote Grandpa? *'Non tutti mali vengono per nuoci'* (Not all bad causes harm).

Life could be very interesting around my father. Do any of my readers remember the glory days of NYU football and the frantic rivalry between Fordham and NYU? Against Georgetown and Carnegie Tech?

One of my father's boyhood pals was Jack Weinheimer, a neighborhood athlete who went on to become a fixture in athletic directorship and assistant football coach at NYU. He is in the NYU Heights Hall of Fame. Both Jack and my father were pals of Frankie Frisch, the baseball immortal known as the "Fordham Flash," who later became a star of the Saint Louis Cardinals. The Frisch family lived in a gracious home on the corner of Perry Avenue and 206th Street just below Saint Brendan's Church.

Somewhere around 1927, the directors of NYU decided the Bronx campus and Ohio Field deserved big-time football. They brought in Chick Meehan, football genius out of Syracuse, and started recruiting football stars from all over the United States, especially the coal-mining areas of Pennsylvania and Ohio.

Through Weinheimer, my father became thoroughly involved with NYU football. Afternoons would find him in the locker rooms and around the trainers' tables under the stadium. We had sideline passes, and every Saturday he would take me onto the field at Yankee Stadium or the Polo Grounds. His pockets were full of tickets to the game, which he distributed to family, friends, and neighbors. He created the impression that he received these tickets without payment. He might have had choice seats, but they did not come free. He had become a patron, a booster of NYU football.

I frequently wonder whether his association with college football and campus exposure was a hidden desire to absorb higher education by osmosis. He was on a first-name basis with all the players as well as other coaches. I remember Bill McCarthy, graceful baseball coach, and Howard Cann, basketball coach. And there was a fabled track coach; he was a splendid gentleman, short and wiry. His name was Scandinavian or German (maybe Von Elling?). I would like to know if someone remembers.

During the off-seasons, these football players would work on my father's jobs. I remember all-Americans Ken Strong and Al Lassman and running backs Frank Briante and Cowboy Eddie Hill. (Tragically, Hill was killed in an off-campus playful lifting of a cop's gun, which accidentally discharged.) Then there was Glenn (or Ed) Concannon, who was almost as huge as Lassman. I saw them working on the new Alexander's Department Store on Third Avenue at 149th Street in what was known as the hub of the Bronx. But I had missed by only a few days their start of work. It was a funny story, and my father came home and told us about it.

When these behemoths arrived on the job, they saw the little Italian laborers plodding their loaded wheelbarrows up the plank ramps. To these athletes, the work looked like child's play. They grabbed the empty wheelbarrows, which looked like toys in their hands, and started running with them, loading, unloading, and laughing at the deliberate pace of the men half their size. Within half an hour, the players had keeled over in their wheelbarrows, exhausted; some were puking. *'Chi va piano va sano, e lontano'* (Who goes slowly goes whole, and a long way). This precursor proverb of the tortoise and the hare was well known for centuries. The work of the laborers was not child's play; it was the deadly serious business, again, of taking care of your body because it represented the livelihood of *la famiglia*.

The laborers continued with their steady plodding, sometimes for as long as ten hours, having the good grace not to laugh at the giants. They knew that in short order, or already, their new friends would learn the realities of life. And they did learn, and their bodies toughened, far beyond what the training fields could do for them. My father enjoyed taking the coaches and the Bronx politicians to the jobs to see his new cadre of what the men called '*i giganti*' (the giants). Bronx County Democratic Party Headquarters was only two short blocks away, on the corner of 148th Street.

These were glory days for the Bronx, for two national football powers were going head to head every season. One year NYU was headed for the Rose Bowl. Only a victory over Fordham would assure the bid. It was not to come. In the annual Thanksgiving Day game at the Polo Grounds, Fordham ecstatically knocked NYU off its perch. The very next year, NYU returned the favor in an unbelievable upset at Yankee Stadium (or was it the Polo Grounds?).

In 1947, almost twenty years later, a feeling of déjà vu came over me as I witnessed a replay of that same scene. It took place in Dumont, New Jersey. We were building garden apartments and all-masonry private homes for Manny Spiegle, president of the New Jersey Homebuilders Association. My brother, Steve, was the foreman. The August sun was making an oven of the excavations for house foundations. We had just lost our father in June, so my recollections are vivid.

My brother had brought a young bull to the job, a friend and fellow local football player named Junior Arata. The near semi-pro league in which Steve and Arata played centered upon the field behind Public School 8, which was the neighborhood school for both of my parents and most of my aunts and uncles when they were young. This was tough football. One of the boys in this league was Art Donovan, who went on to become perennial all-pro lineman with the Baltimore Colts.

Arata needed to make some money as well as toughen his body, so Steve invited him to work as a laborer. His first teacher was *manuale* Antonio (Totò) Fidelbo, who was about sixty-five years old and stood no more than five feet two inches tall, a not particularly powerful-looking specimen. We don't know what his body looked like beneath his clothing because the old-timers never, never exposed their bodies to the sun.

The first thing Arata did when Totò handed him a wheelbarrow and led him to a load of twelve-inch solid cinder blocks was to peel off his clothing to the waist and expose his impressive torso. Totò, not impressed, methodically proceeded to load his own wheelbarrow with the seventy-pound blocks. Arata duplicated the arrangement, ran down the ramp, determined to lift his load onto the scaffolds before Totò. And Arata did—for a while—despite the humid heat, which already at 8:00 A.M. harbingered a brutal day. I could not tear myself away from the show, the similarity to the occurrence twenty years before fascinating me.

The outcome was precisely the same. Despite warnings from Vince Basciano about his exposure to the sun and advice "to take it easy," Arata persisted, wondering how the skinny, little old man could persevere so relentlessly. By 8:40 A.M. it was over. Arata was puking in his wheelbarrow. The worried men pulled him into the shade of the trees that was sheltering me, the water-soaked rags we had already prepared acting as a pillow for his neck and upper spine. We covered Arata with several towels, and the water boy prepared the oatmeal-laden water. The athlete was on the fringe of suffering from heat prostration.

Proper drinking water for the men in summertime was not a casual thing. They had learned that iced water could lead to paralyzing cramps, yet they could not be expected to drink water that the sun had heated to ninety-five or so degrees. The ancient answer was to put oatmeal into it. Scientifically, I can only guess what purpose the oatmeal serves, but I do know the soothing effect of the bulk is immediately obvious. Later, after Arata had learned to pace himself, he went on to pursue a career as a New York City cop.

One of my father's passions was the bicycle races. The sport does not enjoy the huge popularity it once did, but it was an exciting time, especially when the six-day bicycle races came to town. This two-man effort was an international event, and each ethnic group had its favorites. From Italy came Franco Giorgetti, the legend of his time. From France came (Alfred?) Le Tournier, and from Germany the team was Killian and Vopel. I remember Reggie McNamara, a superb sprinter from New Zealand. I wish I could remember more, especially those from the South American teams.

Usually, Madison Square Garden was the site of the six-day races. The beautifully contoured track, banked almost three stories high at the ends, glistened in its shiny maple color. When the cyclists flew around the corners, centrifugal force took them almost to the top. At this point they were riding almost sideways, parallel to the ground. The graceful dipping down of the cyclists to the straightaways, furiously pumping speed after negotiating the curved banks, was a unique thrill, especially when as many as three of them were trying to occupy the lone narrow trail of optimum effect.

Collisions and spills were frequent, resulting in huge skin burns and torn flesh. Fortunately, the boards were highly sanded, polished, and coated so that potentially maiming splinters were not a factor. To afford a break from tedium, usually when the highly attended evening session was in progress, businessmen would post cash sprint awards, the incentives that had brought the riders to these shores. Then the bells would clang, alerting the cyclists as well as the audience. Each team decided which of its partners would represent the team, either one of whom had to be on the track without interruption for the full six days. They rested alternately, spelling each other according to their own team technique.

The sprint races were incredibly fast, and sweaty, distorted faces and taut tendons in the neck evidenced the cyclists' gut-wrenching efforts. To me, these races were far more exciting than watching horses run; it is so much easier to identify with a human being. The downside of the sport, of course, was the tedious six-day length of the race.

Sometimes, again to break the tedium, a new angle was introduced—motorcycles. The roar of twenty or so high-powered monsters rising from the bowels of the arena was deafening and exciting. The object was for the two-man team, a motorcycle leading a bicycle, to race furiously around the track in competition with all the other duos.

The cyclist had to keep his front tire within an inch or two of a bar that extended past the motorcycle's rear tire. You can readily see how perfect the coordination between the two had to be. The cyclist had to anticipate when his partner was going to speed up to pass or dart between two other teams. If he separated his wheel too far from the impact bar, he was eliminated.

Aside from Madison Square Garden, there was the Velodrome, a sports arena across from the very northern tip of Manhattan Island, where the Harlem River swings westward to join with the majestic Hudson. This was just south of Kingsbridge Road and only three miles from our Bedford Park area. Every few years an outdoor track would be installed, and the races would begin.

Those gentle summer nights, out under the lights and the stars with my father, are pleasant memories. My father, the sports-minded enthusiast, was not so frequently violent; maturity was setting in. He would much rather be singing, with that zest for life that surfaced when he was at peace or when we took those Sunday rides:

Tell me, dear,
Are you lonesome tonight?
Do you miss me tonight?
Are you sorry we drifted apart?

Does your heart ever stray
To that bright summer day,
When I held you and whispered, "sweetheart?"

Does your living room sofa
seem empty and bare?
Do you gaze out your window
And picture me there?

Is your heart filled with pain?
Shall I come back again?
Tell me, dear,
Are you lonesome tonight?

Or maybe he would rather be in Camp Jackson, South Carolina, during World War I. There is a uniformed picture of him in this book. Was he thinking:

O k-k-kickety Katie,
My wonderful K-K-Katie,
You're the only kickety girl
That I adore.

W-w-when the m-m-moon shines
Over the c-c-cow shed,
I'll be waiting at the
Kickety kitchen door.

Or, better yet:
Oh, waddya wanna make those
Eyes at me for
When they don't mean what they say?

They make me sad,
They make me glad,
They make me wanna lotta things
I never, never had.

So waddya wanna fool around
With me for?
You lead me on and then you run away.
But I'ever mind,
I'll getcha a lonesome night,

And then you'll surely find
You're flirtin' with dynamite.

So waddya wanna make those
Eyes at me for
When they don't mean what they say?
(fadeout) When they don't mean what they say!
(crescendo) When they don't mean what they say!

And finally:
Ain't she sweet
When she's walkin' down the street?
Oh, I ask you very confidentially,
Ain't she sweet?

Ain't she nice?
Look her over once or twice.
Oh, I ask you very confidentially,
Ain't she nice?

Oh me, oh my,
She's such perfection.
Oh me, oh my,
D'ja ever see such confection?

And I repeat
'Cause she's so darn neat:
Oh, I ask you very confidentially,
Ain't she sweet?

Dad had a smile that could light up the whole world. I could see that he really wanted to be happy like that all the time. And he was happiest when he was doing something for somebody, when he knew his graciousness was appreciated by his sons and his whole *famiglia*.

Dad could not resist the temptation of showing off his exciting and beloved country to new immigrants arriving in America. He would take whole families down to the Hudson River piers that docked the Italian superliners—the *Rex*, the *Conte di Savoia*, the *Biancamano* (appropriately, the *White Hand*)—to greet the newcomers. Without even a stop at home, the confused new immigrant was convoyed up to Starlight Park, near where the Whitestone Bridge is today, or better yet to Playland in Rye, New York. Dad gave everybody a book of ride tickets, including the kids. My father shanghaied the exhausted victim onto the most dangerous and thrilling loop-de-loops, the Dragon and the Thunder-something.

Irrepressible Dad, I think, would gladly have paid for the passage of a stream of *paesani* just so he could enjoy the bewilderment of his recruits' introduction to their new homeland. He wanted to bring joy and assurance to so many.

And, of course, by the next day the newcomer was on the job, already earning his bread for the family he had left behind in Italy.

Dad was the ultimate authority figure. I remember too well the times when the blood drained from his face and a grayish-blue pallor heralded that fierce will and power. Extremes, as we learn as we get older, are never good in any direction. But how do we stop a world from spinning and declare that from this moment on everything will be perfect and there is no need to go through the learning process? Of course, that is ludicrous. So we are left with an imperfect world and imperfect people who are the sum of themselves as well as all the influences upon them, now and in the past.

One summer evening Dad and I left Orchard Beach to travel the seven miles back to our neighborhood in Bedford Park. Dad had to see Dr. Fama, the refuge of all the immigrants in need of medical attention. The subject was political. This dignified and aristocratic man had been schooled in Italy. His stately home, richly decorated in the Italian palazzo style, stood at the corner of Bedford Park Boulevard and Valentine Avenue, only one block from the Grand Concourse. Many of my people, I saw with my own eyes, brought cheese, fungi, their own wine, and other delicacies to Dr. Fama in place of money. No one was refused attention and no one left without his dignity intact.

Dr. Fama held great influence at that time, as Republican county leader at the height of the La Guardia reform movement that had crushed Tammany Hall. Though Dad was a Democrat, he and Dr. Fama enjoyed a mutual respect, probably enhanced by the fact that Dr. Fama had counseled my dad when he was coming up in the world.

After the visit, Dad and I returned to his heavy LaSalle. This time I had been allowed to leave the car to enjoy the luxurious, quiet bronze statuary of Dr. Fama's waiting rooms. As I got in the front seat, Dad slammed my door shut. My hand was still in it.

It is difficult for me to make you understand how or why I, so intimidated by my father's authority, feared his reaction—like I was to blame—that I did not cry out. I find it hard to believe I permitted that, even now. Within two miles we were on Pelham Parkway, and I fainted. It was then my father realized what was wrong.

I have told you before my father could also be gentle. And he was, and back we went to Dr. Fama. I think the greater shock must have been Dad's when he realized that his influence was so strong that he could make someone do something as stupid as what I did. I wish I could tell you that this episode never happened, but it did.

But there were many good times. For example, every summer La Festa (the Feast) came to Villa Avenue. Actually, two different *festas* were organized. One alone was not enough to absorb the nervous summer energy and Neapolitan compulsion that had been building to live our daily lives in the streets. La Festa Sant' Antonio came on June 13. The several weeks of preparation required came just in time to prevent all that youthful energy from exploding like an atomic bomb. But what a waste of good weather!

La Madonna Assunta (the Assumption of Mary into Heaven) came on August 15. The *festas*, each ten days long, were put together by two different organizations—Sant' Antonio by La Società di Sant' Antonio (di Padova), and La Madonna Assunta by an amalgam of all the religious societies: of Mary, of the Rosary and Altar, and of the Sacred Heart. The Saint Anthony Society lended encouragement, as well as the expertise, needed for the gaily colored street lights that formed an arched roof over the length of Villa Avenue, in addition to assistance for the absolutely essential thunderous fireworks.

Back in Naples there would be the Feast of San Gennaro (Januarius); another was La Piedigrotta (the best I can make of the meaning of this feast name is "at the foot of the grotto"). Each little Italian town had its own feast. It was, and is yet, a contest between communities to see whose decorations, enticements, and fireworks imply the most fervent devotion to "their" saint. My people were reluctant to lose that, so we had our own *festas*.

Our immediate competition was from the nearby Arthur

Avenue and 187th Street area, separated from us by the world-famous Bronx Botanical Gardens. Their church and saint was La Madonna Del Carmine (Our Lady of Mount Carmel). Over in a section of Brooklyn, adjacent to the Brooklyn-Queens Expressway, La Festa Del Giglio (the Feast of the Lilies) still takes place. This *festa* comes right from Nola, which is near Cicciano, my grandparents' hometown in Italy. The "lily" is a wooden edifice topped with a San Nicola (Saint Nicholas). The lily is an unbelievable eight stories high, and sits on a huge wooden platform carried by hundreds of men. This frightening scene and parade takes place once a year and is well worth the trip to Brooklyn, or better yet, to Nola.

At our own *festa* there was an elevated bandstand, an immense stage made of scaffold plank that almost blocked the entire tunnel entrance leading to 204th Street. The construction of the bandstand was a community effort, and duck soup really, for there was a superabundance of *scaffaioli* available, including many of my father's own men and relatives. All worked for nothing.

The *banchetti* lining the streets on both sides were the individual stands, again colorfully decorated and lighted, where you could buy a profusion of delicious enticements. There would be *banchetti* selling the doughnut-like *zeppole* (no holes), *sciurilli* (Neapolitan for *fiorilli*), which are zucchini flowers encased in freshly fried batter, and calzones (little half-moons made of light pizza dough and filled with mozzarella and ricotta cheeses).

Then, of course, you had the *salsiccia* stands, some pan-broiling the sausage, sweet, hot, or *forte* (hot-hot), with mounds of fried onions and/or peppers, while others broiled the six-foot-long chains of sausage over charcoal fires. And who could do without the eggplant and mozzarella *panini* (wedges), or the miniature *spolettas* filled with *polpette* (meatballs) floating in fresh tomato sauce? Warm pizza was always available from the copper *termaginos* set up outside pizzerias.

One delight for me was the little stands selling nuts, condiments, and trinkets. The small *nocciole* (filbert nuts) were pierced and made into knotted strings. From these you could fashion necklaces or tiny whips (if you were mischievously inclined); you could also hang strings around your neck and tear off a delicious roasted nut every now and then as you meandered about.

Later you would get into the *gelati* (ice creams) or spumoni (a word unknown in Italy; they call this dessert *cassata*). My favorite was the lemon ice. Two things made it more delicious than it is today: it was made only with freshly squeezed lemons, and the ice was finely shaved shards of real ice. As the evening wore on, it would be time for the tiny cream puffs and *pignoli* (pine nut) cookies.

Then, after the passing of the saint, the fireworks would start—the louder the better. The pent-up excitement was so great that people went out into the streets before nightfall—before things really began. The crowds began to build, and visitors were already selecting the best parking spaces in adjoining streets. The people running the *banchetti* liked this, for business started earlier. Besides, who is to tell you when your own entertainment should begin?

A fanfare of music from the marching band signaled the start, at nightfall, of the parade with O'santo. The double life-sized statue of either Saint Anthony or Mary was taken out of the storefront storage and placed on a huge platform that would be carried by at least forty men.

Why were the statues not kept at Saint Philip Neri Church? The reason the statues were stored off church property is important and deserves an explanation. I will tell you.

The parade would snake its way south along Villa Avenue, and a loud band would precede the completely decorated and lighted platform of O'santo. Every sixty or eighty feet the parade would stop, the music would cease, and the carriers would rest. Actually, the procession could hardly proceed against the crowds lining both sides of the streets. While the parade was at a standstill, those who wished to make an offering to O'santo, and that was practically everybody, would be lifted onto the platform. They would then be lifted farther up to the statue of *O'santo*, onto whose vestments they pinned money. This was particularly exciting for very young children, who were the ones most often selected by their parents and relatives to make the votive offering. It was presumed that the innocence of the child would make the offering more acceptable to O'santo and more likely to produce an answer to a prayer.

Some, however, would deride the whole notion of these feasts and offerings, ascribing the practice to voodoo mysticism and the adoration of craven images. Perhaps they miss the whole point. Why not accept the tradition and enjoy the whole *festa*? Besides, giving makes a person feel good, and there is always the chance that a prayer really might be answered.

Listen to the circus barker: "Step right up, ladies and gentlemen. Cop your bets. The road is hard and long. The voyage is fraught with peril. Avail yourself of all the defenses you can muster. Surely prayer helps; perhaps an amulet or an offering will, too."

These neighborhood feasts have practically disappeared in our country. The few remaining, like the Feast of San Gennaro on Mulberry Street in lower New York, have become strictly commercial enterprises, with a lot of rowdyism and garbage. Yet, if you think about it, you will realize that these feasts still represent an attempt to answer a human desire for close communication with fellow humans, as opposed to the view of the critics who safely isolate themselves in front of their lonely television sets and are busy at work making lists of problems to discuss with their psychiatrists. The *festas* were an affordable emotional outlet for the people, children and parents alike.

My father was the marshall of the parade on several occasions. There were some good practical reasons for this. The whole notion of the *festa* was cause for serious contention between the Italian community and the church, as represented by the now overwhelmingly Irish pastorate of Saint Philip Neri Church. It was not by accident that our church was named after an Italian saint, the founder of the Oratory Fathers, to this day a very powerful influence on society and charities in Naples.

The cornerstone set into the facade of this all-stone church facing the Grand Concourse is incised "1899." It was cut there by the Italian stonemasons who built the huge church, extending the entire block down to Villa Avenue. It you examine the granite and schist blocks, you will see how closely they resemble the huge stones that form the inside lining of the Jerome Park Reservoir, only 1,500 feet to the west. My father's father, originally a stonemason, had come here in 1902, too late to give his labor to the building of "their" church, but he came to know many of the stonemasons who had. My grandfather told me, and the church archives indicate, that all the stone came from the reservoir. These enormous projects took years to complete, and I do not doubt the veracity of the stories.

The immigrants then had both the name and the work with which to feel communion with their *chiesa* (church). But the Italian influence in the administration of church affairs began to wane, primarily due to the lack of vocations among the immigrant youth. It was more logical that the English-speaking Irish Catholics would replenish the supply for the hierarchy.

But this replenishment created a conflict between the two cultures. It was not that one is or was better than the other, only that they were different. This natural situation occurred then, and still does today, for only in our country does the melting pot have a welcome sign hanging on it. That is the source of many of our problems. More importantly, it is the source of our strengths.

Since we live in a real world, and we have no choice but to solve our problems together, whether international, national, or local, then we must not fear being truthful about the differences that separate us. This ventilation is far better than hiding our notions and emotions, which very likely are inaccurate in their isolation. I have become aware that this book is but a pitiful attempt to do just that.

Two extreme, but true, stories are in order. These are historical stories, not criticisms. The first of the two took place in Sorrento, Italy (I also saw this episode repeated on the island of Ischia). It was Sunday, the doors of the church were wide open, and mass was in session. Everyone was bustling, the *comare* were greeting one another, some stopping to show off their children and their *guandierre*[25] which are gaily decorated and beribboned oval platters of pastries and cookies fresh from the crowded *pasticcerie* (confectioners' shops). The hubbub ceased temporarily only when it was time to sing. Then angelic voices crowded the air and the church resounded to the admirable competition. As soon as the chorus was over, the hubbub renewed. Only at the sacrifice of the mass did decorum descend, momentarily. A young dog even sauntered in, inquisitively seeking a young master or

---

25. The "g" is pronounced with a "w" sound in dialect.

perhaps just wanting to see what was going on. No one took exception.

Church thus let in and out in a casual stream. The priest was unconcerned with the noisy competition. There were no somber faces, but little religious fervor was apparent. With few exceptions, the men stood across the piazza, sipping heir tiny but powerful *espressi* at the open-air cafés. But at the moment of their deaths, including the town communists, they would want, and expect, the reassuring transport of Mother Church.

The scene of the second story took place in Saint Brendan's lower-level church early on a Sunday morning. The no-nonsense Father Wickham was celebrating the 7:00 A.M. mass. I was probably around twelve years old.

For those who do not know, the obligation for Sunday mass is technically fulfilled after the sacrament of Holy Communion. Through the years, the practice of communally reciting some extra prayers, which are not a part of mass itself, arose. On this particular Sunday, some of the parishoners, feeling free to leave after the sacrament, started out.

Father Wickham wheeled about, and in a stentorian voice bellowed, "Ushers, lock those doors."

Silence and embarrassment descended upon all, especially upon the "culprits." The prayers continued, and when mass was over, the doors were unlocked. But whatever religious fervor had been felt was gone.

Which way is better? Is it better to practice your religion or to live it? Perhaps more of each? More importantly, these stories illustrate the extreme differences in cultures. In these days of so many people falling away, perhaps it behooves our American hierarchy to review one of the reasons why the Catholic church in Rome has endured for 2,000 years.

This difference in cultures was what was at issue between those organizing the *festas* and the latter-day pastors of Saint Philip Neri Church. The church did not want the seemingly ostentatious irreverence attending the exuberant and public adoration of the immigrants' *Santo*, but the Italian immigrants resented such forced estrangement from "their" church. They felt betrayed.

The schism exacerbated, the statue saints were taken out of

the church and deposited in storefront "clubs," and the church washed its hands of the *festas*. They were to continue.

But let me get back to the festivities. To have a *festa* without fireworks is unthinkable. The more spectacular and louder, the greater measure of success for La Società. That is where my father came in. A special permit was needed for fireworks, and without the sponsorship of the church, the permit was difficult to procure. On several occasions getting it came right down to the wire. The police captain of Precinct 52 would finally succumb to the pressure, though Dad was often forced to exert considerable political influence to obtain it. Again, the matter became a challenge to him. His honor, exposed before his *paesani*, was at stake. His fierce will showed in his eyes. Many a night I spent in a freezing flivver outside Police Inspector Flaherty's house down in the Southeast Bronx.

Dad was now leader of the Bedford Park Democratic Club, which was only a big deal if you started counting votes. More importantly, as the first Italian leader, he had coalesced the three thousand or so votes into a bloc. The Bronx leaders, including Congressman Charles Buckley, were not going to let go of that, especially if you consider that therein lay the possibility of gathering other Italian neighborhood *paesani* into the Democratic fold.

So Saint Anthony always got his fireworks, despite the active contravention of our own pastors on several occasions, and Dad became a semipermanent marshall of the *festas*, especially since Zi Antonio O'Lungo was head of La Società di Sant' Antonio. On Monday mornings Dad's men looked up from their work as their champion arrived on the job.

The fireworks were a measure of the success of the *festas*, and the experts hired to shoot them off played the audience like an opera. First came the startling colors, with just a puff of noise. Then followed the series of multiple explosions, with emphasis on sound rather than light. Then came the crescendo, as light and sound combined in an ascending scale toward the finale. Ears were assaulted by multiple explosions combined with startling arrays and combinations of colors until the profusion of both became almost intolerable. The final blasts were accompanied by both sighs of relief and sorrow that it was all over. But was it? Was this anticlimax?

No! The crowd would not be sent away disappointed: the fat lady still had to sing. After a hiatus of a full two minutes, the darkened heavens suddenly exploded in a sky-filling burst of every type of light and color imaginable, accompanied by a crescendo of rapid bomb bursts, each louder than the one before, incomprehensibly powerful. We all awaited what we knew was coming. That last blast shook the earth. From the nearby Jerome Park Reservoir, where the fireworks were shot, to our own Reservoir Oval on Gun Hill Road in the east, the earth trembled. La Festa was over. But not the excitement or the memories.

In early 1947, I had closed a contract for a soap factory right off Route 46, two miles from the Jersey side of the George Washington Bridge. My father had been with me at the signing, but he died before the work started. It was the first job we would start after his death in June. The "we" was Uncle Joe and I, the two remaining partners.

When the time came to start laying brick, I told Al Stola to wait for me until I got to the job the next morning. I was there at 7:30 A.M. Al had his marks all set on the reinforced concrete frame. I asked Guy Vallese, my adoptive father, to grab a shovel of mortar himself and to accompany Al and me to the far corner where Al was starting. It was before 8:00 A.M., and we were alone. Guy and Al, I think, were beginning to guess what I had in mind. Al also lifted a trowel of mortar from the shovel and laid it along the snapped-line keel mark.

I took the green scapular from my pocket, laid it in the mortar, and asked Al to lay the first brick. Guy and Al joined in when they saw me bow my head in prayer. They knew I was dedicating this job to my father, and in the process, asking for the safety of all our men.

That was the beginning of a tradition. Never, over the course of the next thirty-five years, was a job of ours or mine started without the first block or brick containing the tiny scapular memorializing my father and all those departed with whom we had worked. I can bring to mind sons, sons-in-law, fathers, and dear friends. What had started so privately that day became a command performance. Word spread, and on subsequent jobs the men silently demanded that they be present.

It was contemplatively tranquilizing for all of us to join together in so many emotions. Construction men, who are frequently, almost universally, pictured as rough-and-tumble, hard-drinking, and blasphemous characters, here exposed their obeisance to a greater power and, surprisingly, demanded the right to do so.

I remember Pratt Institute Towers in Brooklyn, which are three 24-story buildings right on the edge of the infamous Bedford-Stuyvesant area, where over thirty men gathered on a hot, dusty morning. Even the vicious Doberman pinscher guard dogs were silent as we quietly assembled.

The petition on the little green cloth now enclosed in a clear plastic cover is simply "O Immaculate Heart of Mary, Pray for us Sinners, now and at the hour of our death."

Embarrassing? The men didn't think so.

The biggest job we ever did, in sheer volume of bricks and blocks, was Linwood Gardens, a complex of thirteen 6-story buildings sitting atop the Palisades in Fort Lee, New Jersey. Each building, which was over a quarter mile in perimeter, had wall-bearing floors. That means heavy masonry walls support the structure, and as a result, each square foot of visible surface has three to four times the volume of brickwork.

The builder was Sidney Sarner, former construction manager out of New York and expert in his chosen work. This was a Federal Housing Administration (FHA) 608 project, an intelligent melding of government incentive with private initiative and direction, and the program which produced most of the decent, affordable housing after World War II. Unfortunately, this program was ultimately massacred by that old combination of bureaucrats, politicians (remember the *mangia-franchi*?), and uninformed do-gooders, like the media, who resented the profits the builders made from placing their mortgages with the banks.

These were the days of cheap money, and the banks were so anxious to possess government-guaranteed mortgages at 4 1/2 percent interest that they paid builders points—not asked points, but paid points. Homeowners know what that means. On large jobs a $20,000,000 loan could generate 2 or 3 percent, amounting to as much as a $600,000 fee. These were dubbed "windfall profits" and became grist for the mills of the do-gooders. Ul-timately, the program was hounded out, and the usual solutions substituted. A series of quasi-socialistic and outright socialist programs were designed, like the FHA 213 project and the New York Mitchell-Lama Cooperatives Program, whose sponsors didn't need to know anything about building. As a result, you had furriers, dress manufacturers, and neighborhood social program leaders as sponsors.

Naturally, the first thing that had to be done was to raise the limits of government-insured mortgages to allow for the inefficient and inexpert builders to survive. The do-gooders could not accept 3 percent for the builders, but for society to pay 50 percent more did not bother them. Besides, by now they were off marching in protest on some other pet activist venture.

The result is what you see today, twenty-five years later: decent housing now costs not $15,000 per dwelling unit but over $100,000, and interest on home mortgages floats around 10 percent, despite subsidized government loans at only 3 1/2 percent and even 1 1/2 percent interest. Reimbursement for inflated land costs, included in mortgages, and special state laws exclusively designed to underwrite defaulted loans of supposedly independent cooperatives, were conceived. One of these is the enormous Co-op City Housing in the Bronx. The typical hard-working family always pays for the socialist experiments, while the smear experts dub them as people "without social conscience" simply because they would rather devote their lives to improving the lot of their own families.

The Linwood Gardens job was almost lost to us. More accurately, it was almost taken away from us. This is a story involving shenanigans, intrigue, and chicanery, which, judging from what you have already read, should be anticipated. Some six months after shaking hands on our deal, but before the site work had sufficiently progressed, Sid called me and worriedly indicated we had a problem. I had as yet no written contract.

When I arrived at the trailer site, Sid took me out in the field. "What do you see?" he asked.

I saw acres of barren rock, with compressors, pumps, blasting mats, and men drilling trenches and trying to sculpt the stone landscape. Even a simple drain line had to be line-cut and blasted through the Palisades' surface.

The most powerful union by far in construction is that of the Operating Engineers; these engineers control all the power-driven equipment on a job. Absolutely nothing moves without this union's approval. On some jobs, where only shoving dirt aside is needed, the unions' interest and involvement is practically nil. On other jobs, like the Linwood Gardens project, preparation for water, sewers, foundations, and utility lines is 100 percent in their control—literally and figuratively.

"Somebody is pushing Dave Leib to get this job," said Sid. Leib was our biggest competitor in the masonry business in New Jersey. "Do you know what happens to me if I don't go along with the engineers?" he added. It was quite obvious. "It's up to you to solve this problem. I can't give you the job if you don't."

"Let me think about it," I told Sid. Again, *'Dice sempre sì, che non è mai peccato'* (Always say yes, for it is never a sin).

I had absolutely no idea what I was going to do, but an opportunity to do a job involving apartments for almost two thousand families does not come along all that often. The fight was on. Dave Leib could not hold a candle to us in expertise or organization. He had been a timekeeper and payroll man, while with us mortar was in our blood. But he possessed a business acumen which far outweighed mine, and apparently he had touched the right nerve. It was obvious who that was. To make things worse, I was fighting Sid Sarner's battle, too. If I were unsuccessful in getting the contract, he would have to pay several hundreds of thousands more. I would not forget that, either.

I had found that forcing a decision to a perplexing problem was not a good technique. The best procedure for me was to put it out of my mind and sleep on it for several nights. This was a heavy game; no lightweight solution would carry the day. My bricklayer-union friends would be of no help.

What was that name from years before? Father Celauro, our "Italian" priest from Saint Philip's had come to my father once for help. The priest's brother, Beniamino, who was a cutter in the cloak and suit trade, wanted something better, more lucrative, and steady. My father helped Benny get a job as an oiler, the second man on a steam shovel (or other heavy equipment) and about as good a blue-collar job as you can get. The main obligation is showing up; the second is making certain the moving parts are oiled or greased. Benny's income increased fourfold. How this all came about is a long story, and an explanation is unnecessary here. Through what connections my father reached out to the source, I don't know, but they were political. And the man contacted had been someone my father admired. That had happened at least fifteen years before.

But what was that man's name? It came to me in the middle of the night. Delaney—Joe Delaney! By this time Delaney had become tops in the vice presidential ladder of the international union. Fortunately for me, I did not know this until later, for had I known I probably would not have had the temerity to approach him. I was still wearing a homburg hat to effect a more mature appearance in those days. How silly that seems now.

I spoke to Uncle Joe. Yes, he remembered my father's efforts to help Benny, and yes, it was Joe Delaney he had contacted. I met next with Tommy Napoli and Guy Vallese. You know, they were my advisers and sounding boards, and even though they sometimes weren't able to do or say anything specific to help me, the very fact that they were there to be consulted helped me clarify my thoughts. Their confidences in my ultimate judgment bound us even closer.

I reached out for Joe Delaney without any trouble at all. His office at union headquarters in New York put me through to Washington. What I had anticipated as a search for several days was consummated in minutes. I was unprepared when he got on the line.

Yes, of course, he remembered my father. "What's your problem?"

"I have to see you personally."

"I will be in New York on Thursday in my office at ten o'clock."

I asked Uncle Joe to go with me. We were ushered in without delay. The large, no-nonsense man said, "Okay, Frank, tell me what's up." I told him about the job and what Sarner had said to me. I will call the delegate Bill, for that was not his name, and there is no need to sully the name of the deceased. After listening for two minutes, Delaney picked up the phone and told his secretary to get Bill on the phone. That took only two minutes more.

When the phone rang, he picked up the receiver and said tersely, "Bill? You're hurting a friend of mine, Frank Puzio. Straighten it out!" Then he hung up and said to me, "Call him tomorrow morning. After you meet, call me." Uncle Joe and I thanked him and left. The total time that had elapsed was less than ten minutes.

Bill and I agreed to meet for lunch at Guido's Restaurant on Polifly Road in Hackensack. At that time, Route 80 did not exist, but it is now the southern boundary of Guido's parking lot. Again, it was proper that Uncle Joe be with me.

After a somewhat uncomfortable lunch where really nothing was discussed, Bill said, "Let's go call Delaney." We left Uncle Joe at the table and went to the upholstered phone closet just inside the vestibule entrance. Bill told me to stick my head in and listen.

"Hello, Joe. I'm here with Frank and we're all straightened out. Here, Joe wants to talk to you," he added as he rose to let me into the booth.

"Frank, is everything okay?"

"Yes, Joe."

"Good luck," and he was gone.

The best was still seconds away. Bill blocked his considerable bulk into the half-open doors and looked down upon me still seated before the phone. With a surreptitious glance to be certain no one was within earshot, he said, taking an envelope from his inner jacket pocket and displaying a packet of one-thousand-dollar bills, "You went to the only man in America who could make me give this back. And this was only a down payment." He had twenty of those bills!

Sid Sarner could not believe the issue had been settled so quickly. Little did he know that his surprise did not even begin to approach our own. His erroneous perception that my uncle and I possessed enormous influence became his reality. I did not dissuade him, and I warned Uncle Joe to keep quiet.

"Sid, you had better take good care of Bill," I told Sarner later. My instincts were not going to fail me now. It was Sid's party: let Sid pay!

I never saw Joe Delaney after that. Several cases of Scotch were returned, unopened. Bill would never take a penny from me, then or thereafter. I will talk about the Linwood Gardens job elsewhere.

In the tumble of so many emotions, then and now, one that has never left me was how remarkable it was that ten years beyond his death, my father's influence, foresight, and sacrifices could still bear dividends. Maybe he was right, after all. *"Pazienza, my son."* I was thinking back to that chauffeur's cap.

On July 13, 1950, I arrived on the job in Kew Gardens Hills, Long Island. We were doing an 846-unit of garden apartments for Gregory, Roth, Schenker. Gregory was a financier—Texas oriented. Roth and Schenker were graduates of the old M. Shapiro and Sons Construction Company, the people for whom my father and uncle did the job in Allentown, which I discussed in "Corner-Man." For the Shapiro organization they, and later I, did work all over the eastern seaboard, as far west as Pittsburgh and State College in Pennsylvania, as well as Detroit, Michigan.

The Shapiro Company had an amazing array of talent. Jim Wolfson went on to become top man at Tishman Construction. Big-name organizations like H.R.H., Uris, Minskoff, Winston, and Gregory, Roth, Schenker all were peppered with former Shapiro men. The sons, Bob Shapiro and Joe Viertel, and brother Jules Shapiro of the original "M." Shapiro went on to form Presidential Construction and Management, in which I still am a stockholder. You may wonder how brothers Bob and Joe came to have different last names. Joe wanted to go to Harvard, and his family reasoned his chances would be better if his name were not so Jewish, like Shapiro. So Joe changed his last name to Viertel, his mother's maiden name. That surely is not a problem today.

I know the date because the day before our son had been born, and when Sam Schiff came to the job looking for me, Uncle Joe told him why he would not see me that day. I did not know Sam Schiff, but he owned (together with a silent partner) the company known as General Builders Supply Corporation—a powerhouse dealer in constuction materials in the New York area. The silent partner (about whom everybody unsilently knew) was Jim Farley, National Chairman of the Democratic party, Postmaster General of the United States, and confidant of

President Roosevelt and his successors.

When I had figured the job, I was told what I would have to pay for the brick, the mortar cement, the gypsum block, and even the foundation cement block, and where the order would have to be placed. The prices were not bad, just a little above competitive, and the JJJ brick were the soundest, best-formed brick made on the Hudson River. These are the Median Weather, the common, dark-cherry-red brick you can see everywhere you look. There were millions of them on this job.

Sam Schiff came back to the site the next day. I approached the chauffeured limousine. Out jumped a gregarious, smiling, big man. My experience has consistently been that top men are big men, not physically but in their lack of pretense. It is not by accident that the leaders of successful enterprises are never overly impressed with themselves and are unerringly gracious. They are *furba*, as you will recall. It would not be inaccurate to say he was *mafioso*, too, with a small "m." It was not beneath him to be kind to me, a young upstart, even though there was no compulsion for him to be so. Sam wanted to have lunch with me in order to let me know that he had known my father and that we should get to know each other. Nor did he forget the congratulations to my wife on our son's birth.

I asked him to give me some time on the job, and he waited patiently, for several hours. He took me to Peter Luger's, a fancy businessmen's restaurant which is now very well known. This place is an offshoot of the famous Brooklyn Peter Luger's.

At coffee time he said to me, "Frank, I knew and respected your father, and I want to tell you something. You will know I am serious about what I say when I also tell you I am a dying man. I have cancer, and I don't have too much time. People stay in this business too long. I have seen the cycles. It is boom and then bust. The more business you do the more the builders are using your money. Become an owner yourself. Do the brickwork on your own buildings."

I took a new, good look at this *mafioso* man, and yes, the ravages of the insidious cancer were beginning to show. I had no choice but to appreciate this man's concern, for I knew we would not meet again. Accidental incidents help shape a man's life. Schiff had confirmed what I had already been thinking. Uncle

Joe had agreed to go along with me on a proposed luxury apartment building in Bronxville, New York. The land was already in our possession.

Schiff brought me back to Kew Gardens. Our good-bye was a silent handclasp. Another legend was passing from the scene. Jim Farley had chosen well. And so had Dad.

Going back in time a little further, before my son was born, I remember the spring rains that came furiously in 1947, especially to the Elizabeth River area of Elizabeth, New Jersey. Alongside the river, we were building six 5-story buildings, for that same Shapiro organization. This was Pearce Manor. There was a lot of talent on that job. Work must have been slow at the time, for I remember all our top men bunched there. Usually they were dispersed to different jobs.

The bricklayer foreman was Tommy Napoli, and Guy Vallese was labor foreman. What a comfortable feeling I still get when I think of my visits to jobs they controlled! Quiet assurance pervaded the entire atmosphere. There would be not one false move made between them, and the work would grow smoothly, without that frenetic nervousness and noise that attends less efficient operations.

Dad had laid the groundwork with the unions; he was to be with us a few more months. We never went into any area without Dad having his friends in the New York unions contact delegates of the local area. The entire family were members of Bricklayers Local #37 in the Bronx, and that was a lot of members. Even my own apprentice card had come from there.

Forty years later, when I told Ralph Belloise I was writing a book about the jobs, he said, "Don't forget to tell them about the scaffold planks floating down the Elizabeth River."

The rains had been torrential for several days. The call from the Elizabeth police came at 4:00 A.M.: our scaffolding was floating down the Elizabeth River, and the erected scaffolds around the buildings were collapsing! How natural that I should have called Guy Vallese! His calm acceptance of the reality was immediately reassuring. He must have been talking to my wife, Emily. She quotes often, "Life is what happens to you when you have other plans."

Immediately Guy galvanized the "foreign legion" into action. All over the Bronx and Westchester men tumbled out of bed, the trucks were warmed up, and the all-night luncheonette on Bedford Park Boulevard and Villa Avenue was overwhelmed. Ralph Belloise manned the telephones and coordinated the stragglers. Even with the abysmal rain, men jumped aboard the backs of open dump trucks as the caravan took off for Elizabeth, which was yet an hour away.

Vince Basciano rounded up the Vitolos on Villa Avenue, Sandy Jackson and his father-in-law, Andy, from Brooklyn, and the Carozzas from Harlem. By 5:30 A.M., even Strawberry was down from West Point. How he did it—pulling a mortar mixer behind his service truck—I will never know. The Storm King Highway must have been witness to a strange whizzing that stormy night.

Uncle Johnny and his two sons, my cousins Sonny and Jamesie, all bricklayers, were there to help. *La famiglia* was in trouble and the ranks closed. From Eastchester, Frank D'Angelica brought Louis Mancuso, Patsy Mosca, and their trucks and calmly assisted Ralph with getting the men transportation.

The early morning scene that greeted the men was disheartening. The river had overflowed its banks, the buildings were hip-deep in water, and the thousands of stored planks, poles, putlogs, and plywood panels were gone; a few visible here and there caught up against banks and overhanging trees.

The Union County police, as well as the local Elizabeth police, were marvelous. The river widened out about a mile downstream, and a dam helped prevent a complete loss. When I arrived on the scene, my men were out in police boats, looking more like fishermen than construction men. There were no coffee breaks that morning as Jimmy Gigolo (his real name is Giglio, for Lily), Strawberry, Louis Mancuso, and Patsy Mosca stationed their trucks on high ground near bridges and banks. The roundup continued for two days, but Gaetano was more concerned about the sagging scaffolds around the building.

I did not have to ask Guy what was worrying him. I knew he was wondering whether, after the water receded and the rebracing was completed, he could trust those scaffolds to support safely the many breadwinners entrusted to his care. Except in this book, no one will ever read about this simple, broken-English-speaking man, and no medals will be made for him. Yet he was a true hero, and I loved him.

At the beginning of this book I said there would be some things that would be difficult for met to talk about. On the early evening of June 11, 1947 I took title to a plot of ground in Bronxville, New York. Emily and I were still living in a sixth-floor walk-up apartment on Perry Avenue in the Bronx. Our daughter, Emilie-Mary, was only six months old.

By a most peculiar set of coincidences, I found at the closing, which took place in a car in Long Island City, that my own father had once held the deed to this very plot, given to him as a guarantee against a personal loan. Neither he nor I was aware of this, since he had not seen the plot I was buying.

After the closing, I drove up the Grand Concourse to my parents' apartment on 201st Street in Bedford Park. Italians put down roots rather permanently. They still lived within one thousand feet of the first American homes they had lived in as children. Dad was in bed, complaining of a "cold" feeling in his chest. His not feeling well took the edge off any joy they could share with me, nor was the coincidence about the property I had just acquired of much interest. Some ten minutes later I left and drove across Mosholu Park to my own family on Perry Avenue. The joy Emily and I shared in these first moments of having our own land was short lived.

Within five minutes of my leaving, Dad was dead. A massive embolism could not navigate a strictured artery. The "good life," the "advantages" to which so many children of immigrants aspired, had forced a change in their eating habits and life style which were different from those of their parents. The abundance of red meat, creams and sauces, automobiles, which reduced the amount of exercise one got, and twenty cigars a day were the rewards. Was this not "why we came here?" Unfortunately, it was not. The consequences, still unknown then, and more unfortunately still ignored by many today, are pernicious.

I told you before about Vince Basciano and his admonition to me at my father's grave, "Don't let people talk!" I was already determined that "they" would not. What I did not tell you, though, within the jumble of grief, was another of my thoughts as I sat beside my mother in the limousine driving us home: "Now I can become my own man." The anguish that this thought should intrude upon me at that moment still haunts me. What kind of a reward is such a thought for a father who devoted his whole life to improving the lot of his family, who has battled, labored incessantly, and persevered without regard to his own wants? How perfect must a parent be to a demanding child who is selfishly stumbling toward maturity?

My father had done it his way, the only way he knew how. If he was tough, violent, and unrelenting, it was because his world had taught him that was the way to survive. *'Meglio che piange tu che io'* (Better you cry than I). Was it his fault that on the deck of that ship, as his six-year-old eyes looked out upon his new world, that his mother should forever chain him thus: *'Dobbiamo trovare lavoro'* (We must find work)? Of course not! It was simply part of the price to be paid for being an immigrant. The rewards are another matter.

But nature is fair. The stumbling child soon becomes the parent. The impossible demands, "I want you and perfection, too," like the voracious chick tearing the food from the parent's gullet, begin anew, and the process repeats itself for another generation.

Grandma said it best. *'Una mama può sopportare cento figli, ma cento figli non possono sopportare una mama'* (One mother can take care of a hundred children, but a hundred children cannot sustain one mother).

Ultimately each of us is responsible for his own actions, for his own handling of the world and the people around him, regardless of the bouillabaisse of influences upon him.

If you think I did not love my father, you are wrong.

Afterthought

I am indebted to my dear friend of many years, Rudy (Rodolfo) Marchesi, concrete contractor, who as a boy in Italy in the 1920's listened to the ancient *'Le Favole di Fedro (The Fables of Fedro)*. I will tell you the fable he told me:

There was a hush throughout the animal kingdom, and the

beasts conversed in whispers: "The king is dying!" Yes, it is true; the lion is in his lair, too weak even to stir."

One by one the animals visited the cave, their fears overcome by their need to know if the lion was really dying. They peered in deferentially, recalling the power that had been there and perhaps still was. Then they flung their revengeful insults and finally their disdainful blows upon the lion.

Even the jackass, more frightened than all the rest, came. His investigating approaches brought only a feeble response from the lion's eyelids. But with each approach the jackass became bolder and bolder. "This is not a ruse; the king is mortally wounded, really. Or is he?" the jackass vacillated. "Now I am before him, within reach of those mighty paws, yet he does not stir. This king is finished; I am greater than he." Now, completely emboldened, the ass turned about and aimed his kick right into the throat of the lion.

With his last gasp of strength, the king raised his head, opened his eyes, and said, *'Ho sopportato pazientemente le offese dei più forti, ma per essere offese da te, che sei la vergogna di Natura, mi fai agognara di morire due volte'* (I have endured with ultimate patience the insults of the strongest, but to be offended by you, who are the shame of Nature, makes me yearn to die twice over).

I often think of my still virile father. How offended he must have been at that Jackass of Death.

Epitaph

"I shall lift up this whole family by its own bootstraps!"
"Nothing can stand before me."
"If you don't like my methods, get out of the way."
There were to be many beneficiaries—only one victim.

Chapter VII

Ricordi e Riflessione
(Memories and Reflections)

I don't clearly remember, but it must have been the summer of 1948 or 1949. We were in Tenafly, New Jersey, building some two hundred units of four-story apartment buildings for Leo Goodman and John Guidera.

Being four stories high, these were unusual buildings, and they must have been the last built in New Jersey. The restricted height was dictated by the municipality, but their ultimate demise was dictated by a more practical consideration—they had no elevators. At that recent postwar period, demand for dwellings was fierce, with returning war veterans and newly formed families; but for those of us still living in five- or six-story walkups in the Bronx and elsewhere, the compromise was not that severe. In a few short years, what we were all willing to live with would become unacceptable to most of us.

This time the tables were reversed. Uncle Louis was the bricklayer foreman and Tommy Napoli was his deputy. Guy Vallese was the labor foreman. Uncle Joe was there, as was I.

Among Guy's hand-picked men was Sandy Jackson. Sandy and Andy Coffey had come north from South Carolina, and only two years before had walked onto the job at Kings County Hospital in Brooklyn. What a find! Sandy was Andy's son-in-law, and they lived together in Brooklyn, more like buddies than father and son, having left their families behind in the Carolinas. Both were very big men, but Sandy was extraordinary. He stood about six feet five inches tall, with the long, lean look and gait of a share-cropper. Below the tan overalls glistened the most magnificent fat-free body. The rippling muscles looked very comfortable in that broad-shouldered, hipless corpus. Sandy was as guileless, retiring, and sweet natured a man as you could find; it was as though he were totally unaware of the powers he could muster.

Guy spotted something he liked in the young Sandy and took him under his own wing. Sandy went quickly from common laborer to mortar man and finally to scaffold man, a position which, between wages and overtime, doubled his take-home pay. Their filial love began to blossom, and it was a joy to watch the rotund, white-haired Guy and the obedient, devoted giant treat each other with ultimate respect. Sandy responded by self-appointing himself as Guy's guardian angel; Sandy's eyes zealously followed Guy around the job.

I have told you before there were always opportunities for conflict among tradesmen on the jobs. Some of the mechanical workers, plumbers, steamfitters, electricians, and others were very careless about needlessly demolishing some of our walls in order to accommodate their own work. Instead of putting in a neat chase or box, frequently they would knock out whole sections of wall. Rebuilding was expensive for us.

This day iron men were on the job. Their steel beams were supported on one end by their own columns of steel in the middle of the building, but these were supported by our masonry walls at other ends.

The iron men were the worst of all, an opinion not mine alone, but rather universal in the construction industry. By now they seemed to enjoy the reputation they had garnered through years, and they definitely had a macho image of themselves which they always seemed compelled to encourage. And they had the tools to promote it—huge wrenches, including spanner wrenches, which had a needle end used to line up bolt holes in the steel.

The iron men were acting their usual rough selves, lifting and banging their steel against freshly laid-up walls, and in the process they needlessly pushed the brick end wall out of plumb. Eagle-eye Guy caught it and walked over to berate the six-man crew. By now our attention had been drawn to the loud voices, and what ensued were their usual responses: "Get out of the way little old man; you're gonna get hurt" and "Go fuck yourself." Then one of the men made the mistake, as at least thirty of us witnessed, of pulling out his spanner wrench and threatening Guy.

The telling takes much longer than the doing. Before anyone was aware, the impressive Sandy was at Guy's side, his eyes already bloodshot, and his scaffold-man's hatchet ready. He reached across the iron man, grabbed him by the biceps, and lifted him clean off the floor, unbelievably with his arms held straight out. We had not yet completely erected the front wall of the floor, and Sandy seemed torn by whether to throw the iron man over the side of the building.

We were all mesmerized, including the other iron men. Sandy's huge, rigid body began to shake, and great globs of perspiration glistened all over him. There was absolute silence; everyone was transfixed by the knowledge that the slightest movement would push Sandy over the edge to destroy the man. His shaking was uncontrollable and frightening.

Suddenly a sharp cry rang out: 'Basta!' (Enough!)

The usually mild Guy was showing his metal. Only he could control Sandy now. His beloved master's voice somehow got through to Sandy, who responded by slowly lowering the man, now ashen and powerless, onto the wooden deck. Sandy's shaking began to lessen, but those wary, bloodshot eyes never changed. For yet another moment the silence prevailed. "Now fixxa the wall," Guy calmly said as he walked away.

For days thereafter, as we replayed the scene, we all agreed that Sandy had never let go of the hatchet. In his fury he was able to pick up that man by the biceps, without the hatchet handle impeding his grip!

Andy went back to South Carolina after about seven years, but Sandy never left Brooklyn. He raised a second family there. I knew him for another twenty-five years. He came to Guy's wake and stayed to the end, every day. He did not cry, and he did not talk. I think I know what he was thinking.

North of Naples, a little more than the distance between New York City and Albany, lies the city of Firenze (Florence), that Renaissance jewel. Great writers have been unable to describe in words the human expressions which flowered in that city, the seeds of which were and are air-sown all over Italy. I will not try.

If you go there, you will find, among other treasures, L'Ospedale Degli Innocenti (The Hospital of the Innocents). This was where the babies born out of wedlock were brought, to be left in the care of the cloistered sisters, who, unexposed to the world, accepted the infants through a turntable in a wall. The whole city knew the turntable was always attended, even in the dead of night. These babies, there and elsewhere in Italy, were given the name Innocenti, and I'm sure you have seen the name in print. Many people bear this name today; motorcycles and automobiles do, too.

This building bears the genius of design of the architect Brunelleschi who built the world-renowned dome on the *duomo* (cathedral) of this building. That was almost six hundred years ago, long before the discovery of America. Brunelleschi's trademark, a series of arcaded porticos, lines the whole exterior. Above the columns in the semicircular arches is imbedded the genius of the three Della Robbias—father, uncle, and son. These roundels bear their own trademark, porcelain-glazed sculptures in blue and white. These sculptures, which all have the same theme—infants in swaddling clothes, in baskets, and in mothers' arms—proclaim the innocence of the child and the succor he or she would gain within.

What is the point? I want you to know that it was not until after World War II, in New York City, in these United States, that the Department of Health finally stopped using the word bastard to describe the circumstances of birth of the Innocents!

Do we have much to learn? Why cannot we, too, have a sensible alternative to destroying partly-formed babies, piling them up in garbage dumpsters, with less thought and dignity than that afforded a bunch of rubber dolls, or cruelly casting them out into an indifferent society, especially since so many childless couples yearn for a baby of their own.

Grandpa would have wanted it—and did!

Back in the late 1940's and early 1950's, we grandchildren of our sacrificial progenitors began to enjoy the fruits of their labors. A number of circumstances came together that made it possible for us to add our own efforts and basic training to the paths they had smoothed before us. Relative affluence was within our grasp; our life styles began to change, thanks mainly to the opportunities inherent in the constitutionally guaranteed freedoms.

This period was a time of unparalleled opportunity, especially in the building and construction industries. I do believe you will not soon see again the unique factors which joined together to make this possible: the tremendous pent-up demand for housing occasioned by the end of World War II; Marshall plans demanding goods of all kinds from America; cheap mortgages at 4½ percent, an interest rate deliberately pegged by the government in order to move the country into a peacetime economy; the federal prime rate at 4 percent and Veterans' Administration loans at 3 percent; the abundance of vacant land at bargain prices, which today would be tagged "ludicrously low;" and a work ethic among the American people which as yet was unspoiled by welfare and other social giveaway programs that later were to teach people it was not necessary to work for a living. Soon welfare was not to be for the needy but for the greedy.

And let us not forget the intact infrastructure of our country, which was relatively untouched by the ravages of the war that had devastated the rest of the industrialized world. Our country and its people were ready. Growth begot growth. Great housing projects begot stores, office buildings, and new factories.

We children and grandchildren of those immigrants were uniquely poised to take advantage of that combination of rare circumstances. By now we were relatively well educated and, better yet, knew that hard work led to the advancement of *la famiglia*. It was once again, '*L'occhio del padrone ingrassa il cavallo*' (The eye of the owner will fatten the horse). Those of us who had learned to work with our hands reached out for bigger things.

For a short while, I went into general construction and then into bricklaying contracting with my father and Uncle Joe.

Rudy Marchesi went into reinforced concrete work, because that's where he had worked alongside his father and *paesani*. He became one of the biggest in New Jersey. Later, as Alba (Dawn) Construction, he became a builder-developer.

Allan Shapiro went into electrical contracting in Paterson, New Jersey. He could not wait to finish his apprenticeship with his Uncle Jake. Today Allan is one of the foremost in his field, recognized nationally throughout the United States.

Dominick Belsole, who had mixed concrete by hand with his father, trucked sand and gravel, first on horse-drawn carts, started up the ladder with Colonial Sand and Stone Corporation, the purchaser of his father's sand and gravel business. Dom ended up as the shining protégé of one of the most influential and prosperous Italian businessmen in prewar New York, Genoroso Pope. On the side, Pope went on to publish *Il Progresso*, the largest foreign-language paper in the United States. He also bought out *La Prensa*, the largest paper in circulation for Spanish-speaking people, as well as the *Italo-Americano*. Dom had ancillary responsibilities with these while he ran the entire New Jersey operation for Colonial.

There were others. Vito Poveromo had been an apprentice boy with my father, part of the young *comparillo* group I mentioned earlier. But he had not been one of the lucky ones to get the gold watch; Dad had not been his sponsor at confirmation. Vito had grown up with Uncle Joe in our Bedford - Park neighborhood of the Bronx. Ultimately, he too became a mason contractor, with Tom Martin (Martini) and later with Curly DeRoberts and Vinnie Lombardi. Practically all of these young men took their union cards with the Bricklayers Local #37 in the Bronx.

Then there was Arthur Grundstein, scion of a New Jersey family that developed a meat-processing plant in Hoboken, which years later was one of the largest in the East. I will never forget that frozen view of a hundred white-smocked butchers taking scores of sides of beef in at one end of an endless refrigerator assembly line and ending up at the other with cuts ready for delivery to butcher shops all over the great metropolis.

The countries of our origins were different, but our ambitions and attitudes were the same. And so were the insecurities that we still carried within. Good thing! In retrospect it was those insecurities that made us "try harder."

Later there was Ben Torcivia, a Jersey City boy and subsequent engineer out of Catholic University in Washington, D.C. I met Ben when he was a young "gofer"—the do-it-all, all-around job clerk, timekeeper, and engineer—on the Camp Kilmer job we were doing for the Arthur Venneri Company of Westfield, New Jersey. This was a huge government-sponsored, barrack-type, temporary housing project on land adjoining the military base. It did not serve too many years for what it was intended. The Korean War came upon us, and the project was pressed into service as military housing.

Ben eventually married Vera, Arthur Venneri's daughter. Later, the Venneri Company came upon hard times and the bonding companies had to finish much government work. By then Ben was intimately familiar with all the projects and was engaged by the bonding companies to finish these jobs. He went on from there by himself. Like us, he put his energies and ambitions to work, and today—forty years later—Torcon Construction is one of the largest general construction contractors in the country. About seven years after the Camp Kilmer job, Ben joined our golfing group.

Another of our original group was Anthony Mazzucca. I spoke about Tony earlier in this book. He was responsible for the "How Many Parts to a Chicken?" story, the one that not only is about hunger and survival, but, better yet, is synonymous with the "waste not, want not" principle that appealed to us.

Tony was an engineer out of Brooklyn Polytechnic, a highly recognized engineering school in New York. It still is. By now he was top man in the Venneri Company, overseeing the field, as well as the bidding for the company. We first met when I was called in to bid on a high school in Union, New Jersey.

Tony and I hit it off immediately; our values were the same, our Italianate tastes were simple, our ambitions were unsatisfied, and we sensed the opportunities and dignity of accomplishment open to us. By then all of our own families were young and growing. We wanted something more. Golf became our passion.

It is easy now to reflect how natural this should have been. Golf imparted a sense of "climbing up the ladder"; it is a gentleman's game, beyond what those in *la famiglia* could even have begun to imagine, a venture into preserves reserved for the rich.

Golf was a statement: "Look, I'm successful!"

First our group played on public and semipublic courses, mostly in Westchester, New York and northern New Jersey. Soon we sought better places—our own clubs. We were to find they were not just for the taking.

By then I had built a home in Bronxville, New York. Some three miles away was Leewood Golf Club, in nearby Eastchester. Don Rice was a member. Don, as had his father before him, sold Cadillacs to my father before the war. He offered to propose me for Leewood but cautioned, "You know, there is a limit on Italian membership—five percent." This annoyed me, but if I was *furba*, as explained earlier, my irritation would not be evident and it wasn't. Realism is a valuable and stabilizing commodity: *'Così è fatto il mondo'* (That is the way the world is made), to requote Guy Vallese. More importantly, I owed it to Don not to embarrass him, for he was trying to be kind.

My check went in, together with the application. After two years of absolute silence, I gave up hope. I sought to join another club, White Beeches in Haworth, New Jersey. My sponsors were two builders for whom we were doing brickwork, John Guidera and Charlie Constanzo. I was accepted, but one major drawback was that I had to travel a long way to the club and thus ended up spending a lot of time away from my young family.

After two more years—a total wait of four years—I was invited to become a member at Leewood. Again, realism overcame annoyance. Five minutes from the house was a mighty big consideration. Besides, there were so many more people subject to really serious prejudice that by comparison mine was inconsequential.

Rudy Marchesi, Tom Viola, and Arthur Grundstein eventually joined The Knoll in Boonton, New Jersey. First Tony Mazzucca, then Dom Belsole, and then Ben Torcivia joined Colonia Country Club in Iselin, New Jersey, while Allan Shapiro went to Apple Ridge, a new club in Mahwah, New Jersey. Dom Belsole later moved from Colonia into Rockland Country Club, some twenty minutes up Route 9W from his home in Englewood Cliffs and just over the New Jersey border in New York State. Eventually, I proposed Vito Poveromo into Leewood. Later, Tony Fonti and Doc Ignaccolo from Apple Ridge were to join our group.

Wednesdays became semi-holidays. We still arose in the mornings on construction time, had our business days lined up by 11:00 A.M., and went off to our round robin of golf at the course selected for our group that day.

The pace was frantic and frenetic. Eighteen holes did not suffice—more often thirty-six was the ticket—and when we finished in the twilight, there was Arthur Grundstein goading us into gin rummy with, "Hurry up, deal the cards; you can shower later." Almost always dinner was served to us in the cardroom, so passionate was the competition and settling of accounts.

Why do I tell you all this? Because the best part of these days were the stories—mostly construction stories.

As affluence began to seep into the formula, we sought to travel, and we made trips to the meccas of golf. Off we went to the Greenbrier in West Virginia, the Homestead in Virginia, Boca Raton in Florida, Pinehurst in North Carolina, Hilton Head in South Carolina, the Canyons in Palm Springs, and the Del Monte Lodge in Pebble Beach, California.

As we became older and smarter, the thirty-six holes went down to twenty-seven. Then, as the stories got better, the game became shorter, and we eventually satisfied ourselves with the normal eighteen. Even the gin games became shorter, despite Arthur Grundstein's proddings, when we realized that what we wanted was to hang out around the fires in the living rooms. We were eight or more adult men constantly reminding ourselves that these were our green years, contrasting our life style with that of our grandfathers in the old country, and being grateful for the differences.

Dom Belsole was, and is, a great storyteller. When he was a young boy living in Fort Lee, New Jersey, there was no George Washington Bridge across the Hudson. The nearest ferry to New York was in Edgewater, at the foot of the Palisades, those magnificent sheer cliffs which confine the mighty Hudson River. That ferry landed on the Manhattan side at 125th Street in Harlem and was known either as the 125th Street or Edgewater Ferry.

Dom's father, John, owned a sand and gravel yard in upper Manhattan on the Harlem River, which divides the Bronx from

Manhattan. In order to get there, he had to hitch up his horse and wagon and work his way south along the switchback roads worked into the face of the cliffs, eventually arriving at the ferry slip in Edgewater. Then it was a wait and a trip across the Hudson, after which he would work his way north and east across Harlem and up Broadway to the northern tip. Elapsed time? Close to two hours.

Dom's father had a big dog named Jack, a mongrel, half or so Saint Bernard, with a lot of collie thrown in. He was John's constant companion and would not leave his master for a moment. Jack's trump suit was loyalty; he even came up with a great plan to be near John. As soon as John's horse took off, Jack would trot along under the wagon, protected from traffic and happy to be beneath his beloved master. Wherever John went, Jack was sure to follow below.

Dom's father also did concrete work, small jobs, especially for friends and customers who bought his materials. One Saturday, John had to go all the way out to Fort Schuyler in the East Bronx. Today, the great Throggs Neck Bridge, which connects the Bronx to Long Island, is there; thus, you can see just how far of a trip that is from Fort Lee, New Jersey. After making the long trip from home to the yard, John would then have to cross the Harlem River and traverse the whole Bronx, clear across the extreme western to the eastern side. This was no small trip, but Jack was right there.

John was doing a concrete sidewalk for a friend, and the job could not be finished that day. John would have to return on Sunday, the next day. So he asked his *compare* to keep Jack there overnight. The next day, when he arrived in Fort Schuyler, his *compare* was beside himself—Jack had broken the halter rope and run away! John was distraught, but hoped Jack would return that day as he worked.

In those days working men did not stop in for a cup of coffee. Instead, they stopped into bars for the nickel beer and free lunch, and that's what John did on the way home, several times. At each stop someone told him, "Hey, John, your dog was here last night. He came in, looked around, and left when he didn't see you. Jack's tongue was hanging out, and as soon as we gave him water, off he went."

When John arrived at the ferry on 125th Street, one of the crew told him, "John, they tell me your dog was here at two o'clock this morning; he hung around for a few hours as if he couldn't make up his mind, then jumped aboard about four." John was elated—there was still hope!

It was dark when John finally arrived at home in Fort Lee, and there was Jack calmly awaiting his master on the front stoop, as if to say, "What's the big deal—surely you expected to see me here?" You would have to know the size and confusion of the Bronx to know what an odyssey Jack had traveled!

Another story Dom used to tell us about Jack was the one we used to call *'O Sofà.'* The property John owned in Fort Lee was large, and among other things stored under the trees was an old-fashioned leather sofa Jack had inherited for his own use. A sofa is called a *poltrona* in Italian, but in an attempt to Anglicize everything, the sofa became *'o sofà.'* The word has even made its way into Italian-American dictionaries.

One day John was not going to the yard on 138th Street and Harlem River. He had a business appointment in downtown Manhattan and did not want Jack trotting along under the buggy. So he tied Jack up to one of the legs of *'o sofà.'*

John started through the property toward one of the streets in the rear. He soon became aware of a commotion behind him, and there was Jack, valiantly pulling *'o sofà'* through the dirt, scraping against trees! John stopped, so Jack stopped, too. The master then said to his dog, *'Porta a sofà a casa'* (Bring the sofa back to the house). Of course, Jack did not move, hoping for more favorable instructions, like maybe, "Okay, jump aboard!"

Finally, John descended from his buggy, untied the ropes from *'o sofà,'* and walked Jack back the half block to the house. John tied up Jack more securely, and *'o sofà'* stayed in its new location from then on. But Jack had earned another A for affection. Such devotion! Among mere humans? Hardly!

These Jack stories were a big part of growing up to Dom and Christine's four children, who now themselves are successful parents.

Dom also used to love to tell the story about the Interborough Rapid Transit (IRT) men, the employees who ran and manned the subway and elevated train lines throughout the city.

Did you ever wonder where subway cars go when they are not running? They go to carbarns, great open spaces of scores of tracks strategically located in the more remote sections of the city. One such carbarn was placed at the extreme northern tip of Manhattan Island. Immediately to the west was Broadway, and the eastern border-walls were across the street from the Harlem River. This is where the Harlem River swings from north to west as it squeezes Manhattan into a tip while it reaches out for the mighty Hudson River, but 2,000 feet away.

On the river itself at 209th Street lay the dock terminus of the barges which fed sand, gravel, stone, cinders, and other building materials to the Colonial Sand and Stone Corporation. Dom worked there for Genoroso Pope, as stated before. And it was natural that Dom should, for he had done the same for his father in the yard his father had later sold to Pope, which lay farther south along this same river at 138th Street. Dom was now an expediter, and he scheduled deliveries of the ingredients which make up our concrete metropolis to customers. He was also the unloading foreman of the barges.

This yard was big and extended out into the river, partly as docks that receive the barges. A traveling clamshell crane rode on railroad track bed that lay parallel to the river. One thing you could always count on in a yard like this was steam, boilered and piped around to power the cranes, pumps, heating system, and scouring devices. The crane and the steam are essential to this story.

Among the expediters, the yard men, the bookkeeper, and drivers, there were always eight or more men gathered in the small office shed during the morning coffee break.

One morning, someone said, "Who is that guy? Every morning I see him come onto the property, amble down to the end of the pier like he owned the place, with his paper under his arm, and use our toilet."

"Our toilet" was a rudimentary affair, a shed added onto the platform located on the underside of the pier's falsework. A wooden stairway, which was also appended from the side of the pier, led down to this platform. The fact that it was below view from the pier itself assured privacy, and this lent a touch of delicacy to the whole process. The shed itself was constructed of corrugated sheet metal, and the plumbing was *au naturel*, a bowl which emptied directly into the Harlem River flowing below.

Dom said "our toilet" was quite comfy, for a heavy metal steam line had been led over and spewed out plenty of heat during inclement weather. It was a year-round station for the employees, including the few office people.

Each morning the mystery of the man became a subject of intrigue. His movements were timed, and from the uniform he wore it became apparent that he was a conductor for the IRT system, whose trains rested across the street from the yard. But as time went on, the man's smug demeanor began to annoy the Colonial Sand and Stone Corporation employees. He asked no permission, offered no thanks, took his lovely time, and offered no apologies.

Finally, the employees decided to "fix his wagon." They held a meeting and came up with a plan. The next day they waited for him. After they were certain he was comfortably ensconced, one of the group stole quietly down the steps to the door of "our toilet." He closed the hasp which was used at night to accommodate the padlock and slipped a railroad spike down through the U-shaped staple. Now the nemesis was securely imprisoned within the corrugated-iron shed.

Up on top, much more was going on. One agent turned up the steam full blast, which began to suffocate the interior of the toilet shed. In the meantime, someone positioned the boom of a crane that had a heavy iron chain attached to the clevis right over the middle of the shed roof.

By this time the shed would be uncomfortably hot, but more was to come. The crane operator raised the chain high over the shed, then dropped it onto the metal roof. The scraping thud was awesome! Dom said that's when the IRT man in "our toilet" made his first attempt to blast through the door. No way! The hasp held fast!

The crane operator raised and dropped the chain again. The sound was frightening, but even more frightening was that the shed began to rock and threatened to fall into the river below! The man pleaded and screamed from within, but the chain kept dropping and the shed kept rocking.

The IRT man's shrieks and attempts to break through the door soon became more wild. Finally, at a signal, the light-footed tormentor who had set the spike stole down and removed it. The man's next shoulder blow from inside flung open the door, and up the catwalk the distraught prisoner flew, with his trousers still halfway down below his knees!

"We never saw the SOB again," said Dom with much satisfaction. "He must still be running!"

In this same yard, Dom used to tell us a story we called "Dunlop Boxes on My Chin." Willie Gallagher was the chief expediter for the sand and gravel deliveries, and he frequently boasted of his prowess as a golfer, especially as a heavy hitter. He kept bragging that he could drive a golf ball across the Harlem River, and with only a five-iron at that. This is an almost impossible feat, for the river is over two hundred yards wide at that point. Dom told him he was "full of shit," and the bantering began.

It so happened that Dom, who had just become a fledging golfer at that time, had a set of partly rusty golf clubs in his car. It was agreed that at lunch the test would be made. There was no way the test would take place before because if Mr. Pope drove up in his chauffeured touring car or if Frank Sisco, Pope's traveling eyes and ears, appeared, they would surely all be sacked.

I mentioned before that a traveling clamshell crane traveled along the set of railroad tracks that lay parallel to the river. The tracks were about four feet higher than the ground itself, so Willie had to move back in order to fly the ball over the obstacle. Dom offered to let Willie use a wood in consideration of the extra distance. Willie, who was ready to tee off, quickly declined the offer.

Dom said aloud, "You guys better move back." As he did so, there were three loud smacks, one as Gallagher hit the ball, and the second as the ball hit the tracks. Dom does not remember the third, for the ball ricocheted off the tracks, flew back, and hit him square on the chin. He does not remember reeling backward, but was told he did. He does remember instinctively reaching for his chin, amazed to see how far out the swelling stuck.

The ball was a Dunlop, a British manufacture, and in those days the balls had rectangular boxes on the surface, not the round dimples you see today. The square boxes were transferred to Dom's chin, and he says it was over a week before the marks receded into his flesh.

That was all bad enough, but it was worse when Frank Sisco later came on the job. The "eyes and ears" already knew, but he wanted to bother Dom with, "What are those boxes on your chin?" Dom gave a sheepish answer, but Sisco's message was clear: "You guys want to fool around and play kid games instead of working." Dom, who had a wife but no money and knew jobs were scarce in those days, then shut up and suffered in silence, but years later we were the beneficiaries of his juicy storytelling.

Rudy Marchesi often entertained us with homespun job tales, too, and they frequently had a scatological twist. Rodolfo had emigrated from Italy as a boy of twelve and, like my grandfather, his father had been forced to come to America years before the rest of his family. Again, like my Uncle Fred, Rudy could hardly remember his father, who had become a *straniero* (stranger), for they had not seen each other for nine years.

Rudy's father had worked in concrete on a hydroelectric dam in Italy, so it was natural he should gravitate toward that kind of work when he arrived here. Rudy's mother had to work, too, while she waited in Italy, so the young boy spent most of his days with his grandmother.

By the age of fourteen, Rudy first worked as a water boy, and then he began handling concrete in between school sessions. By the time he was sixteen, he was screeding and troweling the slabs, as well as setting forms. By then, his family was living in the Italian section of East Harlem on 114th Street, overlooking the East River.

Rudy laughingly tells us that when *la famiglia* did a job in Queens, after Rudy's war service with the Seabees[26] in the South Pacific, they avoided taking the easy route home over the new Triborough Bridge to Manhattan because the toll was a whole quarter. Instead, the packed car went south to the 59th Street

---

26. Seabees was the name given to members of the naval construction battalions (CBs) established in 1941 to build landing fields, airfields, etc.

Bridge (which was free) and then worked its way back north to Harlem. Who would take that trip today, even though the toll is up to two dollars?

On one of these jobs in Queens, there were other family members and *paesani*, including his two future partners, the Crevani brothers, Carl (Rudy's brother-in-law-to-be), and Carl's father. As I have pointed out before, not too many immigrants came from Northern Italy, but some did. Rudy's family and *paesani* were Romagnese, from the province of Emilia-Romagna, high in the hills south of Vorghera and Pavia. Years later, when Rudy and Dominick got to know each other, they found that their families had emanated from the same area. Their French-sounding dialect is incomprehensible to the rest of us.

On every union job there is a shop steward. This worker is appointed by the union delegate (also known as the business agent). The function of the shop steward is to be concerned about protecting the interests of the union and the welfare of the men. Each trade has its own shop steward.

The shop steward has to check the union card of each journeyman on paydays, collect the assessment each worker owes to that local, make certain that starting and stopping hours conform to his whistle-blowing, especially the allowances for walking time, wash-up time, and coffee time. Also, he has to keep the shanty clean. An opportunity for conflict arises, for if the shop steward (who is paid by the boss) decides to exaggerate his importance and refuses to contribute much actual work at his trade, the production average goes down. If the job is a small one, the reduction can be significant.

It is simple human nature at work. Some stewards complete their tasks, lock the shanty, and get to work. Others puff up with their newly acquired authority, and what should be a cooperative effort becomes an adversarial one. It is unfortunate but true that the history of management and labor in our United States has largely been one of conflict, distrust, lockouts, strikes, sabotage, and even severe beatings and deaths. So much energy wasted!

A new day must come, and I see the signs. In the past two decades we have been falling far behind the Japanese and Germans in efficiency, product quality, and cost cutting techniques. The Japanese and German methods that were once derided are now being reassessed and imitated. We now send management personnel to Japan to learn how the Jap-anese form teams of labor and management that strive together for the benefit of both.

But we still have far to go. In the 1988 presidential election, one candidate (Richard Gephardt) was a one-issue candidate: he wanted to protect American jobs—and inefficiency—by installing prohibitive import tariffs, a perfect formula for increasing costs and making goods too expensive for greater numbers to afford. We went that disastrous path once before; remember the Smoot-Hawley Tariffs?

In this day and age, as if we are an island unto ourselves!

Anyway, on Rudy's job there was a shop steward who not only took advantage of his position (by not carrying his load with the tools) but also deluded himself into believing he somehow became the protector of union rights. Frequently this self-delusion has an opposite effect; the union men begin to resent the self-appointed importance displayed by one of their own, and a schism develops. That is what happened on Rudy's job. The steward was ostracized, and for good reason.

In those days most every mason and laborer brought his own *panino* for lunch (as discussed earlier) and, in addition, a bottle of his own homemade *vino* (wine). To keep the *vino* cool, the bottle was often pushed down into the sand. A couple of particularly good wine makers always had a good spot. For example, a loose floorboard would be pried up and the bottles pushed right down into the cool soil.

This shop steward, in the process of sweeping out the shanty, became aware of the daily cache and began tapping the corked bottles, swigging just enough from each so as not to cause alarm. But the men were aware, and it was easy to deduce the culprit.

One victim was known for the especially good *panini* his wife prepared—he had a feast each day. And the culprit daily took to helping himself to a portion. A few others occasionally suffered a similar fate. Resentment grew, and talk started. The men agreed,

'Dobbiamo "acconciare"[27] questo mascalzone' (We've got to "fix" this nasty guy).

The principal victim came up with his own plan. He consulted a man named Brill, the pharmacist back home in Harlem whose store was located at 119th Street and Pleasant Avenue. What the victim needed was a small and powerful substance that would cause severe diarrhea about two hours after ingestion. He got it—in a large quantity. Preparations were meticulous, even the sandwich was pre-cut to encourage easy filching. On the way to work he brought the others into his plan. Shortly thereafter, everyone but the culprit was in on the scheme, and the strategy for the day was laid out.

On a reinforced concrete building, the stairs are not installed until the job has proceeded five or six floors ahead. What remains in the meantime are open rectangles in the floor slabs. Temporary wooden ladders are thus placed upon plank coverings for access between floors. The trap was set.

By now just about everybody knew what had to be done. After an hour or so, the steward would make his appearance on the sixth-tier wooden forms. He would not be ready to work with the tools; he would just oversee and then join in the morning coffee break. He did not notice that the ladders had disappeared, not only on this floor but all the way down to ground level.

The workers watched for the telltale signs of distress. Finally they saw the initial signs. The steward decided maybe he had better get down-stairs. He simply called down for someone to replace the missing ladders. There was no answer.

The shop steward's distress soon became more apparent, and he began to holler. The men on the floor were pointedly oblivious to his dilemma and busied themselves with work, though they exchanged juicy sidelong glances.

It finally dawned on the culprit that he was trapped on the

27.*Acconciare*, which means to fix, is dialect for *aggiustare*, which means to adjust, arrange, or mend. *Acconciare* is the English equivalent of the word straighten when used in the sense of "We're going to straighten that fellow out."

sixth floor with no way down. He began to plead, cajole, and beg—to no avail, and Rudy said sweat broke out all over his face. But the men were not yet ready to relent; they wanted physical evidence, evidence of a lesson well learned.

It was not until his dignity was reduced to tears and the physical evidence began to appear below his coveralls, that the men took pity and replaced the ladders. Whether the physical pain or the embarrassment was worse is moot.

There were no more bottles of wine tapped or parts of sandwiches missing after that, Rudy said. Here it is almost fifty years later and we are still laughing!

I think one essential ingredient of a successful man is his ability to laugh at himself, and that Allan Shapiro can do. Allen told some funny stories of when he first started in the electrical business. He and his Uncle Jake had decided to team up. Uncle Jake had the experience, and Allan had the money. The money was his mustering-out pay from the United States Navy, a total of $650. You can see it was a big operation: two guys with a pair of pliers and some wire, but a lot of desire.

The scene was Paterson, New Jersey in 1946. Paterson was known as Silk City, because the very prosperous American silk industry had settled there from the time of Alexander Hamilton. His vision, a center of water power for the budding industrial revolution, was genius. The Passaic River and falls provided an abundant resource. You will remember that not too far away, atop the Palisades overlooking New York City in Union City, New Jersey, Hamilton lost his life in a pistol duel with Aaron Burr.

Paterson is still known as Silk City, but the silk industry is no more, gone to other climes of greater efficiency and lower wages. Now the city is a repository of abandoned mills, including the loss of world-famous Colt Manufacturing Company, Incorporated. The end of World War II was the beginning of the demise of Paterson.

But at the time, Allan and his Uncle Jake were called in to install an electrical sign in front of a neighborhood candy store. Uncle Jake held the ladder; the neophyte was chosen to do the tough part up top.

Somewhere along the line, Allan touched the wrong things, and a strong current surged through his body. Allan said he yelped as he felt his hair tingling, but he could not let go. Uncle Jake, with the aplomb born of experience (though Allan said maybe with a little unconcern), casually kicked the ladder out from under his nephew. Down he came right into Jake's arm! "It didn't hurt Uncle Jake at all," Allan said mischievously.

Uncle Jake was a real character, with a touch of larceny in his laughable demeanor. Another time they were working in a pitch-black cellar. Jake was a chain-smoker, and the young Allan often had to back up to grab some fresh air. You could always tell where Jake had worked because the panel boxes were filled with the burned-out butts of his cigarettes.

Allan had the flashlight trained on the panel but backed away momentarily to gulp some fresh air. He did not realize that his quick movement had darkened the subject. Immediately a smart smack on the side of the head brought Allan back to attention. While still fouling up the atmosphere with his puffing butt, Uncle Jake nasally said, "Keep your eyes on the subject, kid."

Mainly with Allan's mustering-out pay, the two bought a new panel truck. Most of you can't remember this, but a brand-new Oldsmobile sedan could be had for $980 in those days. I saw Uncle Louis buy one for just that much.

Among Jake's other virtues was his love of gambling. Every Friday Jake would fly off to the Catskill Mountains, the borscht belt of budding Yiddish comedians, and visit Grossinger's, The Nevele, and the Concord Hotels. Naturally, Uncle Jake took the brand-new panel truck; the "kid" got Jake's prewar, broken-down Dodge coupe, whose trunk doubled as a truck bed.

Allan still has a good laugh when he starts talking about Jake's larceny.

One time they were installing new electrical service in the cellar of a small department store in Paterson. Both the electric company and the contractor work in tandem to install electricity in a dwelling. The job of the electric company employee is to bring the service to the cellar wall; the contractor then picks it up inside the building. The electric company employee passes the cable through a metal sleeve installed in the front cellar wall on through to the contractor, who then hooks the cable up to the panel inside.

On this particular day, Uncle Jake was on the receiving end in the cellar, and he saw this as an opportunity to grab a good length of very expensive copper cable from the electric company, Public Service of New Jersey, which is the Consolidated Edison (Con-Ed) of most of New Jersey. Allan still remembers Jake's instructions, "Keep coming, keep coming," as the Public Service man kept feeding cable through the sleeve. Jake kept the excess.

In this same cellar a few days earlier, Jake had told Allan to station himself outside where the steel sleeve came through the wall. "And bring the big carton from the truck," he added. When Allan called through the sleeve to tell Jake he was ready, he almost fell over when out of the sleeve poured men's socks, underwear, pajamas, sweaters, and more of the like. "Even a life-time supply of jockstraps!" exclaimed Allan.

Allan was on the horns of a dilemma. What was he to do with this pile exposed in a dirt trench? In self-defense, he scooped up the loot and stuffed it into the box. The easiest way to divorce himself from it was to throw it all into the truck.

Uncle Jake would hear none of it when Allen suggested they give it all back. "Are you crazy," asked Jake. "How would you explain it to them?"

Allan took note of the emphasis Jake gave to the word "you." Jake had outmaneuvered him again.

Allan, who now runs a very successful business all over the eastern seaboard, still gets a big kick out of telling these Uncle Jake stories, but he adds that he did not think it so funny when, after a year and a half together, he had to go around finishing jobs for which Jake had already pocketed the final payments!

Allan told us another story involving Uncle Jake. When Allan was fourteen years old, just before World War II started, he had worked with Uncle Jake. (By age sixteen Allan would already be in the United States Navy.) Again, the scene was Paterson, New Jersey, and Uncle Jake had a rewiring job in a wholesale fish warehouse, he and Allen arrived early as usual. Allan never gave thought to the second long toolbox that Uncle Jake had brought along with him that day.

But he found out later. The toolbox was empty—that is, it was empty going into the warehouse, but not coming out. During the course of the day's wire pulling, near lunchtime, Uncle Jake pulled out a couple of sandwiches for himself and Allan. This in itself was unusual, but it made sense to Allan a short time later when they remained the only ones taking lunch inside the fish preparation room.

Out came the empty toolbox, and into it Uncle Jake happily placed the most select fillets of sturgeon, lox, whitefish, and snapper, properly bedded in covered ice. Allan marveled at the delicate care with which Uncle Jake tended to his loot. A short while later, the "empty" toolbox made a trip out to the rambling wreck Jake called his truck.

The larcenous Uncle Jake had covered all the bases, including his awareness that Allan was foreclosed from offering any protest. How could he expose his own uncle?

Allan laughingly reminisces about how, when he was in Japan with MacArthur's occupied forces, he used Jake's techniques to collect cigarettes at the American P.X.[28] and sell them in the open market. He says he made a bundle!

Incidentally, over a foursome of pinochle one day, before Rudy, Arthur, and I graduated to gin rummy, we found out that both Allan and Rudy had attended boot camp at the same time in the Finger Lakes region at the Samson Naval Base outside Geneva, New York. Of course, they did not know each other at the time. Moreover, after the war, I did a job of huge warehouses for the Seneca Ordinance Depot immediately adjoining in Romulus, New York.

Some fifteen years ago a new fad erupted in America: bio-rhythms. Machines which were supposed to accurately measure your reflexes suddenly appeared all over the place—in airports, men's rooms, game rooms, and slot parlors. These devices were the rage for a couple of years, but they died the death of all the clever put-ons we periodically fall for.

But in the bricklaying business, I had observed comparable human phenomenon that evidenced itself with such consistency that I believe it deserves some attention. I am not talking about an individual's reflexes or rhythms (which I am certain we all agree vary considerably from day to day), but the collective

28. P.X. stands for Post Exchange. This was a store on the base.

reflexes of a group of people. In this case, it was construction crews, and more particularly bricklaying gangs.

Some days were a joy on the job—all the pieces fitted together. The men were happy, the walls flew up, the job was peaceful and efficient, and the scene was quiet. Those other days, however, were a horror. Everybody was disgruntled, the foremen were cursing, men stepped on nails or tripped over anything in sight, walls leaned out of plumb, mortar was slopped all over the place, someone got hurt. Those were the same days when inspectors would find legitimate causes to criticize the work. And the union delegates coming on the job didn't help, either. Work thus slowed to a limp.

We all know what "blue Mondays" are, but these bad days did not have to be a Monday. When this nervousness and clumsiness pervaded the men, there was no way the day could be a success. And this kind of a day was unpredictable; the weather could be perfect, but nonetheless, a dark cloud hung over the site. These were the days when a "hog" would appear in a brick wall. Remember the chapter entitled "Corner-Man?"

The consistency with which this phenomenon appeared makes me believe considerable work is available for environmental psychologists. You can understand you yourself are not at your best some days, but as to why this should happen collectively is an intriguing question.

I have not mentioned Uncle Al since the beginning of this book. He was my father's youngest brother by about twenty years. A funny thing happened to him (funny for us) on a job in Rutherford, New Jersey. We were building garden apartments along the Passaic River for Joseph Brunetti, an extremely successful builder of thousands of family dwellings under the FHA 608 project, which I mentioned earlier.

Before I relate Uncle Al's story, let me first tell you a little about Joe Brunetti. His story was a Horatio Alger episode in itself. Only a few years before, Joe had been a construction laborer for his brother-in-law, Fred Ingannamort, another builder for whom we did many projects. One day Joe climbed out of a sewer trench, threw down his tools forever, and became a builder. Joe was rough, tough, crude, and knowledgeable. He parlayed his small projects into larger and larger ones. Within six years he was one of the largest builders, buying hundreds of acres on option. His foresight made his success well deserved.

But on this day Uncle Al was working for us as a timekeeper. Intermittently Al's machine-tool business (or his engagement as a drill-tool engineer) would be interrupted by unemployment, so back to the jobs he would come.

I remember Uncle Al when I was in Public School 80 and he was a star cross-country runner for the DeWitt Clinton High School Team on Mosholu Parkway, near Villa Avenue, where we lived. He was always slim as a reed, with a voracious appetite. He moved with quick jerks, as if sparks were popping out of his shoes. But Uncle Al didn't possess much forethought, and hence this story. He was really accident prone. Uncle Joe and I worried about him.

I pulled up to the job one day. Uncle Al was on the side of the street where our men were pouring concrete for cellar foundations; it was lined continuously with parked workmen's cars. Lew Porter, paymaster, was with me on the other side of the street from Uncle Al. I noticed off in the distance that he had spotted us. With that irrepressible energy and enthusiasm, Uncle Al started bounding across the mounds and hillocks toward us, anxious to show off the speed and dexterity of his remembered days as the Van Cortland Park cross-country winner.

As Uncle Al flew toward us, both Lew and I silently wondered whether he would pull one of his stunts. As he approached the opening between two cars, our fears were realized—Uncle Al was paying no attention to the car speeding toward him on his side of the road!

The next scene I will never forget. I see it clearly in my mind's eye, and I thank God it ended up funny. As Lew and I watched transfixed, it all happened together: Uncle Al saw the car; the driver saw him and stepped on the brakes; Al instinctively turned to present his derrière to the car's fender; and the hood and fenders dipped downward as the brakes grabbed hold to conveniently receive a fuller load of Al's rear end. Uncle Al's smile never left his face as he synchronized his leap with the impact of the fender to his ass, and up he went in the most graceful Sitting-Bull position, executing a flying arc that carried him at least fifteen feet down the road!

He landed on his feet, too embarrassed to admit that toothsome grin did not belong on his face. The car driver was furious, and rightly so.

Lew Porter and I didn't know whether we wanted to hug or kill Al, so irresponsible was his escapade. Uncle Al, however, insisted smilingly that "it was all nothing," but I'll bet he was sore for weeks thereafter! Uncle Joe was furious when he learned from Lew that is brother was almost killed.

Irrepressible Uncle Al—he's about eighty-two now—retired from Raytheon, and lives in Myrtle Beach, South Carolina. I see him at family wakes, and those gorgeous front teeth are still laughing, better than Robert Stack's.

A disquieting but true incident occurred with Joe Brunetti, and I tell it only because the reader should know that, contrary to popular notion, all is not peaches and cream in the construction industry; you don't just go into the business and ipso facto make a lot of money. Unfortunately, it is the same now as it was thirty-five years ago when this incident occurred. Once you read this disturbing story, you will know why I opted to tell it.

I was in Maywood, New Jersey on Essex Street in Joe Brunetti's well-appointed office. It was about ten in the morning. Behind this building, and stretching for acres, were the seven hundred or so garden apartments on which Uncle Joe and I were doing the masonry work for Brunetti. We were doing Sections 3, 4, and 5. Sections 1 and 2 had been completed the year before.

Projects of this size were divided into sections because the FHA guaranteed the mortgages, as I mentioned before, and it was wiser to have several banks vie for the deals rather than have one take the whole risk of prudent interest and control. In 1990, the government's stupid action of raising the guarantees on savings books deposits from $10,000 to $100,000 is decimating our savings and loan banks and our federal deficit. Add "easy outs" to politicians' votes, and the chickens come home to roost.

The reason I was at Joe's office was that I needed payroll money to pay my men on Friday. This was Tuesday and, despite repeated promises from Joe, my requisition for the previous month's work was overdue. Two weeks into the current month had passed, and Joe still hadn't paid me. I was getting desperate. Having to wait long stretches to get paid is endemic to the construction industry, and if you have six or seven jobs going on at the same time, with no money coming in, you get more desperate.

Besides the slow pay, there is the standard practice of the retainer or retained percentage. This is an additional amount the builder holds back to guarantee acceptance of the work you have performed. Each month this retainer grows in size, and by the time you complete your work, it amounts to ten percent of the whole contract. Usually, it takes at least a year to collect this retainer.

If you are not making at least ten percent on the work, and you seldom do, you are obviously taking money out of your own working capital to finance the work. This occurs more often than not in the "wet" trades, such as concrete, plastering, brickwork, and tile. The mechanical trades, like plumbing, electrical, heating, and air conditioning, do better, and the reason is obvious. Nothing gets "turned on" with these mechanical works unless the owners pony up. The "wet" trades do not have that control.

Regardless, the real problem is collecting the ninety percent, and that was my plight that day. I waited all day. Joe's personal secretary had reassured me he was still in his rear office. But I also knew he had a private door going out to the parking lot behind the office, where both our cars were parked, and I did not put it past Joe to sneak out the rear door and leave me hanging—even after five or six hours of waiting.

You see, Joe had a reputation, which I think he savored, of being 'pignosa' (tough nut). The word comes from pigna (the pine cone itself) and its fruit, pignoli, those tiny submarine-shaped nuts you see on Italian cookies and sometimes in meatballs. If you have ever tried to extract the nut from one of the hard wooden husks of the cone itself, you can easily understand how appropriate is the appellation 'pignosa.'

I had no choice but to hang in there. There was no other source of funds to pay my men that week. It was panic time. About three in the afternoon, I received a high sign from Joe's secretary; he was leaving out the rear door! I ran out the front and around the back and caught him getting into his car.

Though I am not proud of the way I handled the situation, I do not need to apologize for the lack of niceties.

"You son of a bitch," I said. "I've been waiting all day for you, and you try to pull this! I want my money and I want it now."

"Oh, so you think you're a tough guy?" he answered. "Follow me, and we'll see how tough you are."

"You bet I will," I answered and then jumped into my car.

Down we flew on Essex Street, going west toward Rochelle Park, like two maniacs. About a mile later, at the river, he screeched a right into some empty land and he pulled to the rear of this wooded plot. An apartment building stands there now. I stopped and jumped out of my car, tearing off my jacket as I did so. There was no fear, only fury, as I closed the space between us.

Joe, however, did not get out of his car. I put my hands on the open window, and he said with a smirk I will never forget, "You think you're a wise guy. Follow me back to the office."

I got my money—in full. I also got something else, maybe two things. I know I earned his respect, because thereafter he did not pull any more shenanigans with me, but I also believe he never forgave me, even though I did more work for him.

Joe, as I mentioned earlier, went on to become a very wealthy man. With his foresight, he invested in vacant acreage by the thousands, mostly in the still relatively undeveloped middle and south Jersey areas. This land increased fiftyfold in value as the population pushed south. But Joe died a young man, his ambitions, his volatility, and his girth all contributing to his demise. His son John, who was still a boy when his father died, went on to buy Hialeah Park Racetrack in Florida.

The most important lesson I confirmed from this episode is this: there are people in this world who will not respect you or even trust you until you assert yourself and confront them, forcibly, and sometimes violently. After you do, the air is cleared, and a mutual respect develops. It is a pity that so much energy and time has to be wasted in this way, but there seems to be no alternative. It is always fascinating, though, to watch human nature in action.

It is interesting to note how each of the boroughs in New York had its own concentration of bricklaying contractors. With the exception of the bricklaying contractors on Staten Island, which was relatively isolated before the Verrazano-Narrows Bridge was built, most would occasionally venture into another borough to do a job, especially if a favorite builder or general contractor called on you. Yet the tendency was to stay closer to home, a natural bent since that is where the family grew up, in more ways than one. But there was another natural tendency. The Bronx and Manhattan areas were sort of linked together; likewise, Queens and Brooklyn, which you might call Long Island (for that is where they are) were another couplet.

Exactly why the Bronx became home to the heaviest concentration of "big" masons, I do not know, but I can guess. Most of us were immigrants, or sons of immigrants, so naturally we started out from homes and yards which were inexpensive to buy and maintain. A construction yard to store equipment, scaffolding, trucks, and the like has to be rather large, and Manhattan did not lend itself to that kind of inexpensive land.

The biggest New York masons fell into two ethnic categories (with the large exception of John B. Kelly of Philadelphia): they were Jewish or Italian. Moreover, absolutely every one of them grew from bricklayers who had worked with the trowel.

The Jewish contingent from the Bronx-Manhattan area included Rosen and Rosen (Morris and Izzy), Langer and Langer (Morris and Louis), and Stone and Stone (Albert and Julius).

In the Italian camp were the original LaSala Brothers (Dominic, Andrew, Harry, and Stefano). They lived in the Riverdale section of the Bronx. Not too long later, Stefano broke away, and with his sons he formed the LaSala Contracting Corporation (Frank, Tony, and Andrew). Brother Stephen separately ran Arrow Builders Supply on the Harlem River at Fordham Road. They lived on Rochembeau Avenue, just south of Montefiore Hospital. Just a little later came my family, the Puzios (Frank, my father, then Uncle Joe with him, and later Uncle Joe and me.) Then there was Leon Morano, who later took in his son, Leon, Jr.

At the same time, Palmieri and Sons started. My Uncle Dominick formed it first, then took in his five sons, my cousins Tony, Morris (Mauro), Mike (Michael), JoJo (Joseph), and Rudy (named after Rudolph Valentino).

A little later came the teams of Vito Poveromo and Tom Martin, as well as Cerussi and Verri. Mike Cerussi was the son of Ernie Cerussi, perennial bricklayer delegate from our Local #37.

The Manhattan Irish part included the aforementioned John B. Kelly, as well as Ed (Edward) Hickey, who later took in his sons, Tom and Edward. Another busy group was J. Harry McNally and his brothers.

The Kelly, Hickey, and McNally groups were the envy of all of us because their clients were the likes of Con-Ed, New York Telephone, the New York Stock Exchange, many hospitals, and other big names. As the years went by, this was to change. The law of supply and demand, as well as price and efficiency, were enough to make some of us worthy competitors to any bidding foe.

Meanwhile, over in the Brooklyn-Queens area, the big Giffuni Brothers (Joseph and Andrew) and the big Fisher (Fishkind) Brothers, who included Larry (Lawrence), Marty (Martin), and Zack (Zachary), watched as the challenges came from Gus Nicoletti and Son as well as Tony Perri and Ralph, his son.

After I wrote the above, I was contacted by Dave Spitz, old-time cement salesman now living in Florida; he had read a reference to my book in the November 19, 1990 issue of *The New Yorker*. How happy I was to hear from him! It has been at least twenty-five years since we spent happy times together.

Dave was a perennial fixture in the cement industry, known to every mason contractor and to most concrete and general contractors. He started out in 1931 with the Louisville Cement Company. Right after World War II in 1946, he went over to the Century Cement Company, which was located on the Hudson River in Rosendale, New York, as general sales manager and stayed for twenty-four years. Century concentrated on crushed mortar cement, a naturally cementitious mixture which does not require the additional step of mixing lime with Portland cement. In 1970, Century ceased operations, and Dave was offered the same position with Penn-Dixie, one of the giants of the cement industry. He finished his forty-two-year career there, when back surgery intruded. He now lives happily in Lauderhill, Florida with his wife Grace, and they manage to play nine holes every day. Dave supplied the answers and the following stories to many voids in my knowledge of the Brooklyn, Queens, and Long Island operations.

Gus (Augustus) Nicoletti had an office manager named Edna Levine, who really ran the whole office, including preparing the estimates, buying materials, making payrolls, paying bills, and dealing with unions. She was a legend in Brooklyn.

In addition, another active Jewish group consisted of partners Sam Seltzer, Ruby Smolowitz, and Phil Adler. Dave's wife jokingly referred to them as Martin, Barton, and Fish in reference to the conservative trio made derisively famous by Franklin Roosevelt when pursuing his third term. Joseph Martin was Speaker of the House, Bruce Barton was an advertising executive, and Hamilton Fish was a GOP House Representative from upstate New York. Seltzer, Smolowitz, and Adler could have been the name of a renowned law firm in Manhattan (or was it a comedy act?). They were colorful and everything you would expect from a Brooklyn Jewish group with a sobriquet like theirs.

Then there was the brickwork partnership of Gerace and Castagna, each of whom separately went on to become power-houses in the general contracting business. Their office was on Sheepshead Bay Boulevard. Two other quite active masons who fitted the ethnic rolls were the Mangano family (Italian) and Benny Laikan (Jewish).

Phil Melvin was another character. He owned a construction material supply business, and Court Street in Brooklyn was a comedy zoo where all would gather daily. Phil had the ability to faint at will, authentically, and he used this ability to sell his supplies. Dave reminded me of a story which Andrew and Joe Giffuni had told me years ago at our club on MacDougal Street in Greenwich Village, Tiro A Segno. (Tiro is the oldest chartered Italian club in New York, founded in 1888. The title is an idiom and means the Rifle Range, but it is literally interpreted as Pull at the Target.)

Andy came out of a Brooklyn building under construction, carrying Phil in his arms. Phil had fainted. And why? Because the Giffunis had told him that their next job was going to be given to some other suppliers.

By this time no one took Phil's fainting seriously anymore. Dave Spitz said that this following true story was well known in

Court Street circles. Melvin was purusing a builder who was about to start an apartment building. Phil said to him, "If you don't give me this job, I am going to jump out the window."

The builder answered, "Hold on a minute, Phil. I want to open the window so you shouldn't splatter glass all over my office."

Dave also recalled another scene where Gus Nicoletti, a builder, and Phil were present. They were in the builder's office, and Phil took the liberty of talking to his "landsman" builder in Yiddish.

The builder's face reddened, and he said to Phil, "It is rude of you to do this. I think you should repeat in English what you said about Gus."

Gus answwered, "It isn't necessary. I understand Yiddish—from when I was a kid." Phil was nonplussed. He could always faint if he was embarrassed.

What fascinating times those were! They will never come again; we are all too sophisticated now.

Back in the Bronx, eventually Julius and Albert Stone broke up, and Albert formed a group with Dan Russo and Jim Lionelli, my brother-in-law.

Sibling rivalry exerted its irrepressible force. Langer and Langer broke up, and Morris went on with his own son, Joel. Eventually, Joel teamed up with my cousin Pepe (Joseph) Puzio, Uncle Joe's son. Now Pepe operates alone.

Izzy and Morris Rosen broke up, and Morris went on with his sons, Irving and Phil.

Both the Giffuni Brothers and the Fischer (Fishkind) Brothers went on to become developers of some of the largest and more prestigious office and apartment buildings in Manhattan.

One late night a group of us were in the elegant Columbus Club on 69th Street in New York, and we were talking about the good old days of feverish action in the bricklaying industry. Present, among others, was Larry Fischer, one of the Fischer Brothers—former Brooklyn bricklayers and originally from the Fishkind family. The Fischer empire of high finance and commercial office success is one of those Horatio Alger stories of three Jewish boys from Brooklyn whose scope of success is hard to imagine. How did it come about?

Larry said, "Do you know what was the best thing that ever happened to us?" He answered rhetorically as well as paradoxically, "That was the day the bricklayers' union caught us paying under the wage. They blackballed our family, and we had to quit the brick business. That's how we got started in the real estate development business. They don't know what a favor they did us."

There is no question that Larry was right. The sad history of paying "under the wage" or, to use the uglier synonym, "taking kickbacks," was unfortunately all too common in the days immediately following the Great Depression of 1929 through 1934. Then there was no new work at all.

From 1935 through 1939, until the outbreak of World War II, which stimulated the economy, our country had started to climb back, but very slowly. Work began to appear, but there were not enough jobs to go around. Men were desperate to feed their families or to try to save their homes. This situation applied not only to mason contractors, but to workers in every industry all over the country. The law of supply and demand was at work, as it always is. Contractors, who could not get work unless they bid at absolute cost or below, hoped that somehow they could extract a small profit for themselves, or at least take home a pay envelope every week. At least their equipment would be at work.

The history has already been written: workers offered themselves at wages below union scales, scales which had been set during the heydays of the Roaring Twenties, when everybody thought he could become a millionaire. That was before the stock market crash of 1929. The whole story is ugly, not only the desperation, but the devices and compromises human beings had to make to survive.

The unions could only assume one posture if they were to survive as representatives of the workers: union wages had to be paid, and union rules had to be complied with. This posture, however, was at variance with reality. The government's WPA (Works Progress Administration) was hiring Americans for five dollars per day, just to give men something to do. This was during the days of the alphabet soup of Franklin Roosevelt's New Deal, when the WPA was later replaced by the PWA (Public Works Administration), the CCC (Civilian Conservation Corps), the NRA (National Recovery Act), which was later declared "unconstitutional," and many other experiments.

Whatever it was called, paying under the scale or taking kickbacks behind the shanty or at the neighborhood bar was going on all over. The Fishkind Brothers were not alone.

There is absolutely nothing like the competition of the free enterprise system to distill out the greatest good for the greatest number of a country's citizens. So many fruitless exercises are tried as substitutes, so many brickbats are thrown at the system, and so many people denounce free enterprise in so many ways that I shake my head in wonder. This is the very system that creates the very wealth that permits the socialists and the social do-gooders to play their social games!

I have seen their ethereal "should be's" and "could be's," and I have seen that they make their plans always from afar, comfortably ensconced in a cushy government office, while out in the field those slogging it out in the trenches create the wealth.

Sure, there are those who will put the libel to what I say here: we were efficient, we were hard working, we were independent, we were forced to be ingenious and unrelenting, and the hardships gave birth to pride, to satisfaction, to integrity, to brotherhood, to understanding, and to dignity.

The utter lack of sophistication and abundance of venality, coupled with the amazing innocence that marked our own young ways of life, are still a wonder to me, so far have we strayed into a different world. I pity my grandchildren, and even their parents, who have been led down the garden paths of sex, drugs, hate, filth, abortion, violent crime, and meanness, all done in the name of social justice, but really in unbridled license.

And what do I see so clearly? Most of these evils of society have been caused by the liberal extremists, the minority who believes its function is to ridicule and destroy religion and who hates any form of societal responsibility. They surely don't know human nature.

There was a different way of life back in the 1930's, and it is interesting to note that this was the same period that saw the stock market crash of 1929, the start of the Great Depression. I ask my readers to consider whether poverty and innocence are interdependent.

Immediately preceding our own Revolutionary War, Edmund Burke, British parliament statesman and philosopher, wrote his masterful "Dissertation on the American Colonies," and noted, "Public Calamity is a Mighty Leveler."[29] So was the bombing of Pearl Harbor on December 7, 1941 and the blackout of November 9, 1965; you all remember where you were. There were no kings and no paupers—everyone was affected equally.

I want to tell you about baseball in the Bronx, and other boroughs throughout the city, too, for the neighborhood baseball teams engrossed our youth. There were public ball parks all over the city, and local teams sprouted. Those were for eighteen-year-olds, plus.

In our own neighborhood of Bedford Park, the Willows used bats made of willow wood, just like the ones extant in the Bronx Yankee Stadium swung by Babe Ruth, Lou Gehrig, and others. My father sponsored the costs for team uniforms. Uncle Joe, his brother and later my partner, played second base.

Another team was the Marions, named after Marion Avenue, which was near Fordham Road, east of the Grand Concourse. Saint Mary's Church gave its qualified support to these players. The LaSala family boys, especially Frank, the eldest, were leaders. You will remember I mentioned this family became very successful brick mason contractors before our family made its mark. Also in the Fordham area were the Crescents, who adopted their name from Crescent Avenue, naturally.

Farther south down the area between the Grand Concourse and the Bronx Zoo were the Fordham Clovers, who I think included most of the boys from "Italian Fordham," the Arthur Avenue area south of Fordham College, but still west of the zoo. Down near the Fordham Clovers were the Triangles, who also used church facilities for meetings and suiting up. I can't remember the name of the church, but it was a few blocks south of Fordham road.

North of us were the Wakefields. That's north of the world-famous Woodlawn Cemetery and along White Plains Avenue,

---

29.Burke, Edmund, "Dissertation on the American Colonies" (Harper & Row, 1964).

starting at Gun Hill Road up to the end of the "El" at 242nd Street.

One of the fields these young sportsmen played on was French Charlie's, situated along the Bronx River, which ran south from Westchester Country. This field was immediately north of the administration building for the world-famous Bronx Botanical Gardens, which I mentioned earlier. In order to get to this field for the Sunday afternoon games, those of us from the Webster Avenue and Bainbridge Avenue areas had first to climb down the hills to the valley which contained the main New York Central Lines of the Harlem Division (four tracks wide); then we would go through the fences ripped apart for access and over the third rails.

We were crazy! Those third rails were electrified, and all they had was a wooden plate atop them to prevent electrocution. The sides were exposed. The older boys taught us how to leap from wooden cover to wooden cover. I read about accidents there, but I luckily never saw one.

At the east end of Mosholu Parkway, farther south along those same tracks, was the Mosholu Parkway field, the crème de la crème of ball fields because stadium seats had been installed for at least one thousand spectators. The field was depressed down to the level of the adjacent Bronx River, but Mosholu Parkway was elevated to meet the bridge level going over the Bronx River and adjacent Webster Avenue.

The Woodlawn field was on 233rd Street north across the street from Woodlawn Cemetery. We rooted for the Willows there many a Sunday afternoon. I remember Ralph Belloise, the labor foreman I have mentioned several times, as official score-keeper and statistics recorder. One Sunday he also explained the automatic out of the infield-fly rule. This was knowledge, I will have you know. The automatic out is designed to foil a double play (two outs) by an infielder who deliberately drops an infield fly in order to catch more than one player off base.

One other memory teases about Woodlawn. Some eight idyllic years later, before the start of World War II in Europe, my father did the brickwork across the street on Woodlawn Avenue for "Hungry Joe" McConnell, the builder of two other apartment buildings where our family lived on 201st Street. We were building block partitions in the basement of that apartment building. In those days you did not usually hear radios on construction jobs, but this day we did. It was Jimmy Dorsey playing "Green Eyes," and the vocalist was Helen O'Connell. Oh! "Those cool and limpid green eyes." How could so many years have flown?

There were other fields where those soon-to-be soldiers played. One was Bronx Park; another was Van Cortland Park.

Frank LaSala's later team was the Empires, after the Marions. I remember a trip to Newburgh, New York to watch a put-together of the better players of Empire's team play the Newburgh Athletic Club. A coterie of automobiles—at least twenty—made the memorable three- hour trip for this winner-take-all game. One other memory on that day in this park was then Governor Franklin Roosevelt's speech to the crowd. My mother pushed me to make sure I heard "the governor."

Many of the players on these teams went on to tryouts with the major leagues. I rely mostly on Frank LaSala's memory to resurrect these players. Phil Karish went on to play in the outfield with the Cincinnati Reds, and Lefty Menendez made the Cincinnati team as a third baseman.

Lefty Hirsch, our own Willows' speedball pitcher, a splendid splinter, tried out with the New York Giants on two occasions and was invited to play on the Giants' farm teams.

Lefty Hogebohn was also a pitcher who tried out with several big league teams, and Chick Cicerone (Cicero) was a powerful hitter. In addition, Harry Luboda, a Polish boy and great catcher, later became a dentist and had an office on White Plains Avenue.

There was another standout whose name neither Frank LaSala nor I can recall. His first name was Joe, and he was a wizard ball handler at shortstop. Then there was a right fielder who could hit the ball a country mile. I can't remember his proper name, either, but he had the nickname '*Bruglione*,' a dialectal substitute for '*Imbroglione*,' and it means a "screwer-upper," just like Jimmy Durante sings.

There were so many more, but memory dims with the years. It was sports, sports, sports—good clean fun.

Has the world changed much?

Sadly, it has, and I am convinced those innocent days will not return, ever. My children and grandchildren will never see them.

Tommy Napoli loved *pasta e fagioli* (pasta and beans). Most Americans know this dish as *pasta-fazool* or *pastafazool*. That's what our Irish and Jewish friends called it when they grew up with us in the Bronx because that's what we dialect-speaking Italians called it.

Dietitians used to scoff at this combination of carbohydrates, especially when that hard, crusty Italian bread was added in the deep dish, awaiting the not-too-soupy combination to soak through. But *pastafazool* was the answer to many an Italian mother's (and grandmother's) prayer on how to feed a family of eight or ten—or even twelve—hungry mouths.

How the tables turn! Dietitians today don't scoff at this dish. They have learned that complex carbohydrates—which have no cholesterol, are a good source of energy, are easily digested and are good for you.

Unlike Tommy, I was never a devotee of *pastafazool*. To me, the addition of the beans diminished the luscious tomato sauce and pure pasta. I was, and am, of the purist school. One of my favorite dishes is still the pure *cannellini* beans (white elongated ones) and celery made into a soup, which is then ladled onto broken chunks of hard bread and topped with copious drizzles of olive oil, fresh-dried oregano, and fresh-ground black peppercorns.

And then it goes without saying that I can eat pasta alone (any kind), seven days a week (but not with beans in it). I think one of the reasons is that the not-too-tomatoey sauce keeping the *pastafazool* together is made with a little homemade lard. Those mothers and grandmothers needed something in this dish to make it stick to the ribs, and olive oil was too expensive.

You already know that Tommy Napoli, together with Guy Vallese, was like a father to me when I no longer had one. Tommy was a quiet man, except when the corner men made a mistake, like putting a "hog" in the wall or screwing up the coursing. Then he would take off his brown fedora hat, throw it down on the wooden deck, and stomp on it, first with one foot and then with two, venting his anger and cursing in Italian. He looked like an Indian doing a war dance. We would all watch Tommy's vaudevillian performance—twenty or thirty of us—all the time trying unsuccessfully not to laugh. But he was such a gentle man that he would not curse in English, his easier tongue. That's the way I first remember him, when I was about fifteen years old, on the Garden Bay Manor job in Long Island, which I told you about before.

Do not believe, however, that Tommy could not be tough. He was universally respected. Tommy grew up in Harlem, around 116th Street and First Avenue, and it did not get any tougher than that.

Tommy never had anything to do with the "wise guys," the ones in the rackets, but he knew them, and they knew him. The "good guys" and the "wise guys" had a mutual respect for each other. If you grew up in that kind of environment, you could not avoid having to go to the same school or hang out with the ones who would ultimately choose the "easy" way, the criminal way. But there was an unwritten law: "You do your thing, and I'll do mine. I'll stay out of your way, and you will not bother me or my family." Often we went to the same funerals at Farenga's Funeral Home on 116th Street. How could you avoid running into the "wise guys?" But it was no problem; they lived in a different world.

Today there is too much of the very serious smearing of people with "guilty by association." When you grew up in Harlem, Morrisania in the Bronx, or Bensonhurst in Brooklyn, and when you played stickball between manhole covers ('Jeez, he hit a four-holer'), one of your "spal-deeng" ball teammates could very well grow up to be in the rackets. Does that make *you* guilty of anything? No. Anyway, we were very seldom invited to lunch at the Yale, Harvard or Knickerbocker clubs.

But let me get back to Tommy. The light of Tommy's life was his Kitty, who looked more like his "Wild Irish Rose" than an Italian. They had one daughter, Agatha, who grew up to marry Emil Piscitelli, an apprentice bricklayer with us; he went on, with his brothers, to build apartment buildings in Westchester County.

Tommy was born in Italy, and Agatha told me he came here

as a young boy, when he was around four years old. His natural tongue was English, but he understood Italian like a native.

Tommy's social life was simple: after he came home from work and took a shower, he went for a walk in East Harlem and maybe had an espresso on Pleasant or First Avenues; he and his family ate dinner before six, and then early to bed he went. Kitty, his little daughter, and his neighborhood were his whole life.

Many years passed, and Tommy never left our family employ. He began in 1934 first with Dad, Uncle Dominick, and Uncle Joe; then with Dad, Uncle Joe, and me; and finally with just Uncle Joe and me. In 1962, having worked with just shy of thirty years, Tommy was struck by cancer. The last job he worked on was an eleven-story apartment building that Uncle Joe and I were building for ourselves at the northern tip of Manhattan Island, right next to Columbia University's Baker Field, overlooking the Harlem and Hudson Rivers.

His beloved Kitty had died about three years earlier, and Tommy's life was never again the same. Fortunately, his daughter had married Emil, and both families had moved to Yonkers in Westchester County in 1954. I sensed Tommy's loneliness after his wife died, so once a month I invited him to dinner with us for his favorite meal, *pasta e fagioli*. He loved the way Emily made it, a little on the dry side. Of course, the invitation was always on a Friday. Why? Because Friday was the traditional night for *pastafazool*. Do you think I am kidding? Not so!

Our menus through the week must have been handed out to the immigrants as they debarked the ship. No matter whose home you went to, the menus were the same. On Sundays we had pasta, huge bowls of it, followed by meats cooked in the *pumarolla* sauce.[30] These were usually *braciola* (pounded-thin beef *rollatina*), meatballs made with finely chopped beef, soaked Italian bread that has been squeezed dry, a few eggs, parsley, *pignoli* (pine nuts), and sometimes raisins (raisins were controversial). Then we had sweet and hot sausage, softened in the tomato sauce, always *insalata mista* (a salad), artichokes steamed soft, broccoli *di rape, finocchio* (fennel), and on and on.

---

30. *Pumarolla* is dialect for *pomodoro*, which means tomato.

Monday was *minestra* (soup) day. We usually had cabbage soup flavored with a prosciutto bone. Sometimes it was chicken soup with noodles. Of course, we had the ubiquitous salad. Monday was considered a rest day for the stomach after Sunday's feast.

Tuesday was the closest thing to a blue-plate special: a piece of thin meat—veal or beef—peas, carrots, broccoli, potatoes, and a salad.

Wednesday was bean day, and we usually ate them plain, the way I described earlier. As always, we had a salad and hard, crusty bread.

Thursday was back to pasta. Thursday without pasta was unthinkable. Universally, it was, "Is the water on?" and "Are they ready yet?"

Friday, as I said, we had *pastafazool*, or my version of it. The more affluent also had a piece of fish—usually *baccalà*. *Baccalà* is dried cod that is boiled until the stiffness surrenders, then further cooked in a plain marinara sauce and flavored with garlic and a few hot pepper flakes; sometimes this dish is poured over hard, crusty bread.

On Saturday we had cold cuts for lunch, with dinner according to the size of the exchequer. It could be a pan-fried rib steak or else what we all called a "flat meatball," which is something like a Salisbury steak made from the usual meatball batter. A green salad of escarole, lettuce, and arugula was also put on the table.

Then it all repeated for the next week.

Tommy, the *pasta e fagioli* patron, was a member of our Local #37. Vincent Dee was the business agent (union delegate) in Local #34, and he was a fine gentlemen. He is still alive, though retired. At that time Local #34 had all of Manhattan in its jurisdiction. The Bronx was completely the fiefdom of Local #37. Today, some of Manhattan, starting at the northern side of 125 Street, belongs to our Bronx Local #37, and the rest—south to Battery Park—belongs to #34.

It is required that every union bricklaying contractor report the proposed start of work on any job. That is what I did when we were starting brickwork on Tommy's last job, our own building at Seaman Avenue and West 215th Street. Later, Al Stola was to take over. It was called Indian Park Towers because that was the name of the park it adjoined. This park still stands and runs under the Henry Hudson Bridge, right where the Harlem River meets the Hudson. It is still an exciting spot. The confluence is called Spuyten Duyvil, from the Dutch, and looks out across the Hudson to the majestic Palisades.

When a few days later Dee showed up, by chance Tommy was there with me. I remember Dee was pleased to see his old friend, Tommy, as foreman. I was impressed that Dee arrived on foot, an unusual happenstance. I wondered whether Dee had refused the offer to be supplied a car by his local (and the attendant expense). Such refusal would have been typical for Dee. Don't look for this sort of thing today.

When I review the number of jobs for which Tommy was foreman, I get dizzy. There were hundreds in those thirty years. Off the top of my head I can recall the following: Cheektowaga, Niagara Falls, Buffalo, Norfolk, Detroit, New Britain, Pittsburgh, Hartford, Kingston, Newburg, Kings County Hospital, Staten Island, and Riverdale; going north along the Hudson, Bayonne, Hoboken, Union City, Guttenberg, Fort Lee, River Edge, Edgewater, Bergenfield, Fairfield, Paterson, Bogota, Elizabeth, Newark, East Orange, West Orange, Plainfield, Morristown, Englewood, Teaneck, Tenafly, Jersey City, Raritan Arsenal, New Brunswick, East Brunswick, Fort Dix, Camp Kilmer, Seneca Ordnance Depot, Romulus Naval Depot, and West Point; in New York, the Berkshire Hotel off Madison Avenue, 78th Street and Second Avenue, 61st Street and Lexington Avenue, Park Avenue at 84th Street, 310 and 315 East 70th Streets, three buildings at 69th Street and Second Avenue, and two apartment buildings at Sutton Place (one at the southwest corner of 58th Street and the other at 59th Street facing the East River, which I discussed earlier). The building at 58th Street was built for one of the Greek shipping magnates, Kulukundis by name. The competition for ship bottoms among Jackie O's Onassis, Stavros Niarchos, his brother-in-law, and Kulukundis was fierce. Fascinating times were those.

In each of Tommy's jobs there was dedication, concern, loyalty, a positive attitude, measured judgment, peacemaking, simplicity, calmness, and love. What more can you expect from a human being? By what right are we worthy even to expect a hundredth of such devotion, we who are so weak and undeserving by comparison?

Tommy was in Mother Cabrini Medical Center on 18th Street in New York. It had formerly been the Columbus Hospital, lost in the adjoining massive labyrinth that is now Beth Israel Medical Center. Only by luck could you come across the granite lintel that is inscribed "Columbus Hospital." This was the "Italian" hospital in New York. Deserving or not, it was the refuge to which so many immigrants turned, starting almost a hundred years ago. Most of their doctors were Italian, and the immigrants supposed (I hope rightly) that compassion and understanding would be theirs in their hours of pain and suffering.

Al Stola and I found Tommy in a small single room where one window looked out on the small park across the street. The afternoon shadows of winter were lengthening, and it was quiet, very quiet. Tommy lay in a low bed, which was more like a cot, and if he had had the strength, he probably could have seen the boughs of the trees across the street.

He was partly dressed; I guess it was too late for any treatment. I was glad there would be no more invasions to his body and dignity. Tommy hardly talked, but he seemed to enjoy the silent peace of our presence. He did not cry out.

The hour passed. Darkness was coming, in more ways than one. I leaned over and kissed him for the last time. Only his eyes answered me. We left him in silent resignation. Another Ulysses was on his way home.

"I'm coming, Kitty."